SON OF A
PREACHER

A Hellcat Ace's Memoirs

by
LtCdr Everett C. Hargreaves
VF-2 "Ace in a Day"

Those of us who have survived the infallibility of youth can look back and identify some experience that forever changed our lives. War is one of those experiences. Those who have survived the trauma of combat have forever stamped on their memories those moments when their lives hung in the balance.

World War II was the first true global conflict that touched everyone. Those who lived it experienced life-changing events and each in their own way helped change the course of world history. This then is one man's story. A son of a preacher, who loved God and country, and walked in harm's way for both.

LWB

BAC
Publishers, Inc.

Son of a Preacher - A Hellcat Ace's Memoirs

by Lt.Cdr. Everett C. Hargreaves

Jacket design and book design by Larry W. Bledsoe
All photos and images from author's collection

Edited by Larry W. Bledsoe

Printed in the United States of America.

Published by: BAC Publishers, Inc.
                  1749 W. 13th St.
                  Upland, CA 91786

Library of Congress Control Number
                  2003114173

First Edition 2003

ISBN 0-9655730-3-6

Dedicated to my granddaughter Teresa Hargreaves whose question, "Grandpa, what did you do during the war?" showed the need for us who lived through those historic times to document what really happened for future generations.

Table of Contents

VI

INTRODUCTION

How can anyone not respond to their granddaughter's simple request? It just happened to be an assignment for one of her high school classes. Teresa was studying for another class on history, and the question came up, "Grandpa, what did *you* do during the war?"

My granddaughter, Teresa Hargreaves, is really the one that got me started on my memoirs. She was studying from a book that really had very little text about World War II. And much of what was included was a wrong slant to history, wrongly indicating the United States was the aggressor by dropping those two bombs.

This then is my attempt to answer her question, to correct those wrong impressions that are being taught our children and grandchildren in the very schools that are being supported by our tax dollars. The best way to expose this misleading spin on history for what it is, which is certainly contrary to the interest of this country, is by telling the truth.

So where do I begin? I suppose with knowledge, for it is the source of competitive advantage. You can turn knowledge into ideas and solutions that work for your potential success, along with physical stamina, keen eyesight, and the luck of being at the right place at the right time.

My love of flying has produced many sources of information

that I needed to survive the hazards of combat flying from Navy carriers, where you have just 400 feet to land in, rather than the 10,000 to 15,000 feet runways most pilots have to set their planes down on. Where each landing is considered a potential crash.

The largest source of my knowledge for this book comes from my flight log books, which recorded each flight, its purpose, duration, and type of flying. From my college training programs (CPT) in a little forty horsepower Piper Cub, which provided my original pilots license. My secondary training in a WACO UPF 7, which upon completion gave me a Commercial Pilots License where I could then charge customers for a ride in the air. Then there was the Navy flight training program, which included formation flying and instrument blind flying.

All that provided me with the knowledge to write my memories now. That along with a little memory of growing up during the great Depression years, which Tom Brokaw calls "The greatest generation." I'll also try to insert a comparison of some prices before the economists recommended "good for the country, credit and inflation." For example a 16 oz schooner of beer that was just a nickel then is now $3.00 or more. A loaf of bread was 9 cents and is now over $2.00. A 1¢ candy bar then was larger than a 70¢ candy bar now days. And, a coke or cup of coffee was only five cents then.

I paid for my college education earning three dollars per day on a wheat/oat thrashing gang during the summer vacations. It was hard work, but oh, those noon meals that the farm wives spread out for the crew were really something else to write home about. With a choice of roast beef or roast pork and country fried chicken along with veggies and potatoes, and normally a choice of at least three kinds of pie from twelve inch pie pans rather than the eight inch pie pans of today. My father would let me have the family car one night a week for a date, if I refilled the gas tank. Gas was five gallons for a dollar. Occasionally it was 6 or 7 gallons for a dollar from a gas station if I was lucky. So I was able to keep him happy.

The activities of most veterans from World War II, and more particularly my individual service to my country during the war, lay dormant for nearly 40 years in top secret files stored in archives somewhere in the warehouses of our Pentagon or the war department of Congress. But as time moved on, people seemed to forget the events of the attack on Pearl Harbor. Most of us veterans didn't talk to our families about our participation. We were just getting along with our lives, and the significance of the events diminished with time.

Then in the late '70s and early '80s, as the computer age came abreast of times, many candidates for their Doctoral degrees started analyzing the newly declassified battle reports of the war. They entered much of the information into computers and saved it on computer discs that facilitated the combat information all in numerical order by date and time sequences. Just the touch of a key and a few seconds wait was all it took for the computers to spit out the information that previously would have taken tedious hours of search to acquire.

From there, it didn't take very many more years for historians and the general public to get re-interested in the activities of those who participated in the war. Relatives and family members wanted them to relate their experiences to the younger generation. Some eighth grade teachers, such as the class that Mrs. Linda McAllister teaches at the L. R. Green school in Escondido, CA, were especially interested in having a history day for students so they could interview many of us veterans in one-on-one discussion groups about our participation in World War II. And that led to my granddaughter's request and ultimately to this book.

No one had ever discussed their participation or activity during World War II, for, as I said before, combat records had been top secret. Most of us who had served never realized we'd become an important part of history, until those combat records were declassified.

Then younger professors calling themselves "historians" started getting the wrong slant on history of World War II, calling the Japanese poor victims of the aggressive United States who horribly killed some 15,000 to 22,000 Japanese on every island we retook in the Pacific on our road back. And finally, the U.S.

dropped the First and Second Atomic Bombs to End the Road Back. These historians only considered the fact that approximately 250,000 casualties resulted from those bombs.

They never considered the fact that the Japanese soldiers were so fanatical and willing to die for their Emperor that they would not surrender, but would continue fighting until death. Thus the large number of casualties our Marines inflicted on each Island they retook from the Japanese. Islands that the Japanese had conquered in the Pacific early in the war.

Our Marines lost somewhere between 4,000 and 6,000 in each battle on the Road Back from Pearl Harbor to Bouganville and Espertos Desanto, to Tarawa, to Majuro, to Kwajalein, to Eniwetok, to Saipan, to Guam, to the Philippines, to Iwo Jima, Okinawa and all the other islands. The largest of these islands was probably no more than 25 miles long and 12 miles wide, but it cost the Japanese garrison of some 20,000 soldiers their lives to die for their Emperor.

Those "historians"" also forget that the casualties from the B-29 firebombing raids over Tokyo and Yokohama area far exceeded the number of deaths in Hiroshima and Nagasaki. The relentless firebombings virtually destroyed all of the bamboo shacks and flimsy buildings around the canals of what was known as Tokyo and Yokohama.

Those "historians" also forget the fanatical one-way pilots, known as the Kamikaze, that caused so much damage to our American Fleet of ships during the Okinawa invasion. Some 500 ships were sunk, where thousands of deaths occurred as a result of their "serving their Emperor" with such fanaticism.

What do these younger "historians" think would have happened during the invasion of Japan and its Homeland? It cost our Marines some 4000 to 6000 deaths for every island they retook, which were only three to four miles wide and maybe 15 to 25 miles long. Don't they see the validity of the estimates that at least one million of our Marines and infantry would have died had they invaded Japan? Plus how many millions of Japanese military and civilian casualties would have occurred if we had invaded? Yes, dropping those atomic bombs saved millions of lives on both sides.

Even though the poor Japanese suffered many casualties from the first atomic bombs, they started the war and we finished it as quickly as possible. And with far fewer lives lost than there would have been.

This narration is a result of many years of good intentions, but many frustrations and no one to prod me into accomplishing an actual result of memoirs while I can still remember the war time activities fairly accurately.

It has been quite a while since my granddaughter asked what did I do during World War II. This, hopefully, will give a little insight into Grandpa's being at the right place at the right time, with nerves of steel and eyesight better than his opponent, with the right training, a lot of that Irish LUCK from his 1/16th heritage from Ireland, and a squadron skipper and Task Group Admiral that helped get us to the right spots at the right time for action.

The aircraft carriers in this tale are the ones from which I flew in the conflict or became involved with in the various sea operations and battles described herein. These CV's were among the finest ships that fought the Japanese Navy. The *USS Enterprise* (CV-6) was the greatest U.S. combat carrier that ever sailed in harm's way. She survived more engagements and received more honors than any other warship of that time.

The *USS Hornet* (CV-12) was the successor to a fine ship, the *USS Hornet* (CV-8), which did not live long enough to attain full stature, but was significantly known for being the carrier that launched the Doolittle raid over Tokyo. She established an enviable place in U.S. combat naval history in her short time in battle. As for the new *Hornet*, she proved equal to the proud name and reputation as one of the best of the Essex class carriers that took the battle back to the Japanese homeland itself. She also gained fame as the flagship of that tenacious Cherokee, Adm. J. J. "Jocko Jima" Clark.

The wartime squadrons I served with (VF-2, VF-18, and VF-27) were three of the best, compiling a remarkable combat record. The list of pilots I served with in these squadrons is way too long to elaborate here and so were their heroic records. Suffice it to say that in the truest sense, we were a "band of brothers."

I lived through many harrowing experiences and several frustrating close calls during the first eight months of my combat activity before actually seeing my first Japanese plane. So this book is a combination of personal experiences and factual history arranged in chronological order with some comparisons of prices back then, when we were just coming out from the days known as the "Great Depression," and the inflated prices of today.

This book presents an eyewitness viewpoint for each action. It is a sea story, but not a fantasy. We actually lived it. I have tried to keep every happening as historically accurate as possible. Basic research materials were sometimes sketchy. My personal diary, other notes and orders, letters, battle reports of squadron and ships activity, newspaper clippings, pictures, presentations, speeches, early writings, my own flight logbook, the Odyssey of Fighting Two, the scrapbook of Air Group 27, and other assorted memorandums were all used in writing this book.

A cherished resource is my own memory, for which I have been fortunate and blessed to have retained pretty well through the some 59 years of time.

Naval aviators are considered an elite group requiring physical and mental stamina well above an ordinary person. A famous naval aviator, Adm. John W. Reeves, Jr., put it this way, "Naval aviators, like most specialists, believe that there is something extraordinary about their chosen field. They recognize that this requires of them something above just average, in their concept of responsibility and duty." The concepts of dedication, valor, pride, respect, and loyalty, and exposure to a daily dose of hazards and risks is why Naval aviators consider themselves the best pilots in the world, for they are the eyes of the fleet and set high standards for themselves. This then is my story.

Lt.Cdr. Everett C. Hargreaves

Ensign Carl Hargreaves
with his new "Wings of Gold"
at graduation from Corpus Christi
on March 17, 1943

Chapter One

MY ROOTS

The Hargreaves Family

History reveals the English lineage of ministers in the Hargreaves family from which a young man of 21 volunteered in response to a call from his church for missionary preachers needed to fill the religious needs of people migrating to the wheat fields on the plains of Saskatchewan, Canada. Assistance had been promised for his tuition at a college in Canada, providing the young man would earn the rest of his expenses for theological school at Wesley College in Winnepeg, Manitoba, and spend his summer vacations "preaching" in the missionary pulpits of Western Canada.

My father, Theophilus Crawshaw Hargreaves, thus crossed the Atlantic, enrolled at Wesley College, Winnipeg, Manitoba. After the first semester, he learned that he had to arrange to take his final exams two to three weeks early in order to arrive in the Saskatoon, Saskatchewan area early enough to earn the most money he could planting the wheat seed. His earnings for helping with the planting were still short of what he needed for college and so he had to also arrange with the registrar to enter school late if he wanted to be in there to help harvest the grain.

These shortened semesters required a reduced academic load, to allow for the intense study that he needed to "catch up and get ahead." But, he always made time for participation in the extra curricular activities such as the college's soccer team, theatrical performances, and seasonal ice skating at the Winnipeg rink. It was there that he met a young music teacher who often would waltz with him when waltz music was played at the ice rink. This music teacher, Luella Clare Black, who had graduated from the Toronto school of music, had majored in piano and organ, was teaching music there at the college, and would eventually become my mother.

Dad graduated from college and divinity school to become an ordained preacher and accepted a call to fill a pulpit in Tisdale ,Saskatchewan. After the Sunday morning service, he would then, as he put it, "hitch up olde Dobin" to drive several miles out for an afternoon service in a country schoolhouse. Then on to another farmhouse where people would gather for an evening service.

The winter season was very difficult, especially when temperatures would drop to minus 40 to minus 50 degrees at night. That was before anyone had heard of "wind chill factor." An old buffalo blanket for himself and for his horse along with warming stones usually got him safely back to his "sod house" that he had put together for himself with an add-on shelter for his pinto horse.

However, when the wind would start howling at temperatures that low, especially in a blinding snow storm, he would accept the hospitality of one of his parishioners. This was wiser than attempting the frigid ride back to his cold hut where he would have to stoke up the potbelly stove before he could even begin to warm up. When his room was a little warmer, he would open a window to the add-on shelter to make it a little warmer for olde dobin.

After a couple years of this rugged life, cooking on a kerosene stove and reading by the light of a kerosene lamp (as electricity was a long way off yet in those areas), he was transferred to Lanigan, Saskatchewan, where he spent a couple more years of bachelorhood. The music teacher had moved to Saskatoon, which made for a much shorter trip for courting. It was only a 125-mile train ride.

Before long, they did get married on Uncle Everett's farm

near Foxboro, Ontario. Uncle Everett had raised mom after her mother died when she was just three years old. Soon after the big day the flu epidemic hit, and many of dad's parishioners succumbed to the deadly virus. Both my parents survived, however, and were able to move on to Wadena, Saskatchewan where mom became the church organist and vocalist assisting dad at all his services, funerals, and weddings. That is, except for a few weeks before and after my birth on May 10, 1921. However, after another particularly severe winter, mom insisted the family move to a much warmer climate, closer to her father down in Michigan in the states.

Growing Up

My grandfather, Benjamin Franklin Black, had established a medical practice in Holton, Michigan and learned of a need for a new preacher in Grand Haven, which was only 25 miles away. So we all moved to Michigan shortly after I was one year old. Grand

Uncle Everett Sill's place on river in Canada.
l. to r., Cousin Ewart, author (about age 9), and
Uncle Everett, with other relatives.

Haven had a beautiful church and a lovely parsonage, but it was an older, well-established congregation. After four years there, dad missed the missionary atmosphere of a small town and found a small town in northern Wisconsin needing a pulpit filled. So the family, which by that time included my three-year-old sister, moved again during the summer of 1926.

My first recollections as a youth were of Eagle River, up in Vilas County, Wisconsin where my father was pastor of the Congregational Church. The area was well known for its many lakes and the river that ran through the town of about 1000 people. That was the population during the winter months, which exploded to probably about 25,000 during the summer vacation periods when all the cottages along the shores of the many lakes were filled.

When we arrived, the parsonage was not yet completed, so Mrs. Joe Ellis welcomed us to her beautiful mansion for about a month before we could move into the new parsonage. She was quite a benefactor of the church and saw to it that decorations for what ever season were always placed in front of the alter.

Dad was also very active in many of the community activities, which included being a charter member of the local Rotary club. He participated in several of the youth activities by giving many of us kids swimming and sailboat lessons in the summer. He taught us the intricacies needed for handling a sail boat no matter where the wind was coming from, so we could go across the lake and still get back home again.

Dad also taught us the joys of winter sports. Santa left a pair of ice skates for me one year, and the next Christmas he left a hockey stick and a puck. In winter we had ice skating, hockey, and downhill skiing. Dad made a triangle sail for me to use for ice sailing on the larger frozen lakes before the snows came. We could go for an hour before we would have to put the knowledge gained in the summertime about sailing into practice. We would have to start tacking the wind to get back to the starting point, which might take several hours of tacking back and forth before arriving at the original point. Or we would have to really put out a lot of energy in actually skating back.

l. to r,. the author's grandfather Dr. Benjamin Franklin Black, his mother Luella Claire, his sister Yvonne, the author, and Mr. & Mrs. Putman.

The only problem with sail-skating was watching for cracks in the ice caused by sudden changes in temperature. The temperature could drop to 30 degrees below zero overnight, and those sudden changes in temperature often made big cracks in the ice, which could be quite disastrous if you had not noticed the crack and you took a big spill landing on your knee. That type of injury more than once crippled me for several weeks.

Dad also gave me the experience of supervising the bobbing flags as fish would catch the baited hooks on lines dropped through holes that we had chopped in the ice some 12 to 18 inches thick.

We would skate from one hole to another after warming ourselves around a bonfire built right on the ice. Of course we had to skate to the shoreline to find broken branches, stakes or boards to make the fires with, for warmth to last on our all-day fishing trips.

Our lunches, fishing tackle, and the crowbar needed to chop holes in the ice all had to be hauled out on a sled, at least until the ice became thick enough to hold the weight of the car and all our equipment. Dad would drive the car out as soon as the ice reached about six or seven inches thick. The car would make a wonderful windbreak for those days when blustery winds came up. The winds would make it very difficult to bait our hooks with ungloved bare hands.

Never one to be idle, Dad continued his love for acting by forming a local theater group, performing various plays and renting the local theater for two nights each year when he would even take the part of Scrooge in the annual Christmas story. He also played a very active part in organ-

The author's mother, Luella Claire Black-Hargreaves in 1938.

izing the Rotary club of Eagle River, which eventually led to the friendship of one Col. Jenkins, a veteran of air battles over France and Germany during World War I.

My First Ride

I was a kid of about eight years, when a fellow Rotarian, Col. Jenkins, invited dad to go to the local airport for his first airplane ride. I guess Dad was thinking of me, when he asked the Colonel if he could bring his young son along. The answer came back, "Well, I think you both could probably fit in that front seat, for you both are rather slender. There really is only room for one person but I think the seat belt in the passenger cockpit will go over both of you." The Colonel had a World War I bi-wing plane known as a Jenny that he had purchased to use for barnstorming.

The Colonel made out very well, even during those Depression years, by charging just a dollar for a 20-minute ride at all of the Paul Bunyon parades, the county fairs, and any other special weekend event in the area. Paul Bunyan was a mythical character described in many books about the northern woods. He was a giant logger three times the size of an average person, and he always carried a humongous axe for chopping down the trees. That area was well known for its forests, the lumber industry, and the fortunes that had been generated in the early part of the century. The Colonel also made extra income by giving flight lessons during the week.

Dad, on the appointed day, drove us the five miles south out to Ed Brunswick's "airport." The runway was merely a mowed path, probably 30 feet wide. It ran from opposite corners of a 50-acre clover field that was also used for growing next winter's food for his livestock. In those early days runways were mostly mowed strips. Our small town had no paved runways, it didn't even have paved major roads coming from Three Lakes to Eagle River nor going on up to Watersmeet, Michigan.

Ed's barn was also used for storing the petrol and oil he needed to service the few planes coming in from Milwaukee and Chicago bringing vacationers to their "cottages" on one of the many lakes. John Dillinger and several other known gangsters had more like year-round homes they called "cottages" on catfish lake. Baby Face Nelson also was a sometime visitor coming up in his Ford tri-motor plane. The tie down stakes were all located near the barn and at times there would be four or five planes besides the Colonels.

Upon our arrival, the Colonel gave us a short lecture about not touching anything in the cockpit for he had not removed anything he needed for giving student pilots their lessons and the second set of controls were still active in both cockpits. The Colonel then showed us where to step up on the wing and enter the cockpit and made sure we had the safety belt on and tight before he climbed into the back cockpit. We then heard "switch off" and Ed Brunswick pulled the propeller around twice. Then we heard "switch on" and Ed gave a swift forceful pull on the propeller and the engine sputtered and coughed but did not catch. Again we heard, "switch off" and Ed pulled the prop through again. "Switch on" with Ed giving another forceful pull. This time there was a deafening roar from the engine and from then on Dad and I had to virtually scream at each other for any conversation.

We taxied out to the corner of the field where the Colonel pushed the throttle forward, and we started the bumpy ride across the field to get airborne. Once in the air we headed for the village of Eagle River, and I think Dad was as thrilled as I was to see the river, the church, our house, and the various streets. The road leading to Silver Lake where we went swimming, the country club golf course, the lumber yard and saw-mill before we headed around to see several lakes with their connecting rivers that make up the "chain of lakes." It was so thrilling to see my favorite swimming holes, skiing areas, and my favorite place for ice fishing before we headed back to the airport.

On the way back, I suddenly felt a push on my head. It was the Colonels hand with a note that he was shoving over to me, for we did not have radio or intercom in those days. It said we were now flying at three thousand feet above the ground. I can still remember my father's face with such a look of surprise for he just couldn't believe he would ever be that far off good old terra firma. He certainly was impressed and must have enjoyed the flight as much as I did. After landing back at the field and taxiing back to the tie-down stakes, we climbed out and graciously thanked the Colonel who then said, "See what you've been missing all these years?"

Andy Nelson's Secret Flights

The Colonel then asked if we happened to know Andy Nelson, the local Chevrolet dealer, who was one of his students and almost ready to solo. Andy was the father of Bob Nelson, one of my 6 playmates, so of course I knew him. But we were not to reveal Andy's secretive trips to the airport until after he had soloed and received the new plane that had been ordered.

The secretiveness for lessons was because Mrs. Nelson was not yet a flight enthusiast. However, after Andy soloed, Mrs. Nelson was persuaded into taking a flight with him in his new plane.

The author took first place in a 4th of July parade with his decorated bicycle. (about 1931 at age 10).

Mr. Nelson's son Bob and I were also welcomed to a free flight whenever we could make it out to the airport, which involved our bicycling five miles over sandy back road trails to the Brunswick farm. Bill Brunswick, the airport owner's son, was just a year older than us and we played with him before we would have to catch the school bus for home. He would show us around all the planes that would fly in, and we kind of learned more about the planes, how they were tied down, and what kind of servicing they needed.

It wasn't long before Mr. Nelson talked the City Council into opening up a small runway next to the railroad track just north of town. Then he built a small hangar beside the south end of the runway just large enough for his plane. When he could spare a few minutes away from his business, he would scoot out there, which was probably only about half a mile away.

Bob and I could go that half-mile without any problem. Whenever Mr. Nelson would come out to gain a little more flight experience he would take both of us up for a ride around the countryside, which was very enjoyable. I guess it was from all my flights with Mr. Nelson that I really learned the desire to fly. However, his Chevrolet business slowed considerably during those Depression days.

In the early thirties, the country sank into the depths of a serious Depression and many people just didn't have the money for new cars, even though a brand new Chevy only cost about $750.00. In fact, Mr. Nelson had so many customers repair bills unpaid that he was having a real cash-flow problem and moved to a much smaller building two or three blocks away from his previous garage. He also had to let several mechanics go and started to do much of the auto repair work himself. He had to spend so much time collecting the repair bills that his trips to the airport became less and less frequent. Bob and I kept the prop pulled through and the oil fully loaded so he could just jump into the plane with us aboard for our infrequent rides.

I don't remember where the old OX engine came from, but Mr. Nelson had acquired it and stored it in his garage hoping to overhaul it in his spare time evenings. So Bob and I became grease monkeys by taking it apart, which gave me my first knowledge of engines. At the same time, my father's congregation members were becoming unemployed and not able to complete their pledges. The local sawmill kept making lumber for a while and stacking it up in unsold piles which were neatly stacked ready for the next order once the lumber aged. Construction of cottages on those numerous lakes came to a virtual standstill. With fewer and fewer orders for lumber, the sawmill employees were gradually let go also.

By the middle of 1933, Mom started realizing that her two children should be closer to the larger cities where colleges or universities would be more accessible, as I was already in junior high and my sister was close behind me. Dad, who had already taken a couple reductions in salary, agreed. He started looking around for a pastorate in Southern Wisconsin closer to Madison or Milwaukee where we would be able to enjoy the Art and Music Programs that they would frequently have. There we could see big name artists like Fritz Chrysler playing his violin and many other big name orchestras such as Wayne King, Benny Goodman, Paul Whiteman, Kay Kaiser, Glenn Miller, Tommy Dorsey and others. They played one-hour gigs and had a rest period while the movie was shown. They played for the students at the Orpheum Theater and were open to the general public at a very nominal fee of $1.00.

High School and Growing Desire to Fly

July 1, 1934, saw a humongous moving van back up to our rear door and all our furniture and worldly possessions were neatly stored in it for the trip to Edgerton, Wisconsin, which was 30 miles south of Madison. We took a vacation trip to my grandfather Ben Black in Detroit for a few days.

While there Grandpa got tickets to the Tigers baseball game for our enjoyment. Then one morning Grandpa said he sat up in bed to listen to the news that John Dillinger had been killed! But he didn't remember ever hearing the news! Then we went on to Mom's relatives on their farms near Foxboro, just six miles north of Bellville, Ontario, Canada, before we settled in to finish my last year of junior high and then high school.

Although we had no airport near Edgerton, we had an aviation serial shown for some 20 minutes almost every Saturday afternoon at the local movie theater. That would be my only contact to flying for the next five years until I graduated from high school.

However, my thoughts of becoming a Canadian airman and flying Spitfires really crossed my mind many times in the summer of 1939 and again in 1940 and '41 while I was on my uncle's farm. It was just 10 miles east of the Trenton Canadian Air Force Base. Apparently, we were under the flight path to the student practice area because every day that I was in the field helping my uncle on the thrashing gang those summers, I could hear the planes fly over and would have to stop and watch them.

If Dad had only said yes during the summer of 1941, I would have been down at Trenton starting flight lessons, because it had become my desire to fly. Canada was already training pilots to send

The author's high school senior picture

over to squadrons protecting London during the notorious blitz where the Germans were bombing London. It was natural for Canadian fellows and many American young men who had gone to Canada to join the Royal Canadian Air Force in hopes of getting into Spitfires to help protect London and other coastal cities.

I would help my uncle with his fieldwork while we were visiting, especially with his oat and wheat fields and then with thrashing of the grain on his farm. He would also help other farmers around him who had helped him get the necessary men needed to complete the thrashing process and get the grain and straw into the barns for feeding the livestock during the coming winter. Every time I heard a plane fly over, the urge to fly just kept creeping into my veins.

Each year the month of vacation came to an end all too quickly, as we worked Uncle Everett's fields all day and then would go dancing most every night with my cousin who had arranged dates for us. The time for departure came all too quickly and after saying goodbye to the two families near Foxboro, we headed for Toronto for a real quick visit with another uncle, the Herb Sills family.

Then it was on to Niagara Falls for the most magnificent view of the falls from the Canadian side. At night, powerful spotlights from both the Canadian and United States sides created all colors of the rainbow by using colored filters that changed periodically to enhance the view of the water going over the edge and the mists below.

From there it was on to New Wilmington, Pennsylvania, for me to be dropped off to enter my freshman year at Westminster College. I had my room reserved at the fraternity house for $10 a month and was to wait on tables at the evening meal for my food. Those were the going prices back in those days.

Chapter Two

LEARNING TO FLY

Fraternity Initiation

I had been initiated into the Alpha Nu chapter of Alpha Sigma Phi fraternity during my freshman year at the college. My most memorable incident occurred during the final part of my initiation. I was blindfolded at the frat house after having emptied all pockets and my billfold of any money and then given a total of one dollar in change. I was then driven out on a country road some 10 miles from New Wilmington. My fraternity father let me out of the car at midnight with a letter of instruction to be completed as soon as possible and then return to the fraternity house.

Last one of the pledges to return back would be given additional duties before the final initiation. My letter of instruction was most difficult to read in the midnight darkness by the roadside. But I could make out that I had to go down to Indiana, Pennsylvania and have the parents of the movie film star James Stewart autograph my letter of instruction with the time and date they signed my letter. I lucked out, in that a young farm kid just returning from a date happened along before too many miles of walking in the direction that seemed to have the most light reflecting down from the clouds.

As it turned out, I had actually been heading correctly to New Castle and the young gentleman was on his way home from an evening there. However, he stopped for me as he admitted there was never anyone walking on this back road and I must be in real need of help with a lot of trouble. It was very gracious of him to turn around and take me all the way back into the city and get me headed out on the correct road leading to Indiana.

He certainly deserved a big world of thanks, but wouldn't even take some of the coins I had for a bit of the gas that he would have to use in taking me back into New Castle. He said on the farm they have a big tank for gas and all they had to do was just back the car or tractors up to the tank to fill them up. Of course that was still in the days when gas was five gallons per dollar. He wished me well and turned around and went on his way home again.

I put my thumb out for the next generous driver who came along shortly and fortunately he was heading all the way to Indiana, which is where he was from. He knew of the Stewart name and the Stewart hardware store, but he didn't know if there were any more Stewarts in the town. We had to go get a telephone book at a filling station to get their address. He obligingly took me right out to the Stewart home and again wished me good luck.

By this time daylight was breaking and it was still rather early, but the threat of an additional duty before being initiated set me to thinking. I mustered my courage and knocked on the front door. As luck would have it, the Stewarts were just arising and invited me in to have breakfast with them. They were quite amused at my story and request, which they gladly complied with. I thanked them for their lovely breakfast and their cooperation. Then it was back on my way to New Wilmington. I arrived shortly after lunch with my total net worth of one dollar still in my pocket and was No. 8 of the 21 pledges to arrive back at the fraternity house.

Forty-five years and three months later I mentioned the incident to Jimmy Stewart. We were attending a banquet at the annual conference for the American Fighter Aces where he was to be the guest speaker for that evening. We were at the new Continental Hotel in San Diego, California, and, yes he could remember his folks relating a story of some damn college student having breakfast with them and asking for their autographs. But that was many

Fraterrnity initiation required the author to spend the day with his "buddy."

years ago and we both had to chuckle while relating my side of the story and his response to his folks' amazement.

We were now sophomores and eligible to reside in the fraternity house. My roommates were Hunch Phau (star fullback on the football team) and Rocky Miller (star center of the college basketball team). A second member of the basketball starting five was Tom Patton (our fraternity president) who roomed just across the hall, and the third starter Smoky Dumire was on second floor just below us.

The five starters generally played the full game as we had no capable substitutes. Tom and Rocky would virtually throw up from exhaustion after each game and stay in bed the next day. But they were always ready to play the next game on Tuesday or Saturday whichever the case may be, and wound up their year by playing in the semi-finals of the National Invitational Tournament in Madison Square Garden in New York City. Of course, I had to scrounge a ride and cut classes that week to be in New York to give my roommates the moral support they deserved.

CPT Training

We were having a "smoker" for new prospective pledges the fall of 1940 when I happen to be talking with Dr. Hart, an alumnus of the Pi Phis, which had been the local fraternity that converted to Alpha Sigma Phi, a national fraternity, in the spring of '39. The Doctor mentioned that he was being appointed as medical examiner for the new CPT "College Pilot Training" program that would be incorporated into Westminster's courses come second semester, and that he would like to see a good response from his fraternity. He invited a half dozen of us to his medical office to see if we could qualify. My glasses that I had worn for over five years were tested first to see if I would qualify, as glasses would be a disqualifying point. It turned out to be just pure glass and the Doc let out a sigh of relief after checking and exclaimed them to be virtually useless for I had 20/20 vision, a requirement for pilot training. The rest of the physical was also satisfactory and I got my medical certificate needed for the course.

Ground school got started with the second semester, with Prof. Bert Quick and John Moorhead instructing courses on Tuesday and Thursday evenings from 7 p.m. until 9 p.m. Subjects covered were meteorology, navigation, theoretical operation and construction of airplanes, and CAA "Civil Aviation Administration" rules and regulations.

We were supposed to have had three hours flight time each week in addition to the four hours of ground school. The field used for these flights was at the New Castle airport some ten miles away from campus. This presented a big problem for there was no school bus to take us and we had to use our thumbs to get anyplace close to that airport, provided the weather would allow us practice time in the air after getting there.

Most of our 11 students didn't get the required eight hours dual instruction within the first two months because of the difficulties mentioned. A couple of them needed more than the required eight hours as they seemed to have a problem with depth perception. There was only one runway and the field slopped some forty feet from one end to the other. Landing uphill didn't bother them so much, but when the wind was from the low end, they seemed to stall in and our instructor didn't appreciate the abuse to his plane.

Walt "Tacky" Tackenberg was my instructor and during one of my early instruction periods he was demonstrating the method of recovering from a stall when the engine actually quit. We were over a wooded area and after looking around the only place we

"Tacky," wearing tie and sunglass, showing us our cross-country flights on May 19, 1941 - Westminster College

could find to land was a very small narrow strip next to the humongous cavity of a stone quarry. After landing, Walt was able to get the engine started again. Because it was such a short strip of grass instead of a nice long paved runway, he decided that my extra weight would make a takeoff rather precarious and that he would have to leave me behind and come back in a car for me.

The school coordinator had a problem with my record. Some government clerk had noticed that I was born in Canada but failed to notice that my father had been naturalized, and because of that the school coordinator had all kinds of paperwork to get things straightened out. I was automatically included as a citizen when my father and mother became naturalized citizens of the United States but it took more than just a few phone calls to get the situation cleared up.

The weather cleared a little and I finally got down to the field for my eight hours of dual. Tacky had informed me this period would be nothing more than just practice landings. For me that meant I would spend an hour "bouncing," which was making a landing and pouring the throttle on again for an immediate take off while I still had most of my speed rather than coming to a full stop. Had I come to a full stop I would have had to taxi back to the end of the runway for another take off. After the second bounce I heard Tacky say, "Take me back to the hangar," and in my thoughts I went wild trying to figure what I had done wrong.

When we got back to the hangar he said, "If you feel up to it, you can take the plane up for your solo ride." He got out of the plane and said, "The wind has quieted and you have made two perfect landings," and then waved me to the end of the runway. It was kind of scary as I pushed the throttle forward and started to roll down the runway and thought, "Gee, there won't be anyone with me should something go wrong as when the engine cut out on me before!"

But as I pushed the throttle forward and gained speed going down the runway and finally got airborne, the thrill of accomplishment surged through my blood and I had to calm down to perform as a competent pilot. However, in my elation of being by myself, I didn't feel like just taking off and circling the field and landing immediately. So, I headed for the school to see what the campus looked like from the air, as my fraternity brother Dave Schwartz had done the day before on his first solo.

I circled the campus and dipped my wings over the fraternity house, until a couple brothers came out to wave. Then it was back to the airport and as long as I had a few minutes left in my hour, I bounced a couple times before landing and coming to a full stop and then taxi-

The author minus a portion of his shirttail on the day he soloed.

ing back to the hangar where other students had gathered for their turn to fly. They were all waiting to perform the traditional ceremony of cutting off a piece of the shirttail of a successful pilot after his first solo.

Once I had soloed and was ready for flights without my instructor, it seemed like inclement weather was against me most of the time. I had three afternoon labs for chemistry and only two afternoons when I could even chance going down to the airfield for additional flight time.

The next couple months were mostly rainy with high winds and heavy clouds. Bill Ice, who owned the airport and the plane we used, a large jovial fellow that always had a cigar stuck in his mouth, was not able to let us inexperienced pilots fly even though we had soloed. We were still considered too inexperienced and needed better weather for any flight time at all.

The required syllabus for the CPT program for obtaining our private pilots license had to be followed with every other flight required to be dual time with our instructor. We three Alpha Sigs seemed to have poor weather most of the time, and our progress was slow. By the end of the normal college semester, none of us had more than even half of the syllabus for flight completed. As a

Yvonne Hargreaves in front of the Brimfield Church where their father was pastor in 1941.

result we got special permission from our chapter's faculty adviser for us to stay in the fraternity house so we could at least have a place to sleep while we completed our flight program after the normal class work at Westminster was finished for the semester.

Dave Schwartz who lived in the house just below me on second floor was able to get a family car for us to use for transportation to and from the airport. Even after school let out it seemed like the weather was a big problem. Even though we spent every day at the field trying to get a flight, we had every evening free. Dave would drive us up to Titusville, Pennsylvania, where he had a date with his steady girlfriend, who would always get a friend so that we could double date. We would see a movie or some other activity locally there in Titusville.

It took nearly two weeks to finish enough of the syllabus so that we could take our cross-country flight. Bill Ice scheduled us to fly from the New Castle field up to Edinburg, Pennsylvania, which we accomplished by looking at ground signs with cities and railroad tracks being the most easy to follow. This is called VFR flight. Both of us finally had our ride with the CAA flight inspector and received a passing grade by the end of the third week after school was let out. We all headed home with our private pilot's license in our pockets.

I was all set to take the CPT secondary course during my junior year at Westminster, but upon arriving back at college and registering for the usual required academic courses, I learned we would be two students short of the required minimum. It seems that Bill Ice needed a certain number of students to get approval to purchase a WACO UPF 7 that government regulations specified for the CPT secondary course. I had already attended academic classes for a week when we found out that the secondary CPT program was to be canceled. I hopped over to the college registrar for a rebate of all semester fees and books for the various classes I had signed up for and headed west to Galesburg, Illinois. I had taken my sister, Yvonne, to register for her freshman year at Knox College in Galesburg before I had started east to Westminster for my school year.

On to Galesburg

I already knew that Art Curry, who owned and operated the Galesburg airport, had more than enough students to qualify for the secondary program at Knox College that fall. I knew because I had rented planes from him during the summer to give my sister and my father a ride and let them see what Galesburg looked like from the air before flying down to Brimfield.

It was my sister's first flight and she really enjoyed it, and of course Dad had been up before but not since the time that he and I went up with Col. Jenkins back in Eagle River days. After all, I was a "hot pilot" now with a legal private pilot's license and it only cost $1.50 to rent a plane for an hour. It was well worth that rental fee to see Dad enjoying himself again. For most of the summer I had earned the big sum of three dollars per day slaving away for up to 10 hours a day in the harvest and thrashing gang for oats and wheat, which were the big cash crops of the area around Brimfield and for Galesburg also.

I knew Art Curry already had his WACO UPF 7 and I would be just an additional student for him that fall semester. There was no problem leaving Westminster other than trying to make sure that the registrar of Knox College would accept my transfer and allow me in as a junior, which he did. They accepted all my transferring credits, except the Bible courses I had been required to take each semester at Westminster were not allowed. I had taken so many

The day the author soloed the Waco UPF-7 at Knox, Sept/Oct 1941.

credits during each of the four semesters at Westminster that excluding the Bible courses still allowed me to attend Knox as a junior. All I had to do was promise to study extra hard for a few weeks to catch up the two weeks that I had already missed there at Knox.

I had to sign the required statement again that I would enlist in the Army or Navy Air Corps, should the United States ever become involved in a hostile operation. The big problem was to get my medical examination. The only approved medic was up in Chicago at the Midway Airport. That meant I would have to take a day off from school and board the CB&Q railroad train for Chicago and then find my way from the station out to Midway Airport.

It turned out the doctor for the CAA regional office was in just a small office at Midway. He insisted on putting drops that felt like grains of sand in my eyes for further examination to make sure that my eyes were a full 20/20 and without problems. After my medical examination I was free to go without any substance to put in my eyes to make them clear up. I could hardly read anything up close and trying to find street signs or the bus route signs presented a real problem. I had to ask people standing waiting for the buses what number and where to go or how they would get me to where I had to go to get back to the Chicago Burlington Quincy railroad station.

It was a distance of some five miles, I suppose, from Midway down to the heart of the loop and to the CB&Q station, which I didn't make until much later. It took me the rest of the day to find my way to the station with my eyes in such a condition.

However, I was able to catch a late train after the normal close of business hours heading for Galesburg. I didn't arrive back at school until way late that night and had to be up bright and early for an 8:00 o'clock class the next morning.

When I finally got to flying, the weather again seemed to be against me. I didn't have too many afternoons for flying as afternoon labs at Knox pretty much kept me busy, which meant I would only have a couple afternoons a week for flying. Incredibly most of those afternoons had cloudy damp rainy weather, which of course prevented us from flying in the secondary course where acrobatics were a goodly portion of the syllabus and were so important. Loops with only a 2,000-foot ceiling were very dangerous for a student pilot. Likewise snap rolls, immelmans and about everything else in the syllabus needed more ceiling for us to practice.

Progress on my syllabus was rather slow during the entire fall due to the weather. As fall turned to winter the open cockpit plane required a full insulated flying suit, including fleece lined boots and helmet if I didn't want to freeze, even to circle the field to make practice landings. To get more familiar with a plane required getting all dolled up in the heavy flight suits every time I had a chance to fly.

Pearl Harbor

Thanksgiving came and went. Then after studying all day for an exam on Monday I took enough time to call my father before heading down to dinner. It was my Dad's birthday and I certainly wanted to wish him a happy birthday. It was also December 7, 1941. When I got him on the phone, he asked if I had heard the latest news. Japanese planes have bombed Pearl Harbor this morning with horrible casualties! It's such a tragedy!"

The 8 a.m. exam went on as scheduled and so did the next two classes. At 11 a.m. we were all excused from class to go back to the dorm to listen to President Roosevelt's radio address, which turned out to be the Declaration of War against the Axis and Japan, ending with Roosevelt making his now famous comment, "This dastardly act will live in infamy."

Lunch was served in the dorm shortly after the speech, and then it was time for me to catch the bus for Curry field as it was a beautiful sunny day, a great day for flying, and I had been able to complete only about 40 percent of my required syllabus for the CPT program. Christmas holidays came and we stayed at school to get flight time when there were no classes for those two weeks, but then semester exams came and very little flying was done during that time of review for our final exams.

When we could resume flying, Art Curry insisted we even do the stunts with lower ceilings because he needed the plane for second semester students enrolled in the course. I completed the stunts without incident even doing the loops and barrel rolls, which were all a potential disaster at the low levels, for there was no room for recovery if anything went wrong. I finally got to the syllabus requirement for a cross-country flight, which was to be a three-leg course flying from Galesburg to Springfield heading south and then northeast to Bloomington, and finally northwest back to Galesburg.

Shortly after what became known as "Pearl Harbor Day" all 20-year-old and older students were required to register for the newly established "War Time Draft." A fish-bowl drawing was held later in January to determine our entry date for armed services. My number came out to be number 9 for the registration district I was in and it didn't take long for that number to come up for induction. However, the draft board took pity on most of us actively enrolled in an accredited college and I received a deferment to the end of the school year.

It was early March by the time I had completed most of the syllabus and was ready to go on my cross-country flight. I was waiting for good enough weather to go, when Art Curry told me I should go that Saturday even if I didn't have a ceiling high enough to see too far, because he just had to have the plane for the spring semester's students. True to form, Saturday came and the ceiling was only about 2000 feet and very misty, but the plane was ready and waiting all gassed up for me, and Art said he really had to have me get that cross-country completed.

I received the aerial map with the route I was to take penciled in from Galesburg to Springfield and I donned the all winter flight suit, boots, and helmet all with the fleece lining. I made sure I had a sandwich and something to drink to take along with me on the flight, because it was going to be about a 250 mile dead reckoning flight.

In retrospect, I should have made my own course to fly over to Peoria first and then down to Springfield rather than trying to follow the penciled route that Art Curry had made for me. There were no railroad tracks on the penciled route and there were very few cities for me to use as checkpoints. The only highway was from Galesburg to Peoria going southeast, but that wasn't the route given me to follow. I was supposed to go direct from Galesburg to Springfield.

I set out and flew at about 1,000 feet all the way, because it was so misty and the overcast was so low. There was an occasional cloud even lower than the 1,000-foot level. My hour and 15 minutes went by, and I should have seen the glow from a large town, Springfield, where I would change course and head northeast to Bloomington. However, an hour and 20 minutes went by, 30 minutes, 40 minutes, and still no large town. I became very startled and began to circle in hopes that I could find that large town by myself, but had no luck.

By the time an hour and 50 minutes had ticked by, I just had to find out where I was. I started to look around for a place to land so I could ask questions or directions. No airport could be found and most of the fields had electric wires or were too small, or had something around them that kept me from landing in them. I picked one that looked long enough to land in although it was still covered with snow.

I still had not seen the large city so I kept looking but found nothing better. I could land into the wind on that larger field as it was the only one away from obstructions that looked large enough for me to land in. I started my approach and it still looked good, but as I felt the wheels touching down, I realized it was corn stubble under me. I was bouncing around sliding from one frozen corn row to another as the distance between the wheels of my plane were not matching the exact distance of the corn rows I was going along. The tail wheel kept bouncing over the stubble until I came to a full stop. Then I needed full power to get the front wheels out of that wind roll in order to taxi back to the house at the far end of the field where I would have to get anyway for takeoff.

As I taxied or bounced my way, there was a couple of times I thought I was almost going to nose up, but with a little boost of power from the engine the tail would recede back to the ground. By the time I was able to taxi back near the house, the farmer and his wife had donned their winter clothes and come out to give assistance.

I had no way of starting the plane again and was forced to let the engine idle when I climbed out of the cockpit. When they saw my sheep lined boots and winter flight suit with leather helmet and goggles, they must have thought I was a man from Mars, for they kind of shied away from me. That is until I was able to speak to them and ask what town we were near, as I was lost. It turned out the wind had drifted me quite a bit off course and Springfield was now some 40 miles northeast of where I was. I should have a second chance at seeing Springfield on my new course heading for Bloomfield.

I got back in the cockpit and taxied along the very edge of the field where the windrows weren't quite so pronounced, to a spot that looked like it would give me the longest possible run for takeoff. I got lined up to take off and then stepped on the brakes as I pushed the throttle forward to give me the most possible wind over the wings as the snow would make it more difficult to obtain enough speed for takeoff. Because the speeding engine gave me some wind going over the wings when I started my takeoff roll, it gave me several feet that would have been used up getting the engine up to speed. That extra runway would help me clear the 4-foot fence on the other side of the field.

I sat there for a couple minutes with full engine speed before I released the brakes and started my take off run down that bumpy

stubble row of corn stocks and I was on my way. I was able to clear
the fence without too much to spare but I was in the air and heading for Springfield which I found on my second attempt and set my
course to Bloomfield. I was able to follow the highway from
Springfield to Bloomfield and saw a couple small towns on the
way, so I knew I would have no trouble in finding the airport at
Bloomfield. I had to partially circle the field in order to get to the
runway facing into the wind. I landed without incident and taxied
up to the hangar to have the airport operator sign my flight plan to
prove I had been on the cross-county flight. My fuel supply was
almost at a critical point for making it all the way back to Galesburg
because of the additional miles and time I had flown trying to find
Springfield.

I asked the guy that signed my flight plan to sell me a few
gallons of gas, which he refused to do upon first request as he knew
he didn't have the equipment to get the WACO restarted again after
refueling. I had to practically beg that operator to give me just a
few gallons of gas. I guess it was a good thing he wouldn't pump
a whole dollars worth of gas, for when I reached into my pocket I
could find only 60 cents (college students never had much money
in those days). That would give me a total of only three gallons of
gas at 20 cents a gallon, but that should give me enough gas to get
me back to Galesburg without any problem.

It was a real fire hazard pumping gas with the engine still
running and the propeller still whirling around, but he climbed on
the wing and pumped the three gallons in without any problem as
the outside temperature was low enough that fumes from the gas
were hardly noticeable. After he climbed down from the wing he
must have felt sorry for me and got a bottle of coke to help wash
down my sandwich that I started to eat while he was up on the wing
(coke in those days was only five cents a bottle).

Other prices in those days were a glass of beer, five cents, or
an ice cream cone five cents. A big quarter pound hamburger or a
piece of 12 inch pie cut in six pieces was only 10 cents, and the
movie was only 15 cents. You could wine and dine your date on
less than a dollar bill even after taking her to a movie for an evening

out.

But to get back to my cross-county flight, I guess the operator could sense that I was getting a little nervous at having to buy extra gas and also being well over an hour late in leaving Bloomfield according to my flight plan. I guess he tried to settle my nerves a little bit, for it was probably obvious and his bottle of coke was a gracious thing to do. However, it did settle my nerves a little bit so I would not have to worry about running out of gas before getting back to Galesburg.

The only real problem was I began to worry that Art Curry would probably be calling the CAA to start a search for his missing plane. I was now nearly two hours late for my arrival back at Galesburg. I don't think Art ever learned about my landing in a cornfield, just my extra search for Springfield and a little longer on the ground at Bloomfield but my cross-country was finally finished. That left only my CAA ride with an inspector to obtain my commercial pilot's license.

Chapter Three

WINGS OF GOLD

June 1942 thru May 1943

Naval Aviation Cadet

The next weekend found more students of the flight program completing their syllabus, and Art Curry arranged for the CAA inspector to come to Galesburg for flight tests. We all passed and received our single-engine, land certificates for our commercial pilot's license. To celebrate, we all decided to go to Chicago and enlist in the Army Air Corps during the Easter vacation.

Most of the gang made it with no problems having passed all the exams including psychiatry, physical, math, general aviation requirements and aviation physical - except me. I was standing in front of the officer in charge of the recruitment station, when he said he couldn't accept the fact that I had been born for I didn't have a birth certificate, which was true. There were no birth certificates issued up in the boon docks of Saskatchewan, Canada when I was born and my name did not appear on my father's naturalization certificates. Therefore, my application was turned down, but all the others pilots of the group were sworn in and given orders to active duty. They were to report within ten days after the end of the Knox College semester.

The statement I had signed prior to acceptance in the CPT programs, was that we would enlist in either the Army or the Navy Air Corps. So, I contacted the Navy and learned they would have the same restrictions, but they would accept corrections if I could obtain them prior to my draft deferment expiration.

I got my father to write friends and former parishioners that had been members in his Wadena, Saskatchewan pastorate and Mom wrote her father, Dr. Ben Black, who was then chief medical examiner for the Maccabee insurance lodge in Detroit, Michigan. He wrote back with yes, he had made a special trip up to Wadena, Canada to be there for the birth of his grandson. Maybe for that fact and that he confirmed my birth as May 10, 1921 on his official Maccabee letterhead stationery made it a little easier for the Navy to accept the letter in lieu of an official birth certificate.

Once that had been accomplished, I now had to provide evidence of my citizenship. Dad had written the bureau of immigration and naturalization in their Chicago district office. It seemed like ages even though it probably took only a couple weeks waiting for an answer. When it finally came from Chicago, it said go back to the original court that had issued the original certificate, for any possible corrections needed.

Our family had moved from Eagle River to Edgerton, Wisconsin, and then to Brimfield, Illinois since Dad's certificate of citizenship had been issued. In packing for those moves, Dad had lost track of the actual document. He nervously searched for it, in his study with all the books and notes of his prior sermons and file cases and at first just couldn't find it. Everything was turned upside down and back and forth before the certificate was finally found. He sent it to me at Knox College and I had to forward it to the Navy recruiting station, but they informed me I had to have my name listed or written on that certificate to have some proof that I was actually a citizen.

A letter to the circuit court of Vilas county, Wisconsin with an explanation of what was needed proceeded. A signed certificate with my name actually listed on the certificate or a letter from a clerk of the court stating that she had known Rev. Hargreaves when he had received his citizenship and at that time had a young boy under the age of majority that should have been written on this certificate. The clerk acknowledged that it was her oversight for not having listed Carleton on the Reverend's certificate of citizenship, but her letter didn't arrive until Thursday afternoon of June 4th. On the fifth I called the Navy recruitment station and they told me to bring everything up Monday morning and I would have the week for all the exams to get enlisted into the Navy V5 flight program.

Monday morning, Dad drove me up to Galesburg so I could catch the CB&Q railroad train into Chicago. I arrived at the cadet selection board with my college transcript in hand, the letter from the clerk of courts and the letter from Dr. Black, which satisfied the Navy. Then they started me on all the exams: mental, physical, psychological, and general knowledge. When I finished all those it was late Thursday afternoon and I was told to come back on Friday for my physical exam. It included eyesight, hearing and the aviation heart Schneider test (a heart exertion test to see the length of time it takes for your heart to recover from physical activity to its normal reading).

The college record was to verify that I had at least the two years required of college classes. I passed all the physical exams without problem. Being 6 feet tall, I had no problem being within the Navy's height requirement of 5 foot 8 inches and 6 foot 2 inches for any fellow that was thinking of qualifying for Carrier flight, either as a fighter, dive bomber, or torpedo bomber pilot. It was explained to me that, unlike Army or Marine flying where you had your own plane and could park it next to the runway, on a carrier you take whatever plane is in the spot (flight position you are assigned) and ready to go, and it probably won't be yours, with the proper foot pedal adjustments or the height of the seat adjustment.

I had passed everything during that week of exams except the minimum weight requirement in comparison to your height in inches. I was three pounds lighter than the minimum allowed. The physical had taken all of Friday so the corpsman said he would leave the space for weight blank until I came back on Saturday morning to see if I would qualify by gaining those three pounds.

When I reported back on Saturday morning I had the luck of an Irishman. A little short medic corpsman that had given me my Schneider test pulled me over to the side and said he had never had as high a Schneider as I had and he hated to see me not get enlisted for pilot training because of a difference of three pounds. Therefore, he told me to stay along the side until after the Senior officers left for lunch and he would then weigh me with my clothes on and then expect me to gain at least four pounds over my lunch period and be back so he could weigh me before the senior medical officers arrived back from their lunch.

A visit to Woolworths 5 and 10 cents store produced four pounds of nails that I could scatter amongst various pockets so nothing bulged out. That and the bananas I had eaten provided the necessary weight requirement. At about 2 p.m. when the senior medical examining doctor came back, he signed my enlistment form and told me to wait for a few others to finish their exams and the yeoman would type my orders, I would be sworn in at 3 p.m.

We all raised our right hand and repeated after him our allegiance to the Flag and to the United States. I was then told to go back home and wait for my orders. He said he would see that my orders would send me direct to the elimination "E" base, because I already had a commercial pilot's license, rather than the usual reporting to the Iowa pre-flight school, but that I would still have to go through the entire Navy pilot training program.

I headed for the CB&Q railroad station again and headed back to Galesburg. Fortunately, I was now officially enlisted in the Navy and was told the Navy would take care of notifying my draft board. I would not have to report to the Peoria, Illinois military draft selection board and I would be excused from the next Monday morning requirement, which meant I would not have to be toting a gun during my service days.

The Wait for Flight School

The senior officer in command of the Chicago V5 aviation

enlistment center had told me it would be at least six weeks and more likely two months before I would receive orders direct to "E" base. That I should relax and go back to college if I wanted a few more college credits that summer.

I had often double dated with Roy Strubel during the college year at Knox. He was a biology major and lived in Galesburg and was able to drive himself to class with his family's second car, which he had available for our use in our double dating. After I got back from enlisting Roy talked me into taking a biology course, which he was already enrolled in for the summer. He was the only student and Professor Walten liked the idea of a second student (probably to increase his salary for that summer). It was a three credit course that was about to start and would be completed well within the two months I had before expecting orders from the Navy

Roy and I were having a great time with only two morning classes and one afternoon lab. We used a couple other afternoons for going swimming out at Lake Bracken, and had to study and complete our lab projects on the last afternoon. That left us free for taking our dates out every evening. We were able to see most of the movies that came to Galesburg. Of course the movies cost only 35 cents in those days, so 70 cents got our dates and us into the movie, and because Roy's girlfriend was still under 18 we could not go for a beer afterwards. So we usually splurged by taking the girls to Walgreens' ice cream bar to have the extra large sundaes that Walgreens put out in those days for a total charge of 15 cents each. That made the total cost for each evening's entertainment just a one dollar bill. How times have changed!

Three weeks of very enjoyable living came to a screaming halt when I received unexpected orders to report to the Naval Air Station, Glenview, Illinois, as they had one open billet in class 7-C, which would be starting on July 29, 1942. That left me with no option but to drop the biology course and forget the three credits I thought I would be earning that summer.

However, when I approached Prof. Walten, he suggested having a class every morning and scattering the labs every afternoon for the nine days left before I was to report to the Naval Air

Cadet Hargreaves visited his college friend Roy Strubel the summer of 1942

In September 1942 the author again visited Knox College.

In the fall of 1942 the author in another visit to Knox College. Here he and his friend Roy Struble are on the steps of the ladies' dorm waiting for their dates.

Station Glenview. He would see that we both got full credit for the course, if Roy would go along with it. Roy had no problems with the idea, and we would be taking the final exam on the morning I had to catch the 2 p.m. CB&Q train to the LaSalle Street railroad station in Chicago.

I arrived at the LaSalle Street station in Chicago and had to lug my suitcase to the street car heading for Union station in order to catch the Milwaukee Road train that would make a special unscheduled stop to let me off at Glenview. The conductor was quite obliging to see that I was left off at the dark little pillbox they called a station there in Glenview in those days.

There was no bus or streetcar, and no taxi to get me out to the Naval Air Station. I had to lug my suitcase a couple blocks to the nearest street and then another block to the cross streets that formed the four corners of Glenview. In those days there was only a very small number of residents in homes calling themselves Glenview. The four corners included a grocery store and a filling station on the first two corners and a tavern on the third corner, but I don't remember what was on the fourth corner.

The owner or bartender, when asked, said if I didn't want to walk, that the best way to get out to the naval base would be for me to call the station and see if they would send a car to pick me up. It was already about 11 o'clock and the midnight hour was fast approaching and I had been warned that I must check in by midnight on the 29th.

Navy requirements are that you check in before midnight on the date you had been ordered to report. Because it was already nearly 11 p.m., I didn't think I could walk the three miles to the Naval Air Station main gate lugging my suitcase. I found out the next day I should have just left it at home and brought only my toothbrush and a razor, for the Navy would be issuing everything else I would need and my suitcase would have to be shipped home.

I asked the bartender to see if any of his customers would drive me out to the base, but no one seemed to have a car. So the next five minutes was spent in trying to find the telephone number of the base. When I finally got the correct number and after several attempts, I heard the voice of the yeoman on duty. He was very reluctant to call the motor pool to request a car to pick me up. After several minutes of pleading he reluctantly said he hoped a car would be there shortly to pick me up.

When you are waiting for something to happen, it seemed like an eternity and especially since it was getting closer to that midnight hour when I should have been checked in. It was about five minutes to twelve when the car finally arrived. The driver was not in a very sociable mood for he had been soundly asleep and had to dress, wake up the officer in charge of the motor pool to get the keys to the gate enclosure to get the keys for the car to pick me up.

The midnight bells were already ringing as we drove up to the main gate, but after a short discussion with the century on duty he did clock me in at 23:59 which was my introduction to military time. He agreed that being one minute late to start my Navy career would not look so good on my records. Then he had to wake up a couple other people to find out where my billet would be and in which barracks. Needless to say, I had no trouble getting to sleep once I found my bunk.

Basic Training

Rise and shine came blasting through at 0600, with the comment you have five minutes to muster over on the drill field, which was just across the street. The Marine Sergeant introduced himself and then let it be known that we would be there every morning for a half-hour of calisthenics. He also let us know that after calisthenics we would have 25 minutes to shower, shave, and dress for another muster at 0700 to march to the mess hall.

The mess hall being the cafeteria where we would be eating our meals. At 0800 half of us would be marched to the ground school building, the other half would be marched down to the flightline, where we were introduced to our flight instructors. We were handed several books. One book had the flight rules for the Naval Air Station and a bunch of other books describing the air flight rules pertaining to takeoffs and landings at Glenview, and a book describing the Navy N3N, which was used by the Navy for basic training.

The N3N was very comparable to the Stearman the Army used for basic training. This book explained the construction of the N3N, its flight characteristics, the size of the engine, and had many good pictures of the plane. It had diagrams showing the various parts of the plane, the cockpit controls, and had detailed pictures of the instruments that we would have to know and the limitations that those instruments would indicate.

We spent the rest of the morning reading the books and trying to learn the operation of the N3N. I had already flown the WACO, which was very similar to this N3N, in my CPT course at Knox. It was a good review for me to compare the two planes and refresh my memory as to what the gauges and dials had to read and the capabilities of the plane. Most of the other fellows in that morning class had no idea what flight characteristics meant, as most of my classmates had never flown before.

After spending the morning studying, we were marched up to the mess hall at 1200. At 1300 we were marched over to the supply building for our new Navy clothes which would include flight gear, ground school books and supplies, and our own personal uniforms. The supply people, some of whom were civilians, tried their best to get us fitted correctly, but I soon learned Navy sizes were much different than civilian sizes.

My normal size seven shoe came to be a Navy size 5EEEEE clod hopper after trying on several boots that I floundered in. My dress shoes came to be size 6. We then headed for the clothing racks to get our work uniforms which seemed to fit pretty good and then to a corner of the building where the tailor measured us for our jumper uniforms. But while we were being measured for our whites, we seemed to get swamped with most of the other half of our class.

They had been ordered back for a refit of uniforms that they had been measured for during their morning session at supply. The word had come to supply from the base commander that our class would within a week be reclassified as aviation cadets rather than the seaman 2nd we had been classified as that morning, and he didn't want the expense of being charged two sets of uniforms.

So I had to go back to the tailor to be remeasured for my officers blue uniform instead of the seaman 2nd jumper. The tailor also measured me for my whites. We didn't have much time left that afternoon before the sergeant appeared to march us to our barracks to get washed up for dinner. The sergeant had quite a time trying to keep us in step back to the barracks because of the full load of clothing and flight gear we were hauling back to the barracks to store in our small lockers at the foot of our beds. He came back at 1750 to march us to the mess hall for dinner at 1800.

Our change of classification meant we would get in an increase in pay from the $62.50 per month as a seaman 2nd class to $75 per month as an aviation cadet. And as aviation cadets, we would be wearing officer uniforms instead of the enlisted uniforms and instead of the blue work clothes, we had to go back in and get the khaki work clothes of the officers.

The next morning started as usual with push-ups and the sergeant keeping track of each individual's total before our arms could no longer get us up as high as the sergeant required. Some of us tired rather quickly with the sergeant commenting he would not let us graduate from "E" base if we didn't show drastic improvement in the next three months.

After breakfast my group did not march to the flightline, which would have been our usual program but off to the dispenser for a complete physical with what seemed like a full quart of blood being drawn to be tested for everything under the sun primarily for infectious diseases.

Then without questioning as to how long since our last tetanus shot or even if we'd ever had one, it was just routine that we start down the line of corpsmen, each with a different needle to jab into our arms for the various and sundry inoculations that the Navy provided everyone. By evening time most of us could hardly move our arms. However, after lunch we were marched off to the ground school building where the instructors reviewed our boxes to make sure that we had everything we needed.

The Navy had learned that Morse code was the most difficult for the average Cadet to learn. All the dit-das, or the da-dits, and most certainly the da da da-dit dit dit-da da da that could possibly save our lives out in combat. It was the SOS signal that we could either tap out on the radio or use our hands to signal if in close enough proximity for someone else to read our open hand for the da and the clenched fist for the dit. It was an intensive session for a while before the buzzer rang for us to close the book and the Morse code instrument and head for the next class, which was navigation.

The navigation class started with a lecture on the importance of knowing exactly where we were and what heading we needed to get back to our carrier, which would usually be at least 80 to 100 miles away from the point from which we had been launched. There would be no visual aids out there in the wide expanse of the Pacific Ocean. There would be no cities, or railroad tracks, or highways to follow as guides, just the water. If we didn't know where we were going on paper at least, we could very easily be one of those that got lost landing in the great expanse of Pacific water instead of the carrier we had flown from.

Being able to navigate on paper would more than likely be our lifeline out in combat, for there were no ground reference points, just the vast expanse of ocean, and there's no difference except for the way the waves fall or the mist from the waves' blows. Just the blue water meeting the sky on the horizon.

There would be no mountains or valleys. No rivers or farmlands with crops growing in the fields that would generally have borders facing east and west. At night there would be no lights reflecting up from streetlights that would distinguish small towns from large cities. Day or night there would be no radio beams to guide pilots on cross-country flights, for out in combat it was radio silence. (Late in the war "ultra-high frequency" was invented so that each carrier could broadcast its ZBX codes to assist pilots whose navigation had not been accurate enough to get them directly back to their carrier.)

We soon learned that our "free time" after the evening meal until the 2200 (10 p.m.) lights-out buzzer sounded, had to be used for studying ground school books if we were to get passing grades during our projected 3 months at Glenview. All I needed was a little refresher on most of the subjects that I had learned back in CPT at Westminster and Knox Colleges. I spent most of my evenings studying code and navigation with an occasional look at Navy regulations, which gave me a chance to enjoy a movie over in the base theater once in a while.

The flight line was totally different and I was disgusted and bored. We sat through endless lectures in the ready room and wished they could expedite the demonstrations around the planes, showing all the functions of each control and the correct reading for each gage.

Finally Flight Lessons

The N3N used in primary training was almost an exact duplicate of the WACO UPF-7 I used during my CPT secondary course at Knox college. Although the N3N was manufactured by a different company, the instructor noticed my disdain for his words and acknowledged that I had a commercial pilot's license and two other cadets had private licenses but we were to shut up and learn the Navy way. The other 37 cadets had never been around the plane before and had to gain the knowledge of his instructions. Many of the 37 had enlisted for flight training only because they read about the Royal Air Force pilots having their pick of women that flocked around any man in uniform wearing a pilot's insignia.

We finally started flight lessons after nearly a month of book learning, and my instructor would be Lt. Wilcox. He started me off with a preflight inspection of the plane that the tires were okay and wouldn't blow out on the first landing, and the ailerons and elevators were free of the overnight restrictive devices placed to prevent their flopping up and down during any gust of wind, and that the plane captain had pulled the propeller through a couple times to dispel any oil that would have collected in the bottom cylinder during the time the engine had not been operated.

The lieutenant told me that if this had been my eighth or ninth hop he could have given me a "Clear for Solo," but the chief of training would not have approved on just one dual. So I was scheduled for a second hop the next morning, and I soon learned why. Instead of going out to the auxiliary field "half-day" the lieutenant told me to fly northwest. After about 12 to 13 miles I spotted a small civilian airport and was told to land, and taxi up to the hangar. I was more amazed when he started to climb out of the plane with the comment, let's get a cup of coffee.

There was a nicely decorated restaurant on the 2nd floor of the hangar with a full paneled wall of windows to view the entire runway. The very attractive waitress had already planted three cups of coffee and placed three sweet rolls on the table and as there was no other customers she pulled up a chair to sit between us making sure her skirt road high above her trim silk covered knees. It was evident she was the lieutenant's lady for the evenings and had been expecting us for this get together. After about 30 minutes of chitchat the lieutenant indicated that it was time to be heading back, and that he would see her later.

After two dual flights, the lieutenant thought the chief of training would go along with the "Safe for Solo" and I would have a different check pilot to decide the ready for Solo. The next morning the check pilot came out with Lt. Wilcox who introduced me to him. Then Lt. Wilcox headed back for the ready room.

The check pilot instructions were to go out far enough so I could gain altitude of at least 1000 feet to start my landings from and we would do a few bouncing landings. After my second landing, I started to push the throttle forward but it was pulled back. I then heard the check pilot say through the gosport for me to taxi him back to the hangar and he would let me go as the first of my class to solo. (The gosport is a tube held in front of the speaker's mouth and goes forward to the student's ear piece, which is the only way a student can hear what an instructor ever says.)

Aerobatic Training?

Later, Lt. Wilcox came into the cadets' ready room with a glass of water to toast my success of being the first in class to solo. My elation led to his further comment that he and a couple other instructors still had cadets from the class ahead of us that they could not clear for solo flight yet. He also said that I would technically be scheduled along with those cadets in class 7 B who had not yet passed the next phase of training, aerobatics.

One of the most important and one of the first lessons in the next phase of training was starting from an elevation of 1000 feet, chopping the throttle back to idle, and landing with all three wheels inside a 100-foot circle in the middle of the runway. Lt. Wilcox let me know we could do anything necessary to get both front wheels and the tail wheel inside that circle. We would have to do it eight out of ten tries before we could be passed on from Glenview and head for Corpus Christi for intermediate flight training.

If I misjudged the wind and was coming in short, I could hold off and then stall it in, and hope that the resultant hard landing would get me three in the circle. If I realized I was coming in high, I could slip and slide to lose altitude in a hurry or I could circle just a little wider and then make a sharp turn back into the circle. This whole phase of training was the Navy's way of getting us ready to control speed for future carrier landings.

I had already completed aerobatics training during the CPT course, but would have to demonstrate my ability for Lt. Wilcox. The maneuvers we were to successfully demonstrate were the loop, Immelmann, slow roll, and snap roll, which I was asked to perform without even a demonstration. My instructor must have been satisfied with my aerobatic proficiency because after doing the maneuvers I would hear through the Gosport, "Let's go have some coffee," and I knew that meant Sky Harbor. That very attractive blond waitress was always waiting to pour the coffee when she saw us landing.

I usually had three hops between duels and spent most of the time practicing the three-point landings and was able to get an "up" on both check rides with different pilots. I was now ready for night flying and needed to know exactly where each gauge and dial was located, for there was no cockpit lights in those N3Ns. Only the indicator arms with fluorescent paint could be distinguished in the dark and I had to know if that arm was reading normal or indicating trouble.

I especially had to know the needle-ball, airspeed, and altitude gauges. My depth perception had to change for night landings also, for I no longer had the runway with grass alongside as a guide. There were just the blue runway lights spaced about every 200 feet apart at the very edge of the runway, until I got down to the red light that indicated there wasn't much runway left.

Formation flying was the last phase of training at "E" base. Lt. Wilcox got me teamed with three other cadets from class 7 B and their instructor to show us the intricacies and hazards of flying close to other planes, and what we called a division of four planes. A division of four planes consisted of the lead plane and his wingman and the section leader and his wingman.

The lead pilot was to set the pace and was not to change throttle settings. If he wanted to speed up or slow down he would visually move his head forward or backward so his wingman could see the gesture. If he was going to turn, his head was to have been moved to the side he would be turning to. If his wingman was on his starboard (right) side the section leader should be on the port (left) side. If the division leader wanted to turn, his wingman could adjust his throttle to stay in position if he wanted to stay on the outside of the turn, or he could slide under the leader to the opposite side to keep from jockeying throttle and vice versa.

If I was on the inside of a turn, I could slide to the opposite side, without changing throttle settings. All these movements were necessary because the outside radius is longer than the inside radius, thus it was possible to slide from one side to the other without changing the throttle settings and stay with your division leader. With experience, you got used to the requirements of sliding from one side to the other without changing throttle settings and still be able to stay in formation without always jockeying your throttle. This made it easier and with less compensating moves for the third and fourth pilots to stay with the division leader.

The section leader could do the same, sliding under either inside or outside, but the poor tail-end Charlie, the section leader's wingman, was always adjusting his throttle to stay in position. We had a hop in each of the four positions, all with our instructors riding dual to make sure we did not get into mid-air collisions or let the wingman's propeller slice through the leader's tail or his wings. When we finally came to our check ride, the instructors stayed on the ground to visually grade us on our four passes over the field with each of the cadets in a different position in formation on each pass over the field. I guess we did pretty well, for each instructor gave us a thumbs up, ending our training syllabus for flights at the "E base" phase, at Naval Air Station, Glenview, Illinois.

Lt. Wilcox then contacted the ground school superintendent to see if he could speed up my class work now that I would not be going to the flight line any more with the rest of my class, which was still working on three-point landings in a hundred foot circle. Word trickling back from military sources about combat losses was not good. That, and the stress to speed up pilot training probably forced the ground school superintendent to allow me to attend morning as well as afternoon ground school. I was able to pass my code test that same afternoon.

Then I was able to concentrate on navigation, which would be the standard or usual search pattern looking for an enemy submarine or even an enemy fleet. It involved navigating from point option, the "longitude and latitude spot of takeoff," for a 350 mile flight out, a 50 mile cross leg, and return to the carrier that had probably moved some 80 to 100 miles during the normal four and a half hour search. I had to plot the carrier's movement in direction and speed and consider wind drift. Then I had to plot my own direction of given search, allowing for wind drift and speed and time spent on all three legs of the search and allowing for a potential attack on an enemy ship or a plane.

Corpus Christi

Three full days of concentrated navigation problems gave me a passing grade and produced my graduation from "E base," but the only diploma or even certificate of completion was a railroad ticket to Corpus Christi, Texas. It was a two-section ticket, one from Chicago to Houston, Texas, with a change of trains leaving for Corpus Christi. The bottom half of that ticket was for a train leaving the LaSalle Street station in Chicago that same evening at about 2300 hours (11pm) and provided a Pullman sleeper room for the overnight trip.

The afternoon had slipped away waiting for the yeoman to get the orders completed for my transfer from Glenview to Corpus Christi. Because of the short time left and because public transportation to downtown would not have given me enough time to catch the train, the Navy actually provided a car and driver to get me down to the station on time.

My transfer to Corpus Christi sure put a kye-bosch to my Saturday night and Sunday of liberty. My college roommate happened to live just seven miles south of the air station, in Park Ridge, and George Berquist would drive up to the Naval Air Station to provide transportation for us to the Tamoshanter Country Club, a prestigious club in the northwest Chicago area. We both enjoyed the dinner dance Saturday evenings, for there was usually several ladies also having dinner who enjoyed dancing as much as we did, if we didn't have a date. I was always welcome to stay at Berquist's on Saturday night. Then on Sunday we would go back to the Tamoshanter Club and enjoy breakfast, swimming and playing several sets of tennis along with the scrumptious meals.

George's father was somewhat of a political big-wig in Park Ridge, being its post office superintendent. As such, they were able to have a family membership at the club, which required them to spend a minimum dollar amount each month. Mr. Bergquist didn't mind a bit that we helped him reach that total tab requirement, for at least he was getting something for his money. George was a rather retiring introvert and had no steady girlfriend, so he often brought his brother Jim and his fiancé Betty, who would ask a couple of her friends to be dates for George and myself for those Saturday night dances. But when Betty's girl friends were not available, George and I would go to the club by ourselves for dinner and enjoy the atmosphere.

The overnight trip from Chicago was very pleasant but the trip from Houston on down to Corpus Christi was something else. There was no air conditioning on the train and the temperature was on the warm side, so many of the passengers opened the windows. No screens were on the windows and all the dust and even cinders from the track came up to enter the coach car. There was no dining car and, although the porter brought a variety of sandwiches for us to purchase, there was no coffee.

I was overjoyed when the train finally stopped at Corpus Christi on its way down to Brownsville, Texas, a distance of about 90 miles, which was right on the Mexican border. The Navy had a bus waiting to take all personnel getting off the train that was going out to the base. When we arrived it took a while to get checked in and a billet assigned for the night as the officer in charge had told me I was to be transferred out to an auxiliary field for intermediate flight training the next day. I ended up assigned a bunk in one of the four-man rooms for cadets that were now in the syllabus for instrument flight training, and was ordered to be back at cadet headquarters by 0800 for transfer out to Cudahay, an auxiliary field about 30 miles northwest.

The officer in charge of cadets at Cudahay field logged me in and assigned me to a room. It sure didn't take long for me to settle in the room and with a shower to wash off all the sweat and dirt from that train ride in order to get more comfortable before going to dinner and then a good night's sleep.

The officer in charge had given me a sheet of illustrated instructions, which included a picture of how I would have to have my closet arranged for unannounced inspections. Any deviation would be one demerit, and 25 demerits were cause to wash me out of the flight-training program. Our extra blanket and towels had to be folded a certain way and placed on the shelf in the closet as shown in the illustration. Our blue and white uniforms were to be hung a certain way, and our dress shoes and athletic shoes facing a certain way. Our beds had to be made each day so when the inspecting officer dropped a quarter from about fifteen inches above, it would bounce at least three inches high, and the beds had to be made under hospital bed folding requirements. Our study desk had to be made neat and orderly with no dust to be observed on the inspector's white gloves when tested.

Cudahay was considered an intermediate phase of flight training that would introduce us to heavier and more powerful airplanes. The SNV-1 and the OS2U-3 were more than twice the horsepower and weight of the yellow peril, the "N3N". I was at Cudahay for about three weeks, maybe a little more, before getting orders back to the main base for instrument flight training.

Radio Navigation

Our first day at the main base had us all at sick bay for the usual complete physical, which the Navy was notorious for. Every time we went aboard a new base, we were required to have a new physical. We were then allowed to go over to the link shack. There we were lectured and indoctrinated on the intricacies of orientation, and to radio navigation in order to get back to base from an unknown location. The instructions were actually not too many, but were all so vital when you are up in the soup and your gas supply is dwindling.

The first thing you would have to do is make sure that you knew the radio station that you were listening to and its call letters. Then from the aerial map you would find the direction and distance to the runway from that radio station's high and low cone, which is usually about two miles.

To orientate yourself, let's assume you're flying on a northerly course and the radio signals get stronger, then you're flying towards the station. But if the radio signals fade you should make a 180-degree turn and head for the station.

If you have been receiving the letter "N" (da-dit) in Morse code, you know you are in the south quadrant. Keep flying on a northerly compass heading and the letter da-dit gradually becomes a steady tone from the overlap of the letter "A" (dit-da). That steady tone is known as the "beam" and as the beam's steady tone fades to the "A" you make a 90-degree turn to the starboard. If you fly back to the steady tone, you know you have intersected the Southwest beam. If, after making that 90-degree turn you continue to receive the "A," you must make a 180-degree turn to get back to the Southeast beam.

As the steady tone is reached again, you then make a turn to the right and "bracket the beam." That is, if the steady tone fades to the "A," then turn left till you receive a strong steady beam again. If the steady beam fades to "N," then turn just a couple degrees to the right till you receive a strong steady beam.

Fly the beam towards the station until the beam is interrupted for a couple seconds, which indicates that you're directly over the broadcasting station. That is known as the high cone, and from there you immediately start your descent at a steady 500 feet per minute while continuing to bracket the beam, realizing the quadrants have to be opposite sides after crossing the high cone.

Then you have to calculate the time out on the beam from whatever altitude you are at so that your standard rate of let down at 500 feet per minute would take you down to 1000-foot altitude. After descending to 1000 feet, make a procedural turn of 180 degrees back to intersect the beam and hit the low cone staying on the same heading for the beam.

When you hear the cone of silence you have hit the low cone. After hearing the cone of silence, start a standard rate of decent of 500 feet per minute, which should have you lined up with the runway and about ready to make a visual landing in two minutes. You will have to allow for any drift due to known wind conditions. It is impossible to move the radio station around to have a headwind for all landings.

We started training in the LINK trainer after all the ground school lessons in theory were completed. The link is not an actual plane, but a facsimile of a cockpit with a hood covering so you can't see out, with hydraulic controls built in to give the pilot an actual sensory feeling of rough air or the change of gravity when making turns or changes of altitude. When the enclosing hood came down, you had the sense of being in fog so thick that you couldn't see 10 feet ahead of you.

All you have is the instruments and controls of a plane cockpit plus the on/off switch to get it all started. Wires and control cables from the link lead back to the operator's desk with a miniature instrument to track your flight patterns and every move. The control operator was usually a Navy Wave, who could start you in the middle of a quadrant with just an "A" or an "N", as you would get in an actual flight orientation. She could strengthen or weaken the radio sound from her control box as you oriented yourself. She could control the overlap of the "A" and the "N" to give you the beam and could keep you bracketing the beam as you would normally have to do in the air.

She could also start you at any given altitude, setting your altimeter the same as hers so she could monitor your descents from the high cone to the low cone, and on to the airport. She also had radio communication ability with you in the cockpit to give instructions, as the actual controller would from either a cross-country instrument control station or the control tower at the airport.

Those control stations might give you a mandatory command to change heading or altitude because there might be a plane that strayed from its given course or altitude. The plane could be ascending from takeoff or descending for a landing and is in your course of flight, which, if not corrected, might potentially be the cause a mid-air collision that you would not see until it was too late.

After each session in the link trainer, you normally checked in with the operator. She could show you the orientation sheet that you just finished, for she had tracked your total flight in the trainer. You could get her comments, good or bad, that would help you do better on your next flight in the trainer.

That scale model tracking instrument didn't let you get away with anything. After about ten days flying the link for practice, we started actual flight orientations in the SNJ-1 rigged with a hood that covered the student pilot so he would have no vision of the outside world. We always had an instructor in the front pilot seat. It was a strange feeling being in the air and under the hood, having to trust my needle-ball, airspeed, and altimeter instruments.

I had one hop in the SNJ and one in the link every day from then until December 25th when my instructors thought I was ready for my check ride. It looked like a beautiful day on the ground and none of us realized the upper air currents would be so rough. I took the first flight of the day and there had been no report of bad weather aloft. I had oriented and found the beam while bouncing around, but had trouble staying on the beam because of that rough air. I hit a horrible air pocket just as I should have heard the silence of the high cone. In trying to bracket the beam, I turned the wrong way and could not get back to the beam for the radio quadrants reversed after the cone.

Realizing I had actually passed the cone forced me to make a standard 180-degree turn to get back to the beam. Unfortunately, timing for my let down had been thrown off which would throw my timing for the procedural turn to head back to the low cone, which I also missed in the rough air. Ensign Shaeffer said he wished he could give me a Christmas present, but I had missed both cones due to the rough air. Although I had made correction attempts to rectify, I would have run out of gas before getting to the landing.

He did however, talk to the chief of flight training to cancel all hops for the rest of the day, and said he voided out my down because of the rough air. From then on an instructor was sent up each morning to verify good or bad air currents for student instrument training. It was December 30th before I could get my next check ride and Ensign Harshbarger was able to give me an up on instrument flying and radio procedures. I was given a slip to take back to cadet headquarters stating I could be transferred to an advanced squadron.

Advanced Fighter Training

The officer in charge of the cadet regiment at the Corpus Christi main base admitted to being caught with his pants down when I reported back to his office for reassignment. He had not expected to have anyone from class 10C until at least the middle of January, 1943 for he still had half of class 10B, which was ahead of me, waiting to pass the instruments flight squadron. He admitted to not having even cut orders for that lagging half of class 10B, so billets to their advance squadrons were not filled. Therefore I could make my request and he would cut orders that very day.

I had dreamed of being a fighter pilot and therefore made my request to the advanced fighter squadron out at Kingsville rather than to the torpedo, dive bomber, observations scout, "P boats," or cargo plane advance squadrons. He also gave me a sheet to fill out indicating my preference for a Navy career or Marine Corps duty as I would be measured for my officer uniforms before going to my advance squadron. He also let it be known that in the past, only cadets in the top 10 percent of their class could request Marine Corps duty, and then only if the Marine Corps approved of you and requested your application be sent to them.

However, he also indicated, that because the Marines were suffering rather heavy casualties, 90 percent of my class was to be drafted into the Marine Corps, whether they wanted the red stripes or not. He also handed me a little slip of paper for me to indicate what type of duty I would like. Whether it be duty in the Atlantic Ocean or the Pacific Ocean usually on carriers, so that was not really an option but the choice of duty would be, and he would do everything possible to see that we were chosen for the preference that we had given him.

At that time Navy fighter pilots would be flying from carriers, whereas the Marines generally were based on the islands, in hot, dusty airstrips, and they would have their own planes and a mechanic to keep them running in the best shape possible. But on the carrier, we would have the hangar deck mechanics taking care of planes for us and we would fly whatever plane would be in the spot for takeoff rather than flying our own plane.

I had always wanted to see my paternal relatives, for my father had come direct from England as a 20 year old to become a missionary preacher in the wild west of Canada. I thought maybe the Atlantic Fleet duty would give me a chance to get over to England and see some of my paternal relatives. So, I indicated my preference for Atlantic Ocean duty. After making all these career decisions I was to head for the tailor shop to be measured for my new uniforms, both the Navy dress blues and the white dress uniforms. After my stint in the tailor shop, I was to return to cadet regiment headquarters for my orders to Kingsville and then be ready at 0800 for the bus ride out to check in with the commanding officer for the advance fighter training squadron.

The bus had various items that Kingsville officers had wanted from main base, but I was the only cadet that reported in for the bus ride. The driver dropped me off right in front of the Kingsville cadet regiment office. I checked in with the officer in charge and was given a map of the base on which was indicated the building where I would find my room. I also received a sheet of instructions for my bunk number, desk and closet number with a picture of the way the closet should be arranged.

That arrangement was the same as it had been back at Cudahay. Periodic inspections, unannounced, would be made and the demerits would be issued if anything was not arranged according to the illustrations. I was then told to go find my room so I could get rid of my luggage, have lunch, and then report to sick bay for the usual required flight physical again on reporting to a new base. Everything came out okay, except the dentist found a couple cavities to fill.

All activities seemed to be closing for the day as I suppose the officers wanted to get home early to make preparations for the parties they would be attending to usher in the new year. However us cadets were left to fend for ourselves. There would be a station bus going to town every hour, so I thought I would go into town and find a restaurant to get away from the usual highly seasoned Navy food. I should be able to splurge on a fillet mignon, which was no more than a $1.25 in those days, to celebrate New Year's Eve in Kingsville, Texas.

I would be by myself, for I had not met any other cadet that I had previously known. I was well ahead of my Corpus Christi classmates and way, way ahead of my original Glenview class-mates. What a way to celebrate New Year's Eve, although I was still in hopes of finding a hotel or supper club that might have a dance floor for me to enjoy along with my steak and with someone interested in dancing.

The bus driver had told me he would let me off in front of the best restaurant in town. But I got very disappointed as he drove along the Main Street, for all I could see was old 1860 dirty, dingy bunch of stores. The restaurant looked about the same from the outside, although the fillet was excellent and well prepared. But no dance floor.

As I exited the restaurant, I learned what "Chine Cadet" meant. There was a number of kids, probably 8 or 9 years old, all with a shoe shine box on which you could rest your foot while they polished your shoes. "Chine Cadet, Chine Cadet, only a nickel." I had kept my shoes well shined for my dress shoes were part of the daily closet inspection, which included having shoes "spit-polished shined." However, when that one kid kept following me up the street, saying "Chine Cadet, chine Cadet, only a nickel" over and over, I finally relented and let him do his thing.

While my shoes were getting shined, I decided to get a drink in a bar that looked more attractive from the outside. It was already well populated, but awfully dingy and dirty. I did order a 5-cent schooner of beer, but could finish only half of it before the odor and smell got to me and I just had to leave. While waiting for the next bus back to the base, I was again accosted by the same kid shout-ing, "Chine Cadet, Chine Cadet only a nickel." This time I could tell him he just shined them. Back on the base, I went over to the cadet recreation building to while away my New Year's Eve, and played some pool with other cadets that were also lonesome for home, but were celebrating New Year's Eve the same way I was.

January 1, 1943 brought us weather that was so lousy it was probably a good thing, for many of the flight instructors looked half hung over New Year's Eve celebrations. Besides I had to study the pilots manual and handbook for the SNJ and the station flight regulations for the Naval Air Station, Kingsville.

The SNJ was a heavier and more powerful plane than any that we had flown yet in our training. The most important new control was the lever to pull the wheels up after takeoff, and of course down again before landing. But even with all the book learning and the instructors pounding into our heads to get those wheels down before landing, we still had several pilots landing wheels up. This caused that plane to be out of commission for a new propeller and engine change. The engine change was required because of the sudden engine stoppage, usually causing crank shaft damage.

The instrument flight gauges and controls were about the same as the planes I had been flying, but the gauges and dials indicating engine performance were somewhat different. After reading the complete handbook I went out to one of the SNJ's in the hangar and sat in the cockpit to memorize the location of all dials, gauges, and controls for the blindfold cockpit checkout I would be required to pass before being allowed to actually fly the plane.

Weather conditions remained poor for the next seven days, which grounded all flights because of the low ceilings, gusty winds, and intermittent showers and heavier rainstorms. After the fourth day of canceled flights, I was taken along with other cadets out to the trap shooting range and to the skeet shooting range the following day. This was to help us understand the need to lead our targets, which was a prelude to actually firing the 30 caliber guns that were mounted on the SNJ's.

At first it was just a single bird on the trap range, and then two birds on the skeet range. Even after we started flying, we had an occasional trip back to the skeet range, at least until our proficiency reached 90 out of 100 birds, which came from both houses at the same time. The term "bird" really alluded to the clay disks that were fired one from each of the opposing houses on the skeet range.

When the weather finally cleared, I had three hops, each with a different instructor showing me the capabilities of the SNJ and then testing my ability to land the plane safely. The fourth flight was with a check pilot who gave me a "safe for solo." I was then required to practice several landings on every hop, and when the sky was clear of clouds we could practice acrobatics in this much heavier plane, which was a lot different than doing the acrobatics back at an "E base" in the "yellow peril" (the N3N).

Occasionally, I was assigned to a plane with a hood over the second seat. Another cadet would act as safety pilot in the front cockpit while I had the hood on to keep proficient in instrument flight conditions. After about an hour of practicing under the hood, we would land and trade places so that I would be the safety pilot, and the cadet that had acted as my safety pilot would now be under the hood practicing his instrument flight.

By the end of the month, we were assigned to planes having a 30-caliber machine gun mounted and synchronized to fire through the propeller. We were grouped with six cadets in each flight and a seventh taking his turn at flying the target sleeve on the end of a 1,000-foot towline.

We were all given instructions on how to get the sleeve off the ground so that it wouldn't be dragged down the runway, which would usually caused a lot of damage to it. It could split or tear, and the cloth canvas that was sewed around the metal ring would be so weakened that it might even come off after it had dragged in the air for a couple hours. The tow plane was always the first one off, for the drag of the sleeve slowed the tow plane, and the other six could easily catch up on the way to the gunnery range in the Gulf of Mexico, where all shipping had been warned to stay clear.

The secret to getting a good sleeve in the air was to wait on the end of the runway till the towline was stretched out ahead of it and then attached to the plane. With the actual sleeve 1000 feet ahead of the plane on the runway, the tow pilot would apply full brakes and rev up the engine to full power. Once he has full power without the engine missing or sputtering he could release the brakes, and when he comes even with the sleeve, pop the flaps to give an extra boost for the plane getting airborne.

As soon as you actually feel yourself airborne you need to get the wheels up and then start climbing as fast as possible watching your airspeed indicator for safety sake. After you have reached an altitude of about 125 to 150 feet with your tow line immediately behind you, start a sudden dip back towards the runway. The rippling effect of your towline will pop that sleeve into the air a lot quicker so it does not drag along the runway. After you have reached about 600 feet in altitude you could then retract the flaps which would help give you a little more speed for gaining altitude.

The other instruction a tow plane pilot had to know was how to get the sleeve back to the field and drop it in the designated area. Although for safety sake one of the other pilots in your group was to fly alongside the sleeve as a warning to any other plane that might not see the long towline between the plane and the sleeve.

Gunnery hops ended with all six pilots eagerly waiting for the sleeve to be returned to the hangar from the designated drop area where they could count their hits. Each of the pilots knew the color of paint that his ammunition had been dipped in prior to the hop, and any bullet hitting the sleeve would leave a little rim of that paint in the canvas sleeve, which would be eagerly counted by the other pilots. Of course that towed sleeve was not the size of an actual plane, but you were still judged on the number of holes with your color paint on them indicating your aim had been pretty good, or if lousy, it had to get better before you could graduate.

Bad Food

Our evening meal on Jan. 27 included a portion of beef tongue, which was totally new to me. Never having had it before, I had no idea of what it should taste like, but my best taste buds were telling me it was lousy. However, other cadets around me seemed to be enjoying the tongue, and I tried a few more bites. It just did not entice me to this new selection of beef and I gave up, leaving a good portion of it on my plate.

Our ground school problem to be completed that night was most difficult and concentration for me on that navigation problem was made more difficult with my stomach pain getting worse by the minute. Although I went to bed when lights out sounded, I couldn't get to sleep as the pain just kept getting worse. It got so severe that I had to get up, got dressed, and headed for sick bay to see if the corpsman could give me some medications to relieve the pain.

There was already a number of cadets in sick bay, and the corpsman said he had called all the doctors to come out, for this was getting to be a real epidemic with more cadets reporting into sick bay by the minute. Several doctors finally arrived, questioned all us cadets and gave us something. I don't remember now what it was. That was in the days before antibiotics and all of us were suspended from flight duty while we spent the next three days in sick bay.

It turned out that the tongue we had been served had been improperly refrigerated, and the galley had not prepared them at a high enough temperature to eliminate the bacteria that had developed during storage or transportation.

When finally back on flight line duty we had instructors riding, along in the plane to demonstrate the intricacies of skip bombing as we never seemed to have high enough ceilings to dive bomb. The planes we were assigned had bomb racks installed and loaded with 100-pound water filled bombshells that were thin skinned and would splatter on impact. The bomb release button was on the control stick. We had to judge the bomb's trajectory based on the plane's speed at the time of release and the vertical drop to target. After passing the target we could look back and see how accurate we had been.

Weather was so poor during February and the first week of March that we felt like we were in seventh heaven when we would get a 5,000-foot ceiling. On those infrequent occasions when we did, it made a great day for us because our gunnery hops and instrument proficiency flights had to progress according to the training syllabus. We finished our required gunnery training hops with the tow plane and sleeve at or below 2,000 feet due to low ceilings.

Wrong Turn

We finally got down to the last required syllabus flight. It was a cross-country by dead reckoning rather than by instruments. Delmar Canady, my cadet roommate was to fly out and then I would fly back in the SNJ. The second plane was to be flown by Ralph Hilner and Louis Knight, my other two barracks roommates.

Our instructors briefed us to fly along the coast of the Gulf of Mexico from Corpus Christi, north to the river and then follow it right up to Austin, Texas. When we saw a big city, with the river making an almost 90 degree turn to the West, we would know it was Austin. The airport would be just a couple miles from that bend in the river and on the north side of the river.

The instructor gave us a couple gas chits for refueling so that the Navy would be charged for whatever gas we needed at that civilian airport. We would then change places from the front to the back and the back to the front so each of us would have experience in flying cross-country with reference only to the rivers and cities. He also told us that the civilian airport operator has had other planes from here land there, so he knows he can collect from the government for refueling the planes with those gas chits. We should have lunch in their restaurant and then fly back that afternoon.

Well, as a passenger, I had settled back to enjoy the scenery as Delmar was the pilot and had the aerial map that he was supposedly following. We did find a river, and followed it northwest and there was a city with the river making about a 90 degree turn to the west and sure enough, there was the airport about two miles west of that bend in the river. We received a green light from the airport tower, which cleared us for landing. We taxied in to the terminal area of the airport and an army guy from airport operations came running out yelling, "What the hell are you guys doing here!" which was the first indication that we were not at the Austin airport.

That sentry told us we had landed at the Waco Army Base

and that we were about 90 miles north of where we should have been, if we were supposed to be at Austin. We were taken almost as prisoners immediately to the base commander, who I could see was having quite a time stifling what could have been and outright laugh as he listened to Hilner's account of how we wound up at Waco rather than Austin.

The base commander was quite congenial and realized we were getting hungry by that time. He gave us a pass to go to his cadet chow hall for lunch while he would contact the Navy at Kingsville to see if they would authorize refueling us as our gas chits had been made out to the civilian field at Austin. We were to go back to his office after lunch to learn what his instructions from Kingsville would be for this unscheduled landing, for this was the first time anything like this had ever happened to him.

Delays and red tape used up most of the afternoon before our planes were refueled. Kingsville's instructions to the commander had specified we were not to make a night flight back. The commander turned out to be a real understanding Joe, for he asked if we would like to go into town for a real meal at a supper club rather than at his cadet mess hall. Waco Army Base was very similar to our Navy base with many planes there for their student flight lessons. They had all been in the air when we arrived, which gave us no indication of it being an Army base.

Of course we all wanted and chose the supper club deal, but had no transportation. So the base commander called his orderly

The author's pass to get back on base after dinner in town.

and gave him instructions to find us four bunks for the night, issue us gate passes to get off the base and back on later in the evening. He also got chits for our morning breakfast. Then he called the motor pool for a car and driver.

That driver turned out to be very knowledgeable as to the best 5-cent beers in town. He also knew the best restaurant, which was in a hotel and had a very pleasant sounding orchestra, but I don't remember now how many pieces it had. The dining room was quite well supported and was enjoyed by many of the Waco citizenry having a pleasant evening out.

We enjoyed dining and dancing with a couple girls that were at a table not far from ours. Our delicious dinner cost a total of $1.10 each plus the quarter tip. Wouldn't that be newsworthy at today's prices? Of course we did buy a few more beers during the evening while we were dancing with the girls that had moved over to our table after they had finished their meal. I am sure the driver enjoyed the evening off base also, as we had told him to be back for us by about 2330 (11:30 p.m.), so we could be back at the base before midnight.

We had to get up early in order to have breakfast in the cadet mess hall with all the Army cadets training there. After breakfast we went down to the flight line operations to make sure our flight plan from yesterday had been canceled out so that the CAA would not start a search plan for our planes that had not landed where they were supposed to have landed. Then we made out a new flight plan and filed it for today's return to Kingsville. I was flying the return trip with Delmar Canady in the rear cockpit. I had an easy time just following that river back down to the Gulf of Mexico and then following the shoreline back to Corpus Christi were I turned inland with a heading for Kingsville. I received a green light that cleared me for landing.

We had no more than touched down, and were still taxiing in when we heard on the radio, "Those two planes that just landed are to report to Lt. Woollen immediately." Lt. Woollen was the chief flight instructor. Upon entering Lt. Woollen's office, we noted that Lt. Heisel, the squadron's Executive Officer, was also sitting there.

He made a comment that he had heard all about our fowl up, and wanted to know our version of how in the hell we could have strayed off course by as much as a 100 miles and even landed at an Army air base if we hadn't been flathatting to have missed the correct river to follow up to Austin. To which Delmar stuttered and stammered, "The city from the air certainly looked like the city we were supposed to have landed at and it certainly was an exact duplicate."

Ralph Hilner, who was the pilot of the second plane, then pulled out his aerial map to show Lt. Heisel, who grudgingly said "But you missed the correct river." Hilner came back making the comment that if that was a river "...I'll be go to hell. I thought it was just a little stream emptying into the ocean."

After a few more comments back and forth, the Lieutenant turned to me and said why didn't you keep track of the flight. All I could say was "I had no map," and that I was just a passenger enjoying the scenery and was probably looking at a ship out in the gulf when we went by that first river. All I saw was the river we followed like we were told in the lecture. I saw the almost 90 degree bend in the river heading west, and the airfield was exactly where our instructor had said it would be, on the north side just after a couple miles from the bend as the river headed west.

I could see the lieutenants glancing at each other and then Lt. Heisel finally came out with "Well, for your goof, you each will be given 10 demerits," and I can still to this day see Ralph Hilner's jaw drop about two inches, with his southpaw left hand going to his forehead, saying "Sir, I'm out of the Navy!" Lt. Heisel's comment "Why cadet?" To which Hilner reluctantly replied that he already had 19 demerits. I was still standing in a position to see Lt. Heisel finger running up and down the list of demerits to be given for certain violations on that sheet of paper resting on his desk.

The look and glances between the two lieutenants was amazing, as if to say, they have to be punished with something for their "goof." But the lieutenants' glances also told us that as bad as the Navy needed pilots it would be a shame to wash out a student that had "goofed" on his last flight of his entire cadet training program.

Both of their index fingers kept searching up and down that list of demerits again and again. Pausing once or twice with a nod to the other. Then they went back to the list with another nod of yes or no to the other before Lt. Heisel finally came up with a question for Hilner, "Can you handle two demerits and five hours to march off on the ramp?" Hilner glanced at each of us for our approval. None of us had to worry about the 2 demerits, and would have preferred 10 demerits to toting a gun for five hours on the ramp. Each of us gave our approval and finally said yes, which meant our buddy would not be washed out, could get his commission as an Ensign, and would wear the Navy wings of gold along with us.

Graduation

Those five hours to be marched off on the ramp could be marched only at two hours per day according to Navy regulations, and prevented us from going back to the main base that week for graduation ceremonies. So for the next three days we had to go to the base brig to check out a rifle and march for two hours on the well-trodden marching pad with a rifle on our shoulders. After we'd finished our marching requirement we had two days with nothing to do but play some pool and have a good time going to town for dinners. At least we weren't having to eat Navy chow all the time.

A bus from main base arrived on Wednesday March 15th, bringing more cadets to start their fighter training, and we were to ride back on it to main base. When we arrived at main base we checked in with the officer in charge of cadets who assigned us to our rooms and told us to get over to the tailor shop immediately to try on our new uniforms. The dress blues, whites and the green winter work uniform would cost us $150.

We could write a check for them or have it deducted from our next month's pay for we would now be earning $150 per month plus 50 percent more for flight pay. So the next month's net pay would still give me the same $75 I had received as a cadet. The uniforms fit perfectly and we hauled them back to the barracks. We were then told to report to the drill field at 1600 to practice, so we would "look smart" on Friday when we marched in to receive our graduation diploma and commission as an Ensign.

Marine drill sergeants were there also on Thursday morning and afternoon when the ranks had swelled to probably about 100 cadets coming in from the different advance training squadrons to get their wings of gold at the usual Friday morning ceremonies. The weather had done an about-face from the overcast skies we had had when we were flying treacherous gunnery hops with the tow plane at only 1200 to 1500 feet due to low ceilings. Now we enjoyed a beautiful sky with work crews hard at work and busier than a bee erecting the podium platform and bleachers for the families, parents, and sweethearts that would be attending the Friday morning ceremonies.

Anticipation was so great that Friday morning that I could hardly eat my breakfast, but we had to get dressed and be on the drill field by 0900. We were to be opposite the reviewing stand in full dress blue uniforms that would now have a half-inch gold braid around both sleeves, which at first seemed rather loud and distracting every time I moved either arm.

The Marine sergeants had a list of cadets to graduate and separated the Marine's and the Navy cadets. They also lined us up in alphabetical order so that we would be in the same order that LtCol. Mangrum would be announcing our names as we walked across the podium platform to receive our diplomas. We therefore would be in proper order, and should receive our own diploma when crossing the platform.

Col. Mangrum was the officer in charge of Corpus Christi cadet regiment, and other dignitaries including Capt. Owen, commanding officer of the Naval Air Station, Rear Admiral Alfred Montgomery, Commandant, U.S. Naval Air Training Center, and his Chief of Staff and Superintendent of Aviation Training, Commander George Van Deurs. Each of the dignitaries would give a short congratulatory speech.

One of them pointed out that members of this graduating

class were the cream of the crop, having survived all the rigors of training where at least one-third of the original members that had started failed along the way. They had been washed out of flight training for any number of reasons, which included improper depth perception and unable to land a plane properly, or inability to follow Navy regulations, or disregarding orders, or just lack of inter-

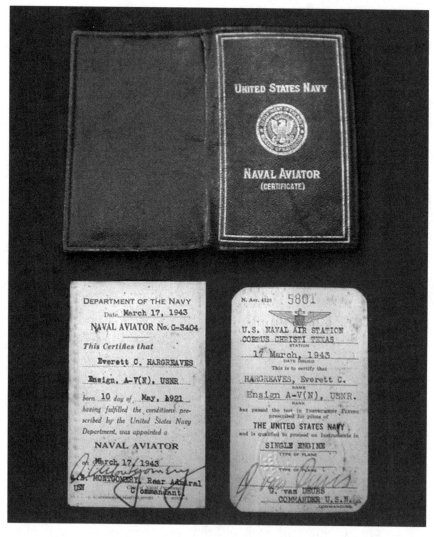

The fruits of his labors - the coveted Naval Aviator's Certificate.

Naval Air Training Center

United States Naval Air Station

Corpus Christi, Texas

Know all men by these presents that

Ensign Everett C. Hargreaves, A-V(N), USNR

*has completed the prescribed course of training and
having met successfully the requirements of the
course has been designated a*

Naval Aviator

*In Witness Whereof, this certificate has been signed
on this 17th day of March 1943 and the Seal of
the Naval Air Station hereunto affixed*

Rear Admiral, U. S. Navy
Commandant

Commander, U. S. Navy
Superintendent of Aviation Training

est in becoming a pilot. Or, they had been killed in one of the frequent accidents.

 We were now eligible to eat in the officers' mess or at the officers' club, and that new opportunity filled the mess hall in a hurry, for by that time it was getting to be a long time since breakfast. Although many of the new Ensigns, along with their fiancees and families, headed for the chapel. Their cadet days were now over and they had fulfilled the Navy requirement of restriction against marriage during cadet training days. Now that they were no longer cadets, they could take the trip to the altar.

 Lunch consumed, we reported back to cadet headquarters for orders, and again we were handed a slip to indicate whether we wanted Atlantic or Pacific duty. Louis, Dewy, Hewy, and myself had finished Kingsville together, and we were now joined by John Heyer who had a Boston accent. He had finished training at Kingsville while we were marching off our penalty for landing at Waco instead of Austin.

 We all received orders to proceed to Miami Opa Locka Naval Air Station for operational training. Our train tickets were attached, and we would leave on the morning train from Corpus Christi with a change at New Orleans and again at Jacksonville, Florida. With our proceed orders we would have three days more than needed just for travel time. We were free to go, so we hopped on the Navy bus going into town, and registered for rooms at the Driscol hotel there on the high side of the cliff overlooking the bay in downtown Corpus Christi.

New Orleans

 After arriving in New Orleans, it was quite a relief to shower off all of the dust, dirt and even cinders from the train ride from Corpus Christi. The Roosevelt hotel had reserved a room with five beds, which Heyer and Dewy did not really want, but were forced to accept because the hotel room clerk said they had no other rooms and they didn't know any other hotel that would have rooms on a

Saturday night.

Many people were still kind of celebrating the end of Mardi Gras. We found out later that the hotel had not really reserved the room. It had been the only one not sold out for the night, and they were just pleased that there was five of us to accept the room. After the shower we dressed putting on our new dress blues for dinner, and headed for the recommended Arnouts restaurant. But when we heard music coming from the hotel's dining room, we decided to eat there and enjoy the big band selections.

It was a large band with probably some 15 or more pieces, and we were doubly intrigued when we saw the dance floor just in front of the bandstand. We ordered, and had finished probably half of our dinner when we were totally amazed with a round of drinks arriving, which we had not ordered. The waiter nodded his head indicating they had come from a nearby table occupied by four very beautiful young ladies who were "just out for the evening" and were just showing their appreciation to actual officers with wings of gold. All they ever saw were cadets, without wings still struggling to complete their "E base" requirements at the US Navy elementary flight field just the other side of Lake Ponchartrain.

Three of the girls worked out at the base and were quite impressed that we had earned our wings of gold. They knew the rigorous effort we had accomplished, based on what they saw the cadets go through every day just trying to learn to fly even at the elementary level.

The two gals that had been most aggressive, had come over to our table to chitchat and had more or less been talking to Louie and Dewy. They suggested that Heyer and Howie move over to their table and talk to the other two girls, as they had finished eating, for it would be more difficult to move all our food over to their table.

I have always been a rather slow eater, but during the time it took to finish my meal, we had exchanged several dances with one or both of the girls on almost every piece the band played. When I finally finished my meal, one of the gals suggested they show us the French Quarters, for it was just a couple blocks away and they could show us how we could still get drinks after the 2:00 a.m. curfew. Many of the decorations for Mardi Gras still hung and were joyously pointed out, for some of them were rather ridiculous. City work crews had not had time enough to take them down as yet.

After having a drink in several bars, one of the gals had a favorite bar she wanted to show us. It was quaint and not very well lit, just like the old-fashioned saloons from the gay '90s, complete with spittoons and a very large mirrored back bar with big round pillars on both ends of the mirror.

At 2:00 a.m. all lights in the barroom were extinguished, the front door locked, and blinds that had been drawn over the front windows were raised. This allowed light from the street lamp just outside on the narrow sidewalk to shine in and would appear to any policeman making his rounds that the bar was dark and empty.

Most of the customers drank up and left, but the gals told us to drink slowly. About 2:20 a door that had been well concealed in the decorations at the rear of the room was opened for us to move to the back room, which was probably well-known by many customers, but "illegal." After a couple more drinks in that back room, we had to exit through a side door into a court, entered the back door of a house next door, and walked through yet another room and out the front door. We hailed a taxi and all piled in to escort the girls back to their apartment, and the four fellows made a date with the four girls for the next evening, with the comment that the girls would see if they could find a fifth gal for me.

The next day was spent visiting a Museum and several historic spots in the New Orleans area, except Heyer hadn't felt too good and elected to stay in the hotel so he could rest up. But before the next afternoon ended, Dewy suggested we hit a drug store and get prepared for a night to remember, he hoped. We were to meet the gals at a family restaurant out on Elm Street, as I recall. We were to take the trolley line to about 50th Street, and look for the restaurant on the left-hand corner.

The place was famous for its Cajun fish, and my catfish prepared Cajun style certainly was a delicacy. The gals had said they would meet as there, and they already had two tables reserved and waiting for us. The gal that had more or less hooked on to Heyer the previous evening was rather disappointed that he was not feeling well and would not be there this evening. So she settled for me as I had been more or less the fifth wheel the night before without a fifth girl for me to escort.

We did, however, have a very enjoyable evening that may have been somewhat extended because of my habit of slow eating. They all had an extra round of drinks while I finished enjoying my Cajun catfish, which I had never had before. After another round of drinks, all agreed it was time to catch the trolley back downtown. After a couple more nightspots, none of them objected to going straight to the hotel. Once my date, that I had wined and dined all evening long, saw Heyer still in bed groaning, she let out a whoop, "There's my Boston accent!" and crawled into bed with him. The others all crawled in beds leaving me as the fifth wheel, still the timid little innocent preacher's boy.

On to Florida

We had to get up early for the girls to get to work on time, and us boys to catch the train heading to Jacksonville, Florida. There was just one big problem, nine of us having turns in the one bathroom. The problem was solved though, when the girls let the boys in first as the train would not wait for us and their timing was not that critical. We said our goodbyes after getting telephone numbers for future reference, checked out of the hotel, stopped at a liquor store to replace the booze we had consumed while in New Orleans, and made the station with just a few minutes to spare.

We had reserved a stateroom primarily to secure our luggage without having to watch it every minute, but also to have a snort when we wanted. When the conductor came in to get our tickets and noticed the bottle, he seemed more interested in having a drink with us than in collecting our tickets. The train was a real "milk run" with frequent stops to pick up new passengers or discharge those that had reached their destinations.

  That conductor was back in our stateroom very shortly after every stop, and taking two or three sips to each one of ours. He must have been a well practiced drinker for he was always able to stagger out to place a step stool in about the right position to assist passengers alighting or stepping up to that high first step of the coach. He even knew of a little town where the depot was on the Main Street and just across the street from a liquor store. He also knew enough to hold the train for us to run across the street to get replenishments before he reached his turn around station to head back west. We often wondered if he was sober enough to have caught his return train heading back to New Orleans.

  The last half of the trip to Jacksonville was at a much slower pace and we were able to go to the dining car for lunch. The afternoon, varied somewhat with fewer passengers in the coach, we could go out there and sit and look out to enjoy the scenery much more so than in that really crowded stateroom that we had. Of course, whenever you wanted a short snort you had to go back to the stateroom.

  It was only a short distance between train stations at Jacksonville, and then as we caught the late afternoon train heading south it would be my first experience at trying to sleep in a Pullman sleeper, which the Navy had provided for us on that all-night trip down to Miami. At first, it was rather distracting. But as I got used to the tick-tick, tick-tick of the sleeper's wheels crossing the butting rails of the track bed, I found myself finally more or less lulled to sleep. After a good night's sleep we finally enjoyed breakfast in the dining car before arriving in Miami.

  The Navy had a bus waiting for us at the Miami train station to haul us bag and baggage out to the Opa Locka Naval Base. After checking in and getting our room assignments at BOQ, we headed for the dispensary for the usual new base flight physical. After completing the physicals we headed for the flight line to meet our new instructors, who shortly thereafter gave us two new handbooks to study. One was for the Brewster Buffalo, the (F2A) and then a book explaining all the signals we would have to know for carrier landings that the landing signal officer (LSO) would be giving us

LSO Signals

Roger - doing okay. Continue as you are for now.

Too Fast - move throttle back a tad but continue otherwise as you are, and watch LSO for him to bring his arm back up to the Roger position.

Too High - bring throttle back a tad and drop the nose until LSO brings his arms back to the Roger position when you should add just a little throttle again.

ROGER

Too Low - add a little throttle until LSO brings his arms back up to the Roger position. Then take a little throttle off again.

Too Slow - you have to add some throttle for you are approaching a stall. When you see the LSO do what a swimmer would call a breast stroke, that is, bringing the paddles to his chest and extending his arms with the paddles straight out and swing them out to the Roger position, and repeat the maneuver again and again depending on the urgency, until he keeps the Roger

Too Fast

Too High

Too Low

position when you might have to take a little power off again.

Get Out of Your Turn - Line Up With The Deck - When you have made a rather sharp turn into the carrier, the LSO knows your ability to land safely. He might even give you a boost with his right foot in giving you a Cut rather than a Wave-off.

TOO SLOW

The Cut - When the LSO thinks he has done all he can to help you get aboard safely, he will from the Roger position move his right arm to his left and pull the paddle across his face. Your response is to pull throttle back to idle, drop your nose, and then pull back on the stick for the tail hook to do its job in picking up a landing wire.

Get Out of Turn
Line Up With Deck

The CUT

WAVE OFF

The Wave Off - add full power immediately, hit the switch to pull the nose up, veer left while gaining speed and altitude to start the whole procedure over again.

in his effort to help us get aboard a carrier. The book also explained the procedures for individual carrier landings and the procedures for four or more planes or a division to break up and make the carrier landings. Also the speeds that we would have to get our planes to, in order to make the landings.

The Brewster Buffalo had been the Navy's first line combat plane just a few years back, although more recently the Grumman Wildcat had replaced it. It was again a step up in horsepower and plane weight, and we now had four 50 caliber guns, which I found to be at the Nth degree of my reach in order to get them charged or safetied. We now had to hand grind the wheels down or up, and that was something else.

The handbook for carrier landings made a lot of sense, for the LSO signals were really quite reasonable and understandable.

The sooner we learned to adjust throttle and plane attitude, the better, for we started field carrier landing practice within two weeks after arriving at Opa Locka. The practice runway was a Navy built up strip out in the middle of the Everglades. I don't know where all the dirt came from to build up that strip some 2000 feet long and probably 80 feet wide, and an extra extension in width for the LSO to park his plane while he was working with us novices. The dirt runway had no cement or blacktop and was kind of dusty, although it had a metal mesh screen to keep the plane's tires from sinking into the dirt too much.

I later learned when I got out in actual combat that the Seabees could use a bulldozer to level the sand and then locked together those metal strips for supply planes to land with supplies even when our Marines were fighting less than a mile away.

I was allowed to fly the Buffalo after proving to the instructor than I could reach blindfolded all the controls without hesitation, and recite minimums and maximums for all the instruments and point to their approximate location. Once that was accomplished we started gunnery practice in a restricted area for shipping out in the Atlantic Ocean. The area was such that when we saw Bermuda about five miles ahead of us, the tow plane had to turn back and head for the Florida coast, and we could make firing runs on the sleeves until he got to about 10 miles from the coast.

Then it was like back in cadet days, when we anxiously waited for the sleeves to be returned to the hangar so we could count our holes from the color of the ammunition that we had used to fire on the sleeve that day. Once a week we still had to get under the hood of an SNJ to maintain our proficiency in instrument flying. After an hour and a half or so we were to land and switch with our buddy that had served as a lookout pilot when we were under the hood, and then he would take over flying under the hood.

It was not all work there at Opa Locka, for we had the base theater for evening movies that were the latest releases from Hollywood, and occasionally had big name performers that would have a one night stand there in the theater. One such entertainment was the good old Victor Borge who had us rolling in the aisles with his masterful performance of jokes and diddling on the piano.

However the next morning when I was on the flight line but close enough to see him preparing to leave for his next assignment, I thought he proved to be the most conceited person I had ever known. He stood there only five feet from the operations door and demanded that the plane be brought over to him so he would have only a very short walk to get on board. His baggage had already been placed in the plane but he would not budge until the plane had been started and taxied over for him. He would have had only to walk probably about 120 feet in the first place, and still had some 35 to 40 feet to walk to the plane when it was moved closer.

After watching Victor Borge's performance that morning, we were scheduled for our first carrier landing practice, so we headed for the carrier, which had been nicknamed "The Ship," out in the middle of the everglades. The LSO became our instructor to refresh our memories of all instructions needed for going aboard the carrier that would generally be heading into the wind, although not necessarily there on "the ship" in the Everglades, which could not be swung around each time the wind would change.

We were to go well ahead of the carrier, dip the right wing, which would indicate to your wing man who should be in a right-handed echelon by that time that you were breaking off to start your carrier landing approach, and he would do the same a few seconds later. The 90 degree turn to the left would be the initial leg of the approach. You would then hit the "wheels down" lever, although in the Buffalo you had to start cranking furiously to get the wheels down and locked. Then the switch for flaps was activated and with both wheels and flaps down your speed becomes controllable before making the second 90-degree turn to downwind and parallel the carrier's course.

You should then be at about 700 feet altitude when the second turn is completed, and by that time you should be opposite the carrier's midship section for a normal landing and at about 100 foot altitude. Then you would start your third 90-degree turn for the crosswind leg into the final turn for the actual landing. When you start your final turn you should be at about 80 foot altitude and 72 MPH and "hanging on the prop." At that point you have only a difference of about 4-MPH between flying and stalling. But you must be down to about that speed when you pick up your LSO, otherwise he will indicate you are too fast, which means too fast for the landing wires on the carrier.

For field carrier landings you should be down to about 20 feet altitude, which means you will be barely above the shrubs and underbrush of the Everglades. At that point you should be watching the landing signal officer for any signal he would give you to help get you in position for a "Cut." When you receive the cut signal you would immediately pull the throttle back to the idle stop position and then it is up to you to line yourself up with the runway and land the plane. The other signal he could give you instead of the "Cut" is a "Wave-off," which he would give you if he doesn't think you are in proper position for a landing. You would then jam the throttle forward for full power to regain regular flight speed as quickly as possible as you would have been only 4-MPH above stall while making your final approach to the carrier. You are then to jog to the left while gaining speed and altitude to start the whole procedure all over again after you have reached at least a 1000-foot of altitude.

Carrier Qualification

My birthday present on May 10 was the LSO's certification that my field carrier landings had been very acceptable, and I was ready for actual carrier qualification. I expected to go to Norfolk, Virginia and check out on the *USS Ranger*, but my orders came through for Chicago, N.A.S. Glenview to check out on the *USS Wolverine*, a converted Great Lakes passenger vessel now with a 550 foot flight deck, used for "green pilots" making their first carrier landings.

After a two-day Pullman berth train ride, I arrived to see a totally different air station from what I had left just six months previously. There was a brand new mile long runway and many more buildings, including a new BOQ (bachelor officers quarters) for all us transient pilots waiting our turn to qualify on our carrier qualifications.

The weather finally cleared on May 28, after nearly two weeks of foul weather when none of us got permission to fly out to the *Wolverine* in Lake Michigan for our carrier check out. Since our last two hops at Opa Locka in Miami had been in the Brewster Buffalo and Glenview had no Buffalos, we would have to go back to the SNJ for our carrier checkouts.

We needed a practice hop anyway because of the length of time since our last flights at Opa Locka and because we needed to refamiliarize ourselves with the SNJ. The weather stayed nice for the 29th, and I finally was scheduled for my carrier landing check out. However, with all the delays they now had the *USS Sable*, and I would be one of the first to check out on the new ship, which was the second carrier to operate from Navy Pier in Chicago.

You can't imagine the thoughts that go through your head when you are finally on the way out to find a carrier somewhere in Lake Michigan. All the way out, I was remembering the comments that so many Navy people had made, "Every carrier landing is considered a potential crash" and I wondered what it was going to be like to make that first landing.

The Navy had considered me qualified, or they wouldn't have scheduled me for check out. But, even though I felt elated to be on my way, the apprehension builds, not knowing what it really will be like on that first landing. I had learned all the LSO signals, and had completed all the field carrier stints, but that was on a stationary runway. This would be on a moving ship, so that my reference points to observe were different. Where I start my initial turn will have to be moved back and where I start my final turn to the carrier where I would pick up the LSO certainly has to be altered.

The instructors had told me I should have sufficient wind over the deck to make the landing and then add throttle for a "bounce hop" just like we did on the field carrier landings. However, the Sable is only 483 long as compared to the 3000-foot runway that we used at Opa Locka to practice our carrier landings. I also had to be lined up perfectly as the flight deck was only 58 feet wide, not like the usual 120 foot wide runways where we practiced our field carrier landings. The wider runways back on the practice field had given us a little leeway, which was now gone.

When I finally spotted the carrier I had to get down to 1000 foot of altitude and pass just to the starboard of the carrier in the same direction the carrier was headed into the wind with my tail hook down. Then I was to go for 10 seconds to get ahead of the carrier before making my initial turn to the port. After making that turn, I had to throttle back, get my wheels down, then the flaps, and descend to 500 feet while making the cross wind leg before starting the second 90 degree turn for the downwind leg. I would continue my descent down to 100 foot altitude and then as instructed, I would start my third 90-degree turn to port when I came perpendicular to the bow of the carrier for the final cross-wind leg.

The carrier would be moving forward while I was on my final cross-wind leg and would place me in the right position for final approach to the carrier. While on the final cross-wind leg my airspeed should be down to roughly 75 knots and I would continue descending on down to about 65 foot altitude, with the gas mixture moved to full rich and the throttle gently forwarded so the plane is virtually "hanging on the prop" to control my airspeed at 72 knots in a plane that stalls out at 68 knots. I would then pick up the LSO at approximately 45 degrees from the carrier and start my final turn to the carrier. My thoughts were all over the place and I wanted to put on a good performance once I picked up the LSO. From that point on to the actual landing, I would have to trust the LSO and follow his signals exactly for a "perfect landing."

Once I had picked up the LSO, I forgot all the anxiety of making that first landing, for my first observation of the LSO was with his arms extended with the paddles being straight out. That meant it was a Roger, and I was doing exactly right. But as I got a little closer on final his right arm dropped to a 45 degree angle, meaning I was a little fast and would have to ease back on the throttle. I did not feel very comfortable doing that, but I was anxious to do what the LSO required as the LSOs really know their business. They can tell if you're at 74 knots or down to the recommended 72 knots.

Within a couple seconds his right arm gradually lifted back to the Roger position again. Then all of a sudden he threw his whole body ahead to the left with the left arm down, and his right arm raised way up and then with a circular motion his right arm came back across his face and down. That meant I had received a Cut. At that point I was to chop throttle completely off and look up the deck and make my final adjustments, because I was on my own now. I had to be heading straight up the deck, for as I found out, you really get jerked around if you are not in the center of the deck when the tail hook engages the landing wire.

The landing wire tends to pull your tail hook straight to the center of the deck from whatever position you are in. The landing wire is pulled out, slowing you to a stop within the distance of about 100 feet and your body is thrown forward against your shoulder harness, which keeps your head from hitting the gun sight. I was sure glad I had remembered to lock that shoulder harness when I was on the downwind leg of my landing.

I've never been in an auto accident but I can imagine the sensation is very similar to hitting an object with your car and your head going to the windshield. You do come to a rather sudden stop when landing on a carrier and you would have quite a headache or brain concussion if it weren't for the shoulder straps.

The force of the wind over the carrier's deck tends to roll the plane back after landing, just enough for the carrier deck hands to come out from the side catwalk of the carrier and disengage the tail hook from the landing wire. A third deck hand comes out in front of you he is in a yellow shirt that indicates he is a taxi director. His hand with the first finger extended and his whole arm is then extended pointing forward to the next yellow shirt who would indicate where I should taxi or park. When he clenches his fists it indicates I should stop, which would be forward of the barriers that had been dropped or lowered in order for me to taxi forward over them. He then came around the end of the wing and hopped up on the wing to ask me to unbuckle myself, get out of the plane and go down to the officers mess for lunch. I had had an early breakfast in order to arrive at the flightline early, so as to be the first to go for the carrier check-out that morning.

It was the first time I had ever been aboard a Navy ship and had to have a flight deck officer lead the way showing me where the officer's mess would be. We went down a couple flights of steps, ladders, as the Navy calls them, to the hanger deck and then another flight down to the level below the hanger deck. It was lunch time, that is early lunch time, for there were several other officers eating early so they could relieve the other part of the crew for their lunch. We went to the serving counter, selected our food and the plate was given to us to take back to the white linen cloth covered tables that had our set up utensils already in place. Before I finished lunch another pilot that had just completed his first carrier landing also joined me.

I found my way back up to the flight deck after I finished eating, and the doctor was there to ask a few questions as to whether I felt ready to make my final seven landings. He asked because so often pilots that had just made their first carrier landing would be so shook up that they needed more time than just a lunch period to recoup. In fact, quite a few pilots would be so shook up that they would have to stay aboard the carrier overnight before he could allow them to continue their carrier qualifications. I assured the doctor that I was totally in control and certainly wanted to make my last seven landings to be a fully qualified carrier pilot. I had waited so long for good weather that I wanted to get going and finish up as soon as I could.

My plane had been wheeled back to about the 354 foot mark for me to climb aboard and get hooked up in the parachute harness, and then the doctor stepped up on the wing to give me a bit of last-minute advice. He congratulated me on my successful first landing, and then said you are about to make your first carrier takeoff. When you come to the end of the flight deck and look down and see nothing but that water below you, don't get rattled, for you should certainly have enough flight speed to stay airborne and climb enough to start your next landing pattern.

It had been a nice day as far as weather goes, but I had been so itchy to get my last seven landings under my belt that I wanted to get going. I got the signal to start the engine, put the flaps down, the fuel mixture gauge to full rich, and the propeller to full pitch. Then I looked out for a signal from the flight deck taxi director. He swung his arm to the right, indicating it would be good for me to taxi up to the flight deck launching officer.

That officer would also check the sound of the motor and that the flaps were down before he would give me the wind-up signal to put full throttle on. Before that, he had given me the signal to hold my brakes, which is with both fists clenched up in the air above his head. After I had applied full throttle it was up to me to read my instruments and gauges to make sure they all were reading correctly, then to nod my head and wait for the launching officer to give the signal to go.

His left hand changed from clenched fist to an open palm moving in a circle to indicate he wanted full power. Then his right hand changed from a clenched fist to an open palm with his forefinger indicating that direction down the flight deck to the bow of the carrier. And I could now release brakes and start my run down the deck for takeoff.

After releasing my brakes and starting my roll down the

flight deck for takeoff I began to think, gee, I have just 350 feet to build up sufficient speed for takeoff instead of the usual three to five thousand feet on a regular runway. As I passed the carrier's island, I looked down at the deck and it didn't seem like I was really building up enough speed. This is deceptive because the carrier is moving into the wind and that automatically gives you an additional 30 knots of airspeed over the wings. The wind flowing across the deck always makes it more difficult to walk around on the flight deck because the wind is either pushing against you when you are walking into it or it is giving you an additional boost when walking with the wind.

The tabs for the elevators which control normal flight either up a slight bit or down a slight bit had been set so that the plane would increase altitude just a bit and as speed build up. I suddenly realized that I was airborne even before I crossed the end of the flight deck and saw that there was nothing under me accept the blue water below. Then I had to loosen the shoulder straps in order to reach down and flip the lever for getting my wheels up, which would help increase airspeed. Then I hit the switch to get the flaps up, to give me additional flight speed for gaining altitude.

I was then supposed to adjust my flight path by jogging to the right to prevent my propwash from going back on the carrier flight deck affecting the next pilot's launch. Then I was supposed to fly straight ahead gaining altitude to 1000 feet before making my first left 90 degree turn to start the procedure all over again. Wheels down, flaps down, shoulder straps locked and on the second landing with nobody else in the traffic pattern I could make a bounce landing for another go around. After coming to a complete stop the wind would roll me back enough to disengage the hook from the landing wire and then I had to hit the switch to raise the tail hook. I would still have enough room on the flight deck for another takeoff because I was at a point some 350 feet from the bow of the carrier. This would give me a full run on the flight deck for takeoff.

After the 8th landing, I was instructed to head back to Glenview and arrived about mid-afternoon. Upon reporting to the chief of training, he informed me he already knew I had completed my qualifications, as the ship's radio had informed him and his only comment was, "You had a great checkout. Report back here at 0800 tomorrow morning for orders."

Dewy Knight, my roommate ever since we had been at the advanced squadron in Kingsville, also successfully passed his qualifications later that day. We both had to report to the pilots ready room the next morning for our orders. Orders were handed out shortly after 0800 on May 30, 1943 and we both let out quite a whoop and holler for Dewey had received orders to ComAirPac, San Francisco and I got my orders to report to ComAirLant, Norfolk, Virginia. Our orders were just what we had wanted as Dewy wanted the Pacific so he could see those grass skirts blowing in the wind, and I wanted the Atlantic duty in hopes that I would be assigned to a squadron protecting the convoys going over to Europe. Maybe I'd be able to have a day or two in Liverpool, or London, or Leeds, or Southampton where some of my paternal relatives lived.

Chapter Four

FIGHTING TWO (VF-2)

June to November 1943

First Duty Station

My proceed orders gave me three days plus travel time so I could make a quick trip down to Brimfield, Illinois to see my folks and up to Edgerton, Wisconsin to see Lorie, my girlfriend, before having to head back to Chicago to catch the train for Norfolk, Virginia. On board the train I had my own private stateroom, which the Navy had provided for me. Out in the regular sleeper part of the pullman were half a dozen chief petty officers on their way to Norfolk from the Great Lakes Naval base where they had been stationed.

As I remember, they had quite a bet going to see if they could get this officer snockered, for they took great pleasure in a chug a lug passing the bottle around. I had a couple snorts with them but felt myself get a little woozie and forced myself to retire to my stateroom for the rest of the night.

At breakfast the next morning they were all quite jovial and ready to start at it all over again, but fortunately the train arrived in Norfolk in a short time. There was no Navy transportation, so we had to ask streetcar conductors which car to get to take us out to the main gate of the naval air station. We checked in and went our separate ways, for I had to go to BOQ and they headed for the chief petty officers quarters.

I asked the desk clerk where I would find the ComAirLant office after I had been assigned my room in BOQ. The ComAirLant yeoman who checked me in seemed to be so busy. His explanation was that a raft of fellows had just arrived from Pensacola for orders and that it would be a day or two before he could get around to completing my orders for assignment to a squadron. This delay gave me a chance to see a couple of the latest Hollywood movies at the base theater, for my only requirement was to check in at 0800 each morning until I received my orders. This gave me a chance to relax and do a little sightseeing around Norfolk in addition to the evening movies.

My orders were waiting for me when I checked in on the third morning. They read for me to report to VF-2, which had just been commissioned at the naval air station Quonset Point, Rhode Island. The squadron was in the process of being transferred to the naval air station at Atlantic City, New Jersey, which was where I was given transportation to meet the skipper of the fighting squadron.

The yeoman then explained that VF-2 would be a 36-plane fighter squadron, which would be going aboard a larger carrier probably out in the Pacific area of combat. It would have 36 new Hellcats fresh from production at the Grumman plant up in Bethpage, New York. This kind of deflated my expectations of getting to see my father's relatives over in England. But the news that we would be flying the new Hellcat gave me a big boost of ego, for the Hellcat had to be a lot easier to fly than the old Brewster Buffalo that we had had down at Opa Locka.

The Yeoman had prepared railroad tickets for me to go from Norfolk to Philadelphia and then from Philadelphia back down to Atlantic City. I left the ComAirLant office and headed for the streetcar taking me back down town and to the railroad station. The coach cars were almost filled to capacity, so the Porter said I could leave my bags in his locker room, which would be one thing less to hang on to during the trip. It was an all-day trip stopping at every small town to let passengers off and others back on.

When I arrived in Philadelphia, I decided to buy a ticket to go on into New York City as I was on proceed orders again. This would give me a chance to see my old buddy George Berquist, who was now enrolled in the Navy V12 program at Columbia University. The V12 program was for college graduates and was better known as a " ninety-day wonder program" giving the graduates a commission.

I had purchased railroad tickets from Philadelphia to New York that turned out to be on the Pennsylvania Railroad. When we arrived in New York, we were apparently several floors underground, as the train had gone through a tunnel under the New York Harbor and come up for its stop directly under the Hotel Pennsylvania. The number of people standing in line to get registered for a room that night was awfully long. Since I did not know where else to go, I went to the end of the line and in just a very few minutes one of the hotel porters came to me and said to follow him. He took me up to the registration desk to shorten my time in line. He said that that was a policy of the hotel for servicemen not having to stand in line. I thanked him and proceeded to fill out the registration card and he then took my bags and showed me the room I would have for the night and told me where to get the best meal for the most reasonable price. I certainly thanked him profusely and gave him a little extra tip for all the help he had been, especially in getting me out of that humongous line at the registration desk.

I called Columbia University and asked to speak to George Berquist. After a few minutes wait my buddy's voice came back on the line informing me that he had an awful lot of studying to do yet that evening, but he would be free for us to have lunch the next noon time. That gave me a chance for a good night's sleep and then time in the morning to find my way out to Columbia University. It certainly was good to see George again and learn his latest aspirations, and of course he was all-curious as to my Navy training after I had left Glenview the previous fall.

We had to talk in a hurry, for he had to get back for afternoon classes and informed me that the professors usually gave them so much homework every evening that we would not be able to have an evening together during my visit to New York. I still had one day to visit around New York and could see Madison Square Garden again where my Westminster basketball team had played in the national invitational tournament back in March of '41. Of course, I had gone to New York to see my fraternity brothers, who were three of the starting five. After lunch, I did a little sightseeing around New York and its many museums.

The next day I had to pack and catch the train back to Philadelphia where I would use the Navy ticket to get down to Atlantic City. When I arrived the Navy had a bus that took all arriving Navy personnel out to the naval air station. I found out we would be the first squadron to actually fly and operate from that base as it had just recently been opened after being hewed from the forest land about 10 miles west of Atlantic City.

I checked in with the air station and then went to the ready room to meet my new skipper. He turned out to be Lieutenant Commander Bill Dean, who had been my senior officer in charge of training back at the advanced squadron in Kingsville, Texas. He welcomed me to the squadron and introduced me to the few pilots that had already checked in, and then gave me the handbook for the FM1 (Wildcat) to study. He also handed me diagrams for the station's air traffic discipline around the new air station at Atlantic City. He also showed me where my locker would be for my flight gear, in the room next to the pilots' ready room, then said I would have to go down to the station flight supply office to check out all my flight clothing that would be needed.

It was summertime, but the supply clerk insisted on checking out all the winter flight gear in addition to our light summertime flight suits. We then had to haul it all back to our locker. We really had quite a time there at the supply warehouse, which turned out to be so new that they were very short on many of the things we were supposed to obtain, except those winter flight suits.

They had marine boots, but not my size. The leather gloves were about five sizes too large, and the cloth helmet was way too small even for my average size 7 head. I couldn't even get it on when the radio cups were put in. The rest of the gear fit fairly well.

Nolan Herrigan, whom I had just met in the ready room, was there getting his gear, also. He had his car and suggested I pile my stuff along with his in the car before we headed back to empty it all into our lockers.

We were issued the FM handbook because our Hellcats had not arrived yet and we had been given 10 FMs on a temporary basis so we would have something to fly while we waited for the Hellcats. The next stop was to the BOQ office for my room assignment and to purchase my officers mess ticket, which was a standard $22.00 charge for the month whether we ate any or all our meals there in the ward room (dining room). Then we were excused for lunch.

After lunch, it was back to the ready room to study, read and memorize the FM handbook. I would have to know the normal, maximum and minimum operating temperatures, the pressures, and the functions of each instrument. I would also need to know the location of all controls and the auxiliary manual control for each function needed to control the plane and the engine in every situation the plane would ever fly in and what to do should they malfunction.

The next day was more studying and memorizing of the handbooks. Finally, we were able to get out to the plane and sit in the cockpit of one of the FMs. We had to be familiar with the controls and where each lever, switch, knob, handle, and gauge was located. I knew there would be a blindfold cockpit check before I would be allowed to take the plane up by myself, for there would be no instructor or anybody else to help in the case of an emergency while in the air. That's why we had to know so much about the plane and its performance.

The FM had much higher performance than the old Brewster Buffalo for it had about 300 more horsepower and a little bit easier control of the guns and hydraulic systems. We had no back seat driver or instructor to help out in any difficult circumstance. I was the pilot in command now, the navigator, radioman, gunner, bombardier, and air discipline master all rolled into one. I was responsible while flying this fighter, to avoid collision with another plane especially during all our formation flying.

We were still way short of the 42 pilots allotted for a 36 plane squadron, but each day saw two or three new faces in the ready room. With only 10 FM's assigned for our use, I had to take turns with other pilots sitting in the cockpit to learn the controls. I finally passed the blindfold test, correctly reaching each control or indicating exactly where each gauge was for the instructor, and then telling him what the normal and maximum/minimum readings should be. Only then was I allowed to go for my first area familiarization flight.

Within a few days, however, we received our first Hellcats. We still had to wait while the station CASU ordinance installed the six 50 caliber machine guns and bore sighted them to the pattern that our skipper wanted. In the meantime, the Hellcat handbooks that came along with the first planes were handed out and of course I had to prepare again for another blindfold cockpit check before I would be allowed my first flight in this new plane. It would be quite a step up from the Wildcats that had only 1350 horsepower engines. We now had 2000 horsepower engines and much easier control for gaining wheels up or down, and a kick knob to charge the guns before use and then to safety them after use.

Introduction to the Hellcat
and VF-2 Shakedown

What a thrill it was to be flying the newest Navy fighter plane. We were all now hot pilots, with most of the plane's controls now activated by a hydraulic knob that was much more accessible than in the Wildcat, with its hand windup and wind down wheels. It was certainly much easier than the long reach to charge the guns of the old Brewster Buffalo, and the almost inaccessible emergency control in the area to the right rear of the pilot's seat.

Although we would get a couple of new Hellcats every few days, we also had new pilots reporting and so the time available in a Hellcat was restricted. Every other flight still had to be in the

Wildcat, which we used for tactical work, including our wild tail-chases high above the boardwalk along the Atlantic City ocean-front. These tail-chases were led by our skipper, Bill Dean. We used the Wildcat for the next couple weeks at least until we got the Hellcats. Then we performed that display of airmanship each Friday afternoon.

The skipper was quite a perfectionist and anybody that fell out of any of the maneuvers he led us on would be given only one more chance to prove his ability. His maneuvers included loops, slow roles, snap rolls, chandelles, with a change of direction when we got to one end of the boardwalk where we would do three-quarters of a loop and a half roll that would change the direction from that which we had just come.

The skipper would do everything that he could think of to find out our flying capabilities and any pilot that fell out of a maneuver the second time could expect orders back to Norfolk for reassignment. By the end of June we probably had some 50 pilots ordered to the squadron and like a baseball team in spring training, this skipper could pick out the best and have the over complement ordered back to Norfolk.

July 4th saw us with a full complement of 36 Hellcats so we were all able to start basic familiarization in the plane. This included stalls, recovery procedures, how fast we could get to 10,000 feet and on up to 20,000 and 25,000 feet. We also had to test ourselves in various acrobatic maneuvers that we knew we had to perform each Friday afternoon. Woe-be-hold the pilot that spoiled the tail chase by falling out of any maneuver, or losing direction from an Immelmann or slow roll, even though we were all new to the Hellcat and had not been able to build up much time in the plane.

The squadron's non flying officers had also reported in by July 4th, which included the AV(S) officers lieutenant Jack Holladay as personnel officer, lieutenant junior grade Tom Morrissey, as air combat information officer, and Lt.j.g. C. P. Barker as gunnery officer. Our new air group commander, lieutenant commander Roy L. Johnson had also come aboard, although he was spending quite a bit of his time with our bombing and torpedo squadrons, which were based on other fields.

A few days later Lt. Jim Stimson arrived on temporary orders to qualify the whole squadron in field carrier landings in our new planes. We would have to qualify as a squadron aboard the *USS Charger* operating in the Chesapeake Bay. It was quite a harrowing experience during the first few field carrier practice hops in our new Hellcats, for the crosswind leg took us just a few feet above the tree tops in the forests surrounding the Atlantic City air field.

The virgin timbers surrounding the NAS Atlantic City were at least 45 to 50 feet tall. Their height left little room for error just prior to picking up the LSO on final leg during our simulated carrier landing. These were all "bounce" practice hops as the runway was long enough for us to get the "cut" to land, and then we get squared away on the runway and then pour on the coal to take off again. We would gain enough altitude for another round at the signal officer. Interspersed with these carrier practice hops were the familiarization flights. We also started doing a few live gunnery practice hops.

July 19th saw the Captain hosting a get to know each other party at the Seaview Country Club for all our officers with their wives or feminine dates for the evening. Our uniform for the evening was full dress whites and the ladies in formal gowns. Most of them looked pretty spiffy in the various colors that appeared at dinner table and on the dance floor.

It was probably the first time that most of us Ensigns had ever actually worn our "whites" as our "greens" were normally worn for any action in the evening. Especially for jaunts to town and the many good times that we had in the Penn-Atlantic Hotel basement bar and dance hall. That's where most of us bachelors enjoyed drinking and dancing with the Army nurses that were in training and staying in a hotel just a block away. They were in training to become flight nurses and all of them enjoyed dancing as much as we did. They had a midnight curfew with the doors promptly locked.

They all looked like queens for our dinner party when they

dressed up in formals. That night they stayed at the Penn Atlantic so as not to put a damper on the evening's celebration by having to get back from the Seaview County Club by curfew time. The country club was some 10 miles north of Atlantic City and would have required leaving probably no later than 1130 to get the girls back to their hotel in time. The food was very well prepared and quite tasty but cooled considerably while most of us enjoyed dancing with our partners to the music of a very good band. The band played all our favorite pieces that night and continued playing until at least 2:00 a.m. for our enjoyment.

We had many grand times at the Penn Atlantic Hotel with drinking and dancing in that basement bar. I can remember one time when "Happy Jack" Holladay had had quite a number of drinks and was in a rather happy-go-lucky mood. He had been kissing many ladies with their lipsticks adhering to his lips, when one lady with rather large breasts that stuck out to a fine point came over to ask happy Jack for another dance. When she leaned over to ask the question and happy Jack turned to listen to her, his lips came very close to the point of her left breast and he unconsciously clamped his mouth around the point of her breast. He certainly was very surprised and very apologetic for his action as she was dressed in a bold all white dress and his ruby red lips left quite a mark around that point which stayed with her the rest of the night to everyone's laughing delight. She was very amiable and I think she had about as good a time that evening as we did, for she just laughed it off and continued having a good time along with several more dances with everybody. She even seemed to know when we would not be night flying and would make an appearance at the Penn Atlantic dance floor for more good times while we were still based there in Atlantic City.

July 22nd found us trying to fly in very fowl weather. There was no ceiling for any of our regular training flights except for the field carrier landing practices that Lt. Stimson was able to conduct. However, even that turned sour as the storm suddenly closed in and the pilots were radioed to proceed over to the Army field at Wildwood. They all had to go on instruments, and only four of the

Captain Dean hosted a "get to know each other" party at the Seaview Country Club for all our officers with their wives or feminine dates for the evening, and what an evening it was.

PARTY
FIGHTING SQUADRON 2
SEAVIEW COUNTRY CLUB-ATLANTIC
JULY 19th 1943

five that had been practicing field carrier landings arrived at
Wildwood. The fifth pilot, Earl "Spider" Evans, failed to arrive at
Wildwood and never landed at Atlantic City. Somewhat later when
the weather cleared, many of us took off on search missions to try
and find Spider. We never found a trace of his plane or a life raft
out in the ocean in the waters off Atlantic City, nor did we receive
a phone call stating that he had arrived at any other airfield.

That evening Capt. Dean called a meeting of all pilots to discuss tactics in bad weather and line squalls and how best to cope
with them. Spider still had not been heard from and it was futile to
conjecture on what had happened. It seemed like we had lost one
of our own so early in our organizational venture. We would miss
the Spider even though we had only been together little more than
a month and a half, for he had always been the life of the party and
gotten to know everyone during that short time we had been together.

Weather cleared a couple days later and us boot Ensigns
were to be taught fighter combat tactics by the senior officers who
had already experienced combat. They had a tour of duty in VF 10
on the *USS Enterprise* down in the Solomon Islands.

One of us Ensigns always had to fly the SNJ, which was the
plane used for towing the target sleeve for live gunnery practice in
a restricted area out in the Atlantic Ocean. A flight of six Hellcats
would be firing on the sleeve when it reached our gunnery area
about 50 miles East of Atlantic City. Again. each of us had our
ammunition dipped in a different color paint so that we could count
our success in hitting the sleeve when it was brought back to the
field.

We really examined that sleeve each time we had gunnery
practice for the one with the least number of holes in the sleeve had
to buy the drinks that night. The Captain then began to require a
minimum number of holes in our target sleeves. If we didn't have
at least five holes with the color of our 50-caliber bullets, we would
be given one more chance to hit the sleeve with that minimum number or we would be receiving orders back to Norfolk and
ComAirLant, just as we would if we fell out of our tail chases over

the boardwalk.

These stiff requirements by the skipper really paid off royally when we eventually got out in combat. There was no other squadron in the history of the Navy with 30 of its pilots becoming aces in one tour of duty, and another seven pilots miss becoming an ace by just one plane. We also set a record of 267 enemy planes shot down, while losing only three pilots in aerial combat. That also was a record with 89 enemy kills to a loss of one pilot, which was much better than the Navy's overall record of 19 kills for each lost pilot who served in combat. Our gunnery practice certainly paid off.

Our days continued with gunnery practice, field carrier landings, and combat tactics, which was primarily the Thatch weave. We had an occasional night flight, and when weather permitting, we had the usual Friday afternoon tail chase of either 16 or 20 planes over the boardwalk. By now people and merchants along that boardwalk were gathering just to watch the early evening performances.

VF-2 Carrier Qualification

The Captain received word on August 8 that his squadrons turn for "carqual" (Carrier Qualification) had arrived. We were expected to have at least 12 planes ready to qualify on the carrier *USS Charger* in the Chesapeake Bay the next morning and the rest of the pilots to follow the next day, after the first group had finished their individual four carrier landings.

The captain decided four divisions (16) pilots would have to get up early and fly down to the carrier. All 16 would then learn what a carrier breakup would be like, with each division making the breakup and the other three divisions at first circling the carrier again until the next trip around for them to breakoff and make their individual landings on the carrier. All four divisions would stay aboard the carrier and one pilot at a time would take off and make his four landings, after which he would stay aboard and probably have lunch while waiting for the other 15 pilots to make their individual four landings.

Everything went well the first day, except our engineering officer, old Charlie Harbert, who was the oldest man in the squadron, had his canopy unfortunately loosened and eventually blew off, injuring Charlie enough for medical attention. He had to delay his last three landings for he was down in sick bay on the *Charger*, and the other 15 finished qualifications and flew back to Atlantic City.

The next day 16 more planes were to fly down in formation for qualification and their learning what a carrier breakup would be like. However, weather turned bad again and a couple of the divisions were unable to find the carrier on the first attempt and flew back to Atlantic City before their gas supply ran out. Of the two divisions that had found the carrier, one pilot had trouble when he dumped in on the *Charger*'s catwalk, which is the walkway on each side of the flight deck similar to a sidewalk in front of your home. This put one plane out of commission and gave the crew on the hangar deck of the *Charger* some good experience in repairing the new Hellcat.

As far as I remember we were the first squadron with the brand new Hellcat to check out on the *Charger*. The aviation mechanics probably didn't have the necessary tools to work on replacing the propeller or to change the whole engine of the plane. Plus, Charlie had to stay in the sick bay for another couple days before he was allowed to take off and continue his three remaining qualification landings and then fly back to Atlantic City.

The following day, the squadron's remaining four divisions were to fly down to the *Charger* for their qualification landings, which were made successfully. The squadron received a compliment from the carrier's skipper that went all the way up to ComAirLant. He said we had a very successful squadron qualification, that we had only one accident, and that all 44 pilots qualified with the fewest number of wave-offs of any squadron that had recently qualified.

Our last tail chase over the Atlantic City boardwalk was

about the middle of August, as the squadron received orders to change our base for training to the naval air station at Quonset Point, Rhode Island. We had an all pilots' meeting before taking off for Quonset, the subject was air traffic rules for our soon-to-be base of operation. We were also briefed on making a 36-plane carrier break off for landing based on the procedures and intervals we had learned when 16 of our planes landed on the *Charger*. Quonset had a long runway that started right at the very edge of the Providence River. The thirty minutes taken to land our 36 planes wasn't too bad for our first attempt, but it certainly would have to improve before going aboard an actual carrier in the fleet where we got down to 19 second intervals between landings.

Training flights continued in tactics and live ammo firing in a new restricted area that was east from Cape Cod with the target sleeve jealously counted each time it was returned to the field. We were all well aware that at the end of the month our skipper would be forced to cut several from the present roster in order to get down to the authorized squadron complement.

Of course other things would be considered besides the gunnery scores, personality along with compatibility with squadron members would also be considered. I'm sure the captain had a difficult time making the decision as to which pilots would be cut during that last month we had at Quonset Point for we had become a pretty close knit group.

Bill Dean had us out on the baseball field, on the tennis courts, and he even threw another all squadron party for pilots and their wives or girlfriends trying to help him decide. Our inter squadron volleyball games headed by old man "Charlie Harbert" on one side and headed on the other side by our executive officer, Mr. Eckhardt created intense rivalry. Even that rivalry helped produce close, compatible friendships, in which the skipper preached, "Be there to help your buddy, for you may need his help at another time." It developed into quite a fraternity. The members of VF 2.

Our social life fared pretty well while we were stationed there at Quonset. During the week, we enjoyed the Bachante Room in the Providence Hotel, and the excellent dance floor of the

Beachcomber supper club. Boston was only 65 miles away, and there were hourly trains leaving Providence that we could get off at Back Bay where the Statler Hotel was. It was a hotel that gave servicemen a reduced rate. Besides, it had a very nice dance floor.

The only problem was, in those days in Boston if you met a compatible girl you couldn't join her at her table, nor could she join you at your table. You had to ask her to leave the room so you could then go to another dance hall together or some other bar down the street together before you could come back through the door at the Statler as a couple. Then you could get a table for two to enjoy the rest of the evening. Only as long as we had entered together and were seated together at the table would the waiter take our order for another drink or dinner.

We had another all pilots' meeting early in September with the skipper telling us that our Air Group commander was pleased with our progress. That he would be recommending to ComAirLant that VF-2 was ready to leave for combat about October 1st at the end of the usual four months training program that all carrier squadrons were given to gel and make ready for combat. However, we would be moving without our bombing or torpedo squadrons as the commander was not pleased with their progress.

Therefore our skipper then warned us to "get our affairs in order" and he especially mentioned that married pilots make arrangements for their families for we would probably be gone for about eight to nine months. He then announced that he and Happy Jack Holladay would be entertaining our enlisted gang, their wives and girlfriends for a party that evening. And he thought it was probably time that the officers all had another party. Happy Jack, our personnel officer, was put in charge of finding a place that would hold some 45 officers, their wives and girlfriends. Then he asked each of us to kick in five dollars to cover the cost of another dinner dance evening so we could have a good band to dance to. He then gave us the bad news. For the next two weeks we would all be changing the days' work schedule. We haven't done enough night flying, so our hours will be moved from eight to five to 5:00

p.m. to 2:00 a.m., which would put a kye-bosch to all the enjoyable evenings we had been having.

Well, we survived the night time hours pretty well, except Al Scheele forgot to put his wheels down on the second night. He was quite surprised to find himself skidding down the runway so low to the ground. He was lucky the belly tanks had not yet been installed, which we would need for cross-country work. He had his shoulder straps locked as should be, and was not injured physically. But he was the recipient of the butt end of jokes of all kinds for a few days from everybody.

After that episode, Capt. Dean decreed we would have a duty officer assigned at the end of the runway with a strong flashlight to verify wheels down and give a wave off in case another pilot goofed the same way Al had done. The control tower was not able to verify wheels down in the darkness during our night flying as they normally did during regular daylight hours.

Happy Jack Holladay found a quaint roadhouse just outside Providence city limits, and although it had a rustic decor, the uniform of the day this time was our dress blues and formals for the ladies. We were a bit farther north now, and after September 1st, Whites became passe under Navy regulations and were not acceptable except in tropical climates, where, I guess, Whites were worn all year long.

Most of us had found very compatible dance partners during the month of evening liberties around Providence. The girls more than willingly dolled up in their long flowing formal gowns for our special and their spatial evening, as we had learned that our time in the states would be limited now, with us heading out to combat on or about the first of October.

Old Happy Jack had done an excellent job in finding this place, for the food was excellent and the orchestra was able to mix somewhat faster music with the slow music that we all appreciated. For a generally informal party, it turned out to be a real success. And, we all got to sleep in, for our next duty would not be until 5:00 p.m. that next afternoon.

During the week of rearranged schedules, the skipper divided the squadron in two groups. Those not playing baseball in the afternoon were expected to be on the volleyball court. My roommate and I chose to play baseball. I welcomed the game, but forget which team scored more total points. But I do remember my roommate and buddy, Chub Eckert, sliding into second base on a hit that most fellows probably would have stopped at first base on. Chub was called safe by the umpire, Henry Fonda.

However, Chub did not get up immediately. He just lay their looking at his arm which had been broken in a couple places, and I was elected to accompany him to sick bay where the doctor would be able to take care of his compound fracture. The doctor straightened it all out and put a big cast on most of his arm and then told us both that he would be with that cast for probably at least eight weeks. That doctor said he would send a no-flight duty slip to our skipper, which would ground Chub for the rest of the days that we would have at Quonset Point. When Bill Dean heard that, he was relieved, because Chub would then become one of those he would have to transfer back to Norfolk and ComAirLant. His job had become a little less restrictive as Chub would still be in the hospital, probably long after we had received our orders to fly west.

Just before shipping out, Chub Eckert, the author's friend, broke his arm and got orders to stay in the States.

VF-2 Heading West

Our skipper received orders for the squadron to fly cross-country on October 3rd. We would be leaving on Thursday. Our non-flying officers, excess pilots, and the enlisted gang were to leave on Wednesday, which meant old Charlie Harbert, our engineering officer, would have a herculean task of preparing in two day's all 36 planes for the cross-country flight. Some were getting very close to the required 100-hour check and others would certainly need a check along the way. Since there would be no maintenance facilities along the way, those planes would have to be done before we left as it would be approximately 16 flying hours from Quonset to the Naval Air Station, Alameda, California.

That 16 hours could even be exceeded because of rendezvous and breakup time when we landed. We would need at least four landings to refuel, and hopefully we would get a meal or two along the way with a couple night stay-overs in hotels. In addition to the 100-hour checks, our planes would need to have belly tanks installed before our enlisted mechanics had to be ready for the troop transport, which was scheduled to leave Wednesday morning.

The belly tanks would be installed midway between the front wheels and would give each plane an additional 150 gallons of fuel, which would then give each plane a total of 400 gallons of fuel. I don't know how our enlisted mechanics were able to complete all the work needed in those two short days. Somehow they got it all done and still had time to pack their own personal gear that would have to be put aboard the transport planes. I think they were able to enlist the help of other mechanics in the hanger that took care of the planes for the station officers. They got all 36 planes ready to go, and everyone boarded the transports on Wednesday. That is, except Chub Eckert, who was required to stay in the hospital on doctors orders and would therefore not be allowed to stay in the squadron.

Thursday came with all of us having to get up rather early to report to the flight line for takeoff on our approximately five hour

Those that made the final cut - VF-2 at Quonset Point on October 3, 1943.

jaunt down to Atlanta, Georgia. Good old Charlie Harbert, being the engineering officer, elected to be the pilot to stay with one of the planes that would not start. We never did find out why it would not start but Charlie thought he could get a station mechanic to help and then catch up with our gang at Atlanta.

Thirty-five of us took off and got rendezvoused to start our long journey, but my division leader Mr. Eckhardt for some reason broke away from the big group in flight and our four planes then landed at Charlotte, North Carolina. Lt. Eckhardt must have had a relative or even his wife that he wanted to say goodbye to, for he disappeared immediately upon landing and the three of us division members enjoyed a nice lunch in the officers BOQ while our planes were being refueled. The three of us were only on our second cup of coffee when Mr. Eckhardt returned and said let's try to catch up.

We got back in the planes, taxied out and headed for Atlanta only to find that personnel there had not been alerted to the arrival of our 36 planes. They had taken so long refueling the 31 planes that had already arrived, that our second leg of the flight to Dallas, Texas would have had us arriving well after dark. The Naval Air station personnel there would not have enough help around at that time of day or night to service all our planes.

The skipper then made a couple quick calls to ComAirLant

to get their approval to have all our pilots stay overnight in Atlanta and then proceed to Dallas the next morning. It was already late in the afternoon when the station's operation officer at the Navy base called for transportation to get our group over to the BOQ to register for rooms for the night and have dinner at the bachelor officers quarters. After dinner, we again enjoyed the station's provision of transportation to downtown Atlanta for a movie and then schnapps at a couple bars the bus driver recommended. With our unexpected evening out most of us agreed that we hadn't better push our luck. We told the bus driver to be back at the last bar he had recommended by 1130 so we could get back to the base for a good night's sleep, as we had to get up for an early departure to Dallas.

Friday morning found us all out at the flight line bright and early, ready for the hop to Dallas, to refuel there and then on to El Paso, Texas. However as we crossed Alabama and into Mississippi the weather started turning foul. As we entered Louisiana we encountered thunderstorms and lightning, so the skipper turned North with all thirty-five of us following to skirt the storm and wound up going quite a distance out of our way.

We had to go as far north as Little Rock, Arkansas before we could turn back heading south on a course to Dallas. We arrived there about an hour and a half later than anticipated. With the storm delay and all, we found another base that was not prepared to service thirty-five planes. We even tried to help the ground crew at Dallas in refueling of our planes, but then the gas truck ran out and had to go to its supply depot and that took forever, it seemed like.

So again, the skipper was forced to call ComAirLant and ask permission for the squadron's pilots to stay over in Dallas. The BOQ on that Naval Air Station was too full for all of us to stay in, so the skipper had to make a few more calls to ComAirLant for authority to have the U.S. Navy pay the expense for hotel rooms in downtown Dallas. The base furnished two large buses to transport us and our personal suitcases or bags from the naval air station to the hotel where they had been able to make reservations at the last minute for all of us.

It was still too early for dinner even after we had all checked in to our rooms at the hotel, which gave us time to change from our flight suits and clean up with a shower and probably a shave before wandering down to the dining room. Many of the tables were already filled and our gang almost completely filled the dining room. The food was very good and we were pleasantly surprised at about 7:00 that evening to see a large band come in for the Friday night dance. Their music was out of this world and very danceable on a wonderful dance floor that had just the proper amount of wax so you could slip and slide just right. We found a number of cooperative dance partners, and we all had a grand time, with some of the bachelors even having the luck of having their dance partners wind up in their rooms for a continued party.

The only problem was, we knew the skipper would be raring to go very early in the morning to make up for all the delays we'd had so far. That forced us to get an early rise at 6:00 a.m. for our breakfast and then the bus ride back to the naval air station. The skipper gave us a short lecture on the bus while we were on the way out to the Navy base. It was for when we got to El Paso to keep our landing speed up a little higher than usual because El Paso is some 5000 foot altitude so that the air would not have as much lift as normal for our landings. He really emphasized those comments in front of the operation room for all of us to hear again.

We were on our way again, even Charlie Harbert who had caught up to us in Dallas. We had a good time flying across most of Texas to land in El Paso where we didn't really need gas yet, but we certainly had to refill in order to reach our next destination, San Diego, California. None of us had any problem with the landing at El Paso, except Al Minges, who couldn't control his plane in the higher altitude and with a slight direct crosswind ran off the runway and flipped completely over on his back.

The crash truck and fire truck of course were dispatched immediately from their hangars to the accident site, and within short order had him out of the plane and on his way to the hospital. He was dazed and completely out of it, with many bruises but no broken bones that were evident. Many of us got a station car and went to the hospital, for we wanted to be there when the doctor could give us a diagnosis of our buddy's condition.

Again, it took much longer than expected for our planes to be serviced by the station ground crews, for in those days, air fields were not used to servicing so many planes all at one time. When the doctor finally came out of the operating room, he told us it would be some time before Al would be able to continue any place, and that we might as well go back to the airfield and continue our journey to San Diego.

By that time we thought it was about snack time, if not a full lunch. Our skipper waited at the hospital trying to find out Al's actual condition and whether he would have to be dropped from the squadron roster. It was mid-afternoon before the skipper learned from the doctor that it would be many, many days before Al could be released for any flight duty, which meant we had seen the last of our buddy, for he would have to be dropped from the squadron's roster.

We had had so many delays and interruptions that our skipper felt he just had to get the squadron over to San Diego that same day. With the late departure from El Paso, the skipper knew it would be a night landing at the Naval Air Station, San Diego, but he was bound and determined to get there on the date given by ComAirLant for us to arrive at San Diego. So our 35 planes took off from El Paso heading for our destination.

While we were still climbing to the usual 20,000-foot flight altitude (it takes a lot less gas in thin air than it does at lower altitudes), I noticed a beautiful canyon below. With the sun setting and casting shadows on the otherwise bright sunlit eastern ridge, it made the gorge look like what I imagined the Grand Canyon, which I had never seen, would look like.

As we crossed from New Mexico into Arizona, one of the divisions reported to the skipper that he had an oil leak problem and would be required to land while he still had enough oil to keep the engine running. Otherwise, it would freeze up, forcing a dead stick landing. Thirty-two of us continued on, and as darkness set in, our running lights had to be turned on long before we arrived for the night landing at San Diego.

On to Alameda and Mom Chung
Doctor Margaret J. Chung "Mom"

Our arrival was much later than the station had anticipated and personel then on duty at the station had been secured long before. The Naval Air Station at San Diego did not have lighted runways, so we were forced to make landings by the aid of some smudge pots that were put out to form a runway. In fact it wasn't even a blacktop or cement runway, it was just a grass sod field. When the skipper realized that, he cautioned everybody over the radio to make virtually a carrier landing with our speed well under control so we could set down almost at the very edge of that small field. There were no taxiways either, so after we had landed we had to skirt around the rim of the field to get back to the hangar. Fortunately, we all landed without mishap.

The skipper went into base operations and there waiting for him was another set of orders for the squadron to fly up the coast of California to the Naval Air Station, Alameda. However, it was much too late for any more flying, as our gas supplies would not support the distance from San Diego to Alameda. In fact, it was about noon the next day before our thirty-two planes were refueled and ready to go again. We were all bused up to BOQ and registered for the night. After having the cooks wakened to prepare a late evening meal for us, we enjoyed a few drinks over at the "O club."

After breakfast we were bused down to the flight line and had to wait just a little while for them to finish refueling the planes. Again, we practically had to use a carrier takeoff where we were bouncing over the rough sod on that small field. We all got airborne, rendezvoused, and headed for Alameda. We arrived just in time for lunch and then had to go back to our planes. We sat in the cockpit in order to control any emergency that might arise while they were being towed by tractor over to the pier. There, a CVE (baby flat top) was waiting to hoist our planes aboard.

It seemed like an awful long time for my turn to be towed

over to that pier. Time goes so slow when you are waiting, as we were free for the rest of the day after our planes arrived at the pier. We were also free on Monday and didn't have to be back at the BOQ until Tuesday morning by 0800. The skipper had hoped that our second DC-3 transport would have arrived by then, with much of the squadron's equipment and tools, and our enlisted complement: the aviation mechanic chiefs, the radioman chief, the gunnery-ordinance chief and the non-flying officers.

The pilots from the planes that had been towed over to the carrier in the first group had already headed into Oakland for liberty, and some of them went across the Bay Bridge to San Francisco. Those of us in the third group to be towed were just arriving back at BOQ when the skipper, who already was one of Mom Chung's adopted sons, announced he was going over to Mom's. He said she would welcome any and all of us from VF-2 that wanted to go along with him.

We certainly were welcome at Mom's, with snacks and drinks flowing freely around her large circular bar on the second floor of her home. Her medical offices were on the ground floor. Mom came up to greet us after her last patient for the day had left her offices. I found her to be a very gracious lady, and she made us feel right at home with the comment that she was so honored to see one of her bastard sons again and meet some of his pilots that were "going to set all Navy records," she hoped. It was positive thinking on her part at that time, although it did come true during our tour of duty in combat.

Mom Chung was a single lady and had been very influential in getting the WAVES chartered by Congress and approved as a branch of the Navy. She also made an effort to honor famous or well-known flyers. She adopted Claire Chennault as her first "bastard son." Others like Billie Mitchell, Hap Arnold, Adm. Marc Mitscher, Adm. Jocko Clark were all added to the list. I believe Bill Dean was No. 34.

All of her sons had an open invitation to visit her whenever they were in the San Francisco area. The bar on second floor was always open, as Mom had a full-time bartender, and we certainly did enjoy her hospitality upon our arrival on the West Coast. After the skipper had introduced us and made us well-known to Mom, he announced that he and Happy Jack Holladay had reservations up at the top of the Mart. The skipper also told us we certainly were welcome to go back to the BOQ, but he thought we would enjoy the St. Francis, for it probably was much more to our liking. It had a large dining room with a super ballroom that usually had very good dance music, and certainly would be more in tune with our pocketbooks.

Our last two days in the States should be royally celebrated, and we did. Sightseeing around San Francisco was good with so many places to see, wonderful meals at the St. Francis, and we danced both nights away. The only problem was having to get up so early on Tuesday morning to get back to the base on time. We all chipped in for a taxi cab to help us get back to the Naval Air Station on time. It was clear across the bay and we would have to use the Bay Bridge to cross from San Francisco to Oakland and then on to Alameda. Then word came out that the carrier was going to be leaving a day later because it now had to load more Hellcats and then load all remaining space with P-47s. That meant we wouldn't even have enough room to catapult a plane from the flight deck.

We could have gone back to BOQ, but the six of us decided to check the bus schedule going into Oakland, then across the Bridge, and back to the St. Francis for one more night of good food and dancing. Even though it meant we would have to get up very early on Wednesday morning to be back in time for the 0800 muster, with bags and all luggage ready to be loaded on the carrier shortly thereafter.

The four planes that had been forced down in Phoenix had arrived the day before and had already been put on the carrier so even those pilots would have another day for sightseeing and a good time around San Francisco before we pulled out. However, the weather seemed to be turning sour, with mostly overcast skies and an occasional drizzle that put a damper on any outdoor sightseeing. We had to find a museum to be inside and away from the drizzle and even had a good time visiting some of the department stores in downtown San Francisco. Of course, we were looking forward to another night of dancing and good food at the St. Francis.

The only thing wrong with this extra day that was granted us was that we would have to blow the whistle early, for we couldn't always depend on finding a cab to take us all the away over to Alameda Naval Air Station. And we could not take the chance of being late, for we were afraid the skipper would find some kind of a penalty for us.

We made it back to BOQ on time the next morning, and after getting our bags from the storage locker, we headed for the carrier. We waited a few minutes after boarding, which was the first time I had ever climbed the "ladder" leading up to the hangar deck. The skipper showed up shortly with stateroom number assignments for the senior officers, but us junior officers, Ensigns of the Navy, we had to go down to the junior officer's bunker room (JOB). There were about 20 of us in each of the two JOBs, which would be our quarters for the voyage to Hawaii. All we had was a single cot type bed with sidebars stacked three high so we did not have much clearance for climbing into bed. All we had to store our personal effects including our uniform bag was a very small locker. Any other gear would have to be kept in our parachute bags and stowed up on the hangar deck.

We didn't have much time to snoop around or see much of the carrier before the bullhorn announced, "All going ashore leave now." We all headed for the flight deck to see the Navy tugs waiting and ready to push or pull the carrier away from the dock, which they did at about 1000 hours and we were soon underway. The steady quiver-throb of the carrier's engines was a different feeling than I had ever experienced before. It seemed to vibrate the whole carrier. Then we started to move quietly into the bay and headed for the Golden Gate Bridge.

Off to Hawaii

It was quite a spectacle with the San Francisco skyline on the port side and Alcatraz Island to the starboard. Looking ahead, it seemed like the carrier would never be able to clear under the Golden Gate Bridge, but we eventually steamed under it with a lot of distance from the topmost radar screens of the carrier to the bottom of that Golden Gate Bridge.

It had been a cloudy day with occasional showers, but after we cleared the channel from San Francisco Bay it started to rain hard. The farther we proceeded into the Pacific Ocean, the higher the waves became, and the rain started coming down in good deluges. Approximately five hours into the ocean, the carrier started rolling slightly at first. As the waves kept getting higher, the carrier really started rolling from one side to the other and some of my squadron mates were finding their way up to the catwalks that surrounded the flight deck, or searching for the traditional barf bag.

I was still okay and feeling good as long as I didn't get a whiff of someone else's throw up, and headed to the wardroom for dinner. Our dinner plates with food on them even started to slide on the white linen tablecloths, and I had to put the sidebars up on the table to keep the plate from spilling into my lap. The roll of the ship continued, and even got worse while I was eating.

Then all of a sudden the cupboard containing ready-to-use silverware let loose from the straps holding it to the bulkhead (wall) and went smashing across the room to hit the bulkhead on the opposite side. When it did, the whole cupboard smashed to pieces spilling silverware out on the deck, and it didn't take long before the silverware was sliding all over the room as the carrier rolled from side to side.

We had no flight duties on this trip to Hawaii, and I couldn't even drum up enough buddies to play a game of bridge or even an acey ducey game. They were up in the catwalks heaving over the side of the carrier or they were trying to catch up on some sleep that they had missed during the last nights in San Francisco, so I decided to hit the sack myself.

The weather had cleared during the night, and when I got up on the flight deck I noticed we were all by ourselves. No DDs (Destroyers), or even DEs (Destroyer Escorts) floating with us for protection from enemy submarines. We were on a zigzag course so it would take considerably longer to make the trip to Hawaii, which was to be our first stop according to the skipper when he called an all squadron pilots' meeting.

And, of course scuttlebutt started as to where we were really heading. We were without our bombing and torpedo squadrons so we knew we wouldn't be going on a large carrier requiring a full air group. Possibly to Munda or Rabaul, but the skipper said he didn't know. He did say that he was going to offer our services when he was in his conference with the Admirals of the Pacific Fleet to go wherever a fighting squadron could do some good. And that he expected us to make the best record of any fighter squadron during our tour of duty.

The compass course from San Francisco to Pearl Harbor is approximately 235 degrees. But with the zigzag course we were cruising, we would sail roughly 250 degrees for one hour and then 195 degrees for the alternate hour. Instead of a four-day jaunt, we took over six full days before we had our first glimpse of land. Unlike our leaving Alameda, it was a bright, beautiful sunny day greeting us to the Hawaiian Islands. As we closed in on Oahu, the water changed from a cobalt to azure hues and then to a dirty blue with some crude oil floating as we entered the channel leading to Ford Island. That is, after we passed the gates that allowed ships to enter the channel leading to Pearl Harbor.

There was quite an armada of carriers docked along the shore of Ford Island. There were also many battleships, cruisers, and destroyers in the anchorage beyond the island and the gutted ruins of the battleship *Arizona* that had been sunk and destroyed on the day the Japanese attacked Pearl Harbor back on December 7th 1941. It was still resting on the bottom with its superstructure charred and rusting and was one of the few ships the Navy had not had a chance to resurrect or refurbish.

Navy tugs helped push our carrier in to the dock while our gang from VF-2 stood on the flight deck enjoying the music being played by a Navy band. As the gangplank was lowered, the band swung into the tune of "Aloha," then "Anchors Aweigh," and then on to other military marches.

Hawaiian Air Defense

The skipper was the first one down the gangplank, heading for ComAirPac to try and find out what the next leg of our trip would be, and to curtail the speculation we had been guessing at since we left the states.

This was Monday, Oct. 18, 1943, and we had taken a full six days for the crossing, and still didn't know where we would be sent for our first combat action. Scuttlebut ran rampant, for none of us really felt like we would enjoy being based on some island with all its dust. We guessed it would be Guadalcanal in order to participate in the taking of Rabaul, for without our dive bombers and torpedo bombers we could not expect to board a carrier in a fast carrier task force.

Squadron morale took a small nosedive when the skipper returned with the news that our planes were to be off-loaded as we were scheduled to become part of the Hawaiian defense operating from NAS Barbers Point for about six weeks. He also informed us that he had volunteered the services of his squadron for any and all types of missions. The sooner the better, for he had seen to it that we had undergone an intensive training in the States and were fully ready for combat.

The all pilots' meeting came to an end with all our JGs and us Ensigns headed to the bunk room for our gear and then up to the hangar deck for our parachute bags. They would have to be carried off the carrier and loaded on a truck that was waiting to haul it all over to Barbers Point. The truck would be taking the long way around the entire basin of Pearl Harbor. After loading our gear, we were to go to a designated pier for transportation of all personnel heading for Barbers Point.

It was an old scow that took us from Ford Island west across the waters to an obscure stream that was almost covered with dense underbrush. Because of the underbrush it was a slow ride, but we wound up close to the point with busses from the base waiting to take us to our accommodations. Our luggage would take quite a while to arrive. After getting our billet assignments, there was only one thing to do. Head for the O club. And, the party began with the bartenders mixing pineapple in every drink we could think of. It was evident they wanted to promote Hawaii's main agricultural crop.

Our planes were to be unloaded from the carrier by winch, and then the canvas covers that had protected the engines from salt water while on the way over from the States had to be removed. All we had to do for the next few days was check in each morning to see if the planes had been unloaded and were ready to be flown from Ford Island over to Barbers Point. It was actually a Marine Air Station from which the Marines flew prior to the start of this war. With no flying assignments, we were able to go into Honolulu and enjoy the sandy beach. However, I was totally disappointed the first time I saw the Waikiki Beach, which had a distance of only about 25 feet from the line of buildings to the water's edge.

There was a small "O gauge" railroad train that came to the main gate of Barbers Point and would take us all the way around Pearl Harbor and into its station in Honolulu. We could walk from the station to the Royal Hawaiian hotel, or if we were really lazy, we could catch a city bus that would take us to the Moana Hotel.

Like I said before, I was totally disappointed upon seeing the beach of Waikiki. I had heard the song "On the Beach at Waikiki" so often while I was a student in high school, college, and even during my training to become a Navy pilot. It was a total let-down for me after having gone swimming so often on the eastern coast of Lake Michigan at places like Grand Haven and Ludington, Michigan while visiting my grandfather in Muskegan.

I still believe those beaches in Michigan were ten times better than the beach of Waikiki with at least 100 feet of sand between the water and the nearest auto parking spaces. But the Moana hotel was beautiful and I don't remember if we received a special rate or not, but when you compare today's rates of $150 or more per night against the $5.00 a night we paid back in those days, that made it quite a bargain.

The rooms were nice and the dining room served excellent food and had a wonderful wooden dance floor. The only trouble was, there weren't very many women around to dance with. Just a few Army nurses from Hickum Field. All other women and dependent families had been transported back to the States. It was for their protection because of the possibility of a Japanese invasion of the island.

We had a good time riding that "O gauge" railroad into Waikiki Beach each day and back at night. We had a whole week of swimming before we got the word that our planes had finally been hoisted overboard and taxied over to the hangar area on Ford Island. We never did find out why it had taken so long for the flat-top to unload our planes and make them ready to fly back to Barbers Point.

Thirty-six of us pilots were loaded into a bus and headed for the landing where we would take the ferry across to Ford Island. The skipper had told us before we took off that he had no restrictions. If we wanted to go sightseeing around the island, he would have no objection.

He was going to a meeting that would probably last all afternoon long with the "big wigs." When he did return to the pilot's ready room he gave us the latest scoop. We will have a practice session with "Butch" O'Hare's Bombing Six and Torpedo Six squadrons on the *USS Lexington*. "Butch" didn't want his fighter squadron, with nearly 50 percent replacement pilots that had never flown the Hellcat before, to go on the next operation.

An experienced landing signal officer, which us pilots knew as a flag paddle waiver, was sent over to Barbers Point to refresh our memories of field carrier landing practice again, for it had been well over a month since we had checked out on the carrier in the Chesapeake Bay. We would be going aboard the *Lexington* to give those aboard it and two CVE carriers a mock amphibious landing experience.

We would be covering the Marines landing onto the sandy shore of Maui, which would give them some experience in preparation for the next combat operation. Field carrier landing practice was intense for the next two days. Then we flew out to the Lexington for an overnight stay and practice landings as kind of a qualification all over again. Then our 36 planes flew back to Barbers Point from the *Lex* and the *Lex* slid back into Pearl Harbor for the night.

The next morning our whole squadron of non-flying officers and our enlisted men boarded the *Lex*, although they did not take their tools or equipment with them. Then our thirty-six planes rendezvoused with VB-6 and VT-6 and flew out to the *Lex*. By that time, it was about 100 miles from shore.

This operation was to give us and the air group an actual combat situation, with live ammo. We were given vectors from the carrier fighter director to fly out to investigate a " bogey." We also had to fly CAP (combat air patrol) flights, which meant we had four planes at 10,000 and another four plane division at 20,000 feet waiting for a vector from the carriers fighter director.

We also escorted our bombers and torpedo planes to their assignments over the Marines going ashore during their mock attack. The only thing missing were the actual meat ball (Japanese) planes to fire at, although we did have a few target sleeves to fire at. And, of course those sleeves were toted back to Barbers Point for us to verify our hits. Our dive bombers and torpedo bombers of Air Group 6 also had some practice. The carrier let out a 1,000-foot rope with a sled that was probably 30 feet wide and 50 feet long to represent a ship for them to use as a target.

Things went well on this "cruise," with Butch making it known that we were now his fighter squadron for Air Group 6 on the upcoming operation. Our flight deck discipline had improved so much that when our planes were launched for our return to Barbers Point we set a new record for the carrier. It was the least amount of time that it had to be heading into the wind while launching all 90 planes of our group.

VF-2 headed for Barbers Point, which was approximately 100 miles. VB-6 and VT-6 headed for Kaneohe Marine Air Station. We were not required to move our personal baggage, for we figured we would be flying back out to the Lex again within a few days and heading for the next combat operation.

The skipper was called in for another conference on Ford Island with the Admirals in charge of the Pacific Fleet. When he returned he told us we'd better get over to the Lex and retrieve any personal gear we had left aboard, for we would be going aboard the *USS Enterprise* (CV-6).

Chapter Five

FIRST COMBAT

Aboard the USS Enterprise
November 9ᵗʰ to December 10ᵗʰ, 1943

Nov 19   Invasion Gilbert Islands - Makin, Tarawa
Dec. 4   Raid, Marshall Islands - Kwajalein, Ebeye, Roi

The "Big E"

A
lthough the "Big E" was not in port yet, it was expected within the next few days, and we were told to be
ready to go aboard it on November 9. During the interim, we were
to get some very fine grain sandpaper to smooth the paint on the
wings of our planes and then use a high-grade wax on them in
hopes that we might pick up an additional mile or two of top speed.
It might come in handy for escaping a Japanese Zero.

The *Enterprise* arrived from the States on the 6th in almost
new condition for she had come direct from the stateside repair
shipyards that had rebuilt the entire flight deck and ready rooms
just under it. Also, much of the officer country after the Japanese
bomb exploded on the flight deck during the Solomon's operation
earlier that year.

Our enlisted complement and chiefs immediately started
gathering all their tools, equipment, and spare parts that had to be
transferred to the hangar deck of the *Enterprise*. Their personal
gear also had to be taken aboard, but most of us pilots could find a
place for a parachute bag in our Hellcats.

Our enlisted personnel and all non-flying officers had to be
aboard on the eighth. Our thirty-six pilots would be flying out to
the *Enterprise* after she cleared the Pearl Harbor channel. We were

surprised to see that the landing signal officer we had for the practice field carrier landings at Barbers Point was the LSO on the *Enterprise*. Bringing us aboard the *Enterprise* would be different than flagging us around on the field carrier landings but those landings had given him a little experience with the various pilots so that he would know a little more about the pilot's ability.

Our arrival on the *Enterprise* was somewhat unceremoniously. It took a good hour and a half to land all the fighters. Two fighters had signaled for emergency landings because the readings on their instrument panel were not giving the correct readings. Johnson had to be waved off twice, but got a cut on the 3rd Pass, only to have the newly installed belly tank let loose. The spilling gas ignited and created quite a fire on the flight deck, causing the flight deck crew to use practically all the prepared and available foam before the flames were extinguished. Johnson was not injured, but the plane was pushed overboard for the fire had completely damaged it.

The second emergency was Ozzie Osborne, who couldn't get his belly tank to drop and was therefore not allowed to come aboard because there was very little foam left or available in case of another fire. He finally ditched, or made a water landing in front of a destroyer that picked him out of the water. Now we had lost a second plane and Ozzie was forced to become a "tin can" sailor for a while.

Tires blown out due to hard landings could be replaced in a short enough time for the next hop. But planes damaged when the deck crew taxied one of our planes into another were lost for several hours, for the mechanics would have to take the planes down to the hangar deck to replace the propeller on one and repair the tail elevator on the other. That was par for the course? We sure hoped for better days to come. Then it was the SBD dive-bombers' turn to come aboard with the TBF torpedo bombers to follow, which pretty well finished the afternoon.

After flight quarters were cleared, most of us Ensigns were ushered down to the junior officers bunkroom where we would be lodging while aboard the *Enterprise*. The weather was starting to close in on the task group, which now consisted of another carrier of the CVL class along with a couple battleships and a couple heavy cruisers in addition to the 21 destroyers scattered in a circle around the perimeter of the whole Fleet. Our all pilots' meeting that the skipper had wanted in the ready room was delayed until the next day, so we still didn't find out what operation we were taking part in or where we were really heading.

On November 11, Armistice Day 1943, only the task group Admiral knew where we were headed, and he had not even informed his intelligence officers, the air group commander, or the squadron skippers. So we still had not found out the battle plan or where we are heading.

We were informed that the Admiral would not reveal his orders to anyone, for they had been sealed when he received them from ComAirPac. They would not be opened until we were well on our way and there was no chance of any more mail leaving the ships of the task force that could possibly be picked up by enemy submarines and spoil the surprise of our attacks. Thus, giving the enemy's eyes or ears little chance of obtaining any information they could pass on that would counter our surprise attacks.

Our days were spent in the ready room reviewing the use of our plotting boards for navigation problems of time, distance, and headings to targets from our point of launch. And then being able to navigate back to our carrier that would be moving some 20 miles per hour away from our launch point.

Our navigation had better be damn accurate for there are no towns or highways, railroad tracks, or hills or mountains to visually check to help recognize your flight location, as there are on cross country flights back in the States. Just a never ending expanse of blue water meeting the horizons on all sides, once you leave your carrier for the target and while heading back to that elusive carrier. There would also be no windsock to help gauge the direction and force of the wind. Only your sharp eye could judge the direction of the waves breaking and the mist and the spray coming from the crest of the waves some two to three or even four miles below your altitude.

During the day we had recognition classes to occupy our time. We practiced recognition of Japanese planes we would most likely encounter. The fighter pilot that isn't the first to recognize an enemy plane will usually not be the one to survive, as the enemy would have the advantage of position if he sees you first. Our skipper seemed to be trying to give us the best chance to survive our tour of combat.

Entering the Combat Zone - CAPs Begin

The delayed pilots meeting finally became fruitful with the information that we are on our way to the Gilbert Islands. The skipper and Tom Morrissey our ACI (air combat intelligence) officer for the squadron had been in conference with Rear Admiral Radford most of the morning and were now at liberty to review our destination. The skipper had given us the Gilbert Islands and then turned to Tom Morrissey who went on to explain D-Day would be November 20th and we would be going in on D minus 1 escorting our bombers and torpedo planes.

In the meantime our squadron would be flying CAP "combat air patrol" starting tomorrow. One division of four planes would be in the air above our task group ready to investigate any bogey that our fighter director had picked up on his radar screen. Then as we got closer to the target area we would have a second division in the air, one at 10,000 feet and the other at 20,000 feet. CAPs were to be in the air continuously from sunup to sundown in four-hour on station stints.

The skipper called another all pilots meeting after dinner and thanked us for our efforts during the four months of organizational training back in the States. He went on to tell us that he had already promised Mom Chung that she could expect us to set all records for a navy fighter squadron during its tour of duty. He also stated he hoped our training would see us all through the period of combat we would be experiencing beginning the next day.

The skipper went on to say that combat is combat, and casu-

alties do occur. That some of us will unfortunately not be returning home to loved ones at the end of our tour of duty, which would
be approximately six months. He also stated history has proven
that pilots do get shot down, which was the reason our VF-2 had
been selected to serve in Air Group Six. We should each try hard
to make sure it's the enemy who gets shot down and to watch our
rear, for that's where the Japanese would like to be. He then said
be careful, good luck, and God bless. He went on to say he hoped
he would never have to write a bereavement letter to any of our parents or loved ones.

"First Strike"

Reveille would get us up bright and early at 0230 hours!
After dressing and having breakfast, I reported to the fighter ready
room to see the schedule for the day. My division had drawn the
first CAP, which would be the squadron's first combat flight.
However, we were still far enough away from the targeted island
that we really didn't expect any action.

We brought our plotting boards and navigation charts up to
date, and at 0430 when the ready room squawk box uttered "Pilots
man your planes," we headed for the flight deck. I headed for the
starboard catapult for I would be flying wing on my division leader
and therefore would be the second plane catapulted while the carrier was still swinging around into the wind for the others to fly off.

In order to get to the starboard catapult I had to cross the forward elevator. I had crossed most of the elevator from the port side
and was nearing the starboard side, when all of a sudden, with my
right foot just barely touching on the flight deck, which was flush
with the elevator level, the elevator suddenly started to drop out
from under me. I had not heard the loud noise that was mandated
at the control box when the elevator is to be moved either up or
down.

With my helmet on, which had the radio cups already
installed ready for flight, all noises were apparently blocked out,

and I had not heard the warning siren. And, apparently someone down on the hangar deck had to bring an item up topside and hit the button to activate the elevator's downward motion almost coinciding with his activating the alarm button without enough of an interval between the two buttons. Without that interval, I was caught with my right foot barely on the leading edge of the flight deck and with my weight still on my left leg.

The sudden drop of the elevator found me struggling to grab the railing that was rising as the elevator headed downward. My plotting board was in one hand and with the other I tried to grasp the railing but could not hold on and slipped backwards into the cavity created by the falling elevator. I found myself falling some 25 feet.

Fortunately, the elevator comes to a cushioning, slowing motion before it is locked in the bottom position, and I had landed on the elevator on my back as it was in that process of cushioning into its bottom position. My plotting board hit the deck and spilled my pencils and papers and other contents all over the deck. A couple of the hangar deck crew came running up to me yelling, "Stay still, we'll get the doctor, stay still!" They had seen me falling and hitting the deck.

I stayed still for a few seconds, but didn't feel any broken bones and then I realized I had really not been injured. I started gathering up my plotting board and supplies that had been scattered around and then got back on my feet. I stayed with the elevator going back up to the flight deck and even had to wait a couple seconds for the protective railing to let down enough to walk past it. I continued my jaunt over to the plane that I had been assigned to fly on this hop, which was sitting on the starboard catapult.

Watch and experience! That incident could very easily have put me down in sick bay with life-threatening injuries after falling 25 feet. But I didn't want to join my buddy, By Johnson, who was already down in sick bay after having been operated on the previous day for a sudden attack of appendicitis.

My incident had not delayed the launch at all. After climbing into the Hellcat, I got my parachute harness hooked up with the help of my plane captain, secured the plotting board in its place under the gun sight, and hooked the radio cord to my helmet cord. I was ready to start the engine when the air officer announced over the flight deck bullhorn to do so.

Once power had been established with the engine running smoothly, I was given a signal to spread the Hellcat's wings and check the locking device. Next was to check that the propeller control was in low pitch, the carburetor mixture in full rich and the flaps were down. I waited a few seconds for Mr. Eckhardt, my division leader, to be launched and about five seconds later I received a signal for full power, with both the launching officer and myself listening for a smooth running engine. Then I got the signal to get my thumb braced behind the throttle. This was to make sure I would not lose power during launch should the throttle snap back to a lower setting due to the forward thrust of the catapult.

Then the all-important signal to get my head back against the headrest. I had been warned that the sudden thrust forward of the catapult as it propels you from zero to 72 knots in the distance of only 80 feet could crack my skull if my head was not already back against the headrest. It was quite a different feeling, the first time you experience a cat shot. I assume it is like an automobile accident in reverse, where the car comes to an abrupt stop and your body is thrown forward against the steering wheel and into the windshield.

Once you are clear of the flight deck and are in the air, you have to strain forward in your effort to reach the wheels up lever that will help reduce wind resistance as soon as possible. A soon as you gain a little altitude, you are supposed to jog right so that your prop wash will clear the carrier to the starboard and not effect a pilot that is flying off the flight deck. Then as you gain a little more altitude and speed you can hit the flaps up switch to gain even more speed without changing the throttle setting.

As the number 2 pilot of the division, I would fly straight ahead for three and a half minutes to give the third and fourth planes flying off the carrier a chance to join up expeditiously. The number 3 plane would fly for three minutes and the No. 4 plane for little more than one minute. The division leader would have made a 180 degree turn and started back toward the carrier for us to join up in formation on him, before turning to a heading for the target.

In this case we do not have to wait for other fighters nor even our dive bombers or torpedo bombers. All we have to do is climb on up to the 10,000-foot level and make wide circles around our fleet in anticipation of getting a call from the fighter director. However, this flight had no calls to go out for investigation and we in boredom kept circling the fleet and waiting for our relief to come up so we could head down for our carrier landing.

We had another predawn launch on the 19th. This time we would be launched along with another division of fighters to escort our bombing and torpedo squadrons to a target on Makin Island. When the word came down to the fighter ready room to man planes, I was again assigned to the starboard catapult, and made sure I walked around the elevator this time on my way to the plane, for I wanted no part of falling 25 feet again.

We got launched and circled the fleet while our bombers and torpedo planes flew off the carrier and formed up with their formation for the flight into the target. When we are escorting our bombers and torpedo planes we have to criss-cross them to compensate for the difference in our speed from their lower normal speeds.

We were approximately 200 miles from Makin, and on our way. Anticipation was building that we would see some Japanese planes. Although we did have some antiaircraft shells come up at us, it was an uneventful flight. After hitting the target and about two-thirds of the way back to the *Enterprise,* we straighten out and stopped the weaving above our torpedo and bombing planes. We headed for the carrier so that we could land ahead of them and let them come straight in for their landings instead of them having to circle the fleet while us fighters landed first.

Our division had a CAP later that afternoon and again no vectors for a Japanese plane, but after landing aboard we learned that Tex Harris' flight had drawn first blood for the squadron by shooting down a Japanese "Dave" (a single engine observation

VF-2 in USS Enterprise ready room. Bunks on wall when pulled down were our bunk for the night when we had to stand night fighter duty.

plane). But we didn't see anything at all during our hop.

The skipper called for a debriefing meeting that evening to review our first day of real combat. He had bracers (one ounce of brandy or one can of bear) for calming our nerves as he reviewed the accomplishments for the day. Knocking out the five inch guns around the Kings Wharf and other bomb hits or strafing hits that had started several fires helped reduce the anti-aircraft as those positions were targeted. With all of that the skipper announced our squadron had used over 12,000 rounds of 50-caliber ammunition during the day. He congratulated the squadron's pilots for a very successful first day of combat and then started to let us know what our tentative schedule would be for the next day.

"Tarawa"

Reveille was at 0230 hours. This is D-Day and again we have a pre-dawn launch. Our bombers set the course and although I thought we were to hit Makin Island again, we were heading for Tarawa and got to see the blasts resulting from the battleship's 16-inch guns shelling the landing area prior to the Marines going in. We were escorting our bombers which had picked out a few targets the battleships had missed, and we thought our strafing efforts had pretty well quieted Japanese gun emplacements that our Marines would have to face when it came time for them to go ashore.

We could see the transport ships unloading the first wave of Marines that would be going ashore. They were getting into their little landing barges, which were circling and waiting for other landing barges to be filled with Marines that would then join up with the barges already circling, waiting for orders to head for the beach. These barges were supposed to be shallow water craft that would take them from the transport ships into the beach where we could see many craters from all the bomb hits and from blockbuster shells shot from the battleship's 16-inch guns.

However, we later learned that the Japanese had been very well dug in and still had several machine-gun batteries that were able to slaughter nearly 3000 of our Marines wading in from sand bars where their landing barges had been caught during that first wave. They had been caught many yards away from the actual beach because our admirals had failed to consider the effect of the ocean tides.

The flight in itself had been routine for us, but I guess my turn to create excitement had arrived, for in landing aboard, I had caught the number four wire, but my tailhook sheared off leaving me to float on up the flight deck and into the barrier. Fortunately, I had followed procedures correctly with my shoulder harness locked, which saved my head from being split open on the gun sight from the sudden stoppage because the barrier does not budge. It is there just for that purpose of catching runaway planes from plowing into other planes already parked forward.

The flight deck crew was right there to help me out of the nosed up plane, and the firefighters in their asbestos suits were there in two seconds ready to have foam hit the plane if fire had broken out. The plane would normally have been disengaged from the barrier cable and taken down to the hangar deck for an engine and propeller change, which the mechanics could do in about three hours. That included all wires and tubes and other connections that had to be made for the cockpit dials and gauges to be hooked up correctly.

But in my case, we still had many planes coming back from the target that should be landing. The urgency to get them landed and "turned around" (refueled and re-armed) was great, for the next scheduled strike would be required to go about as planned. The flight deck crane was brought over from its normal storage place between the five-inch gun housings. It was so large that it easily picked up my plane, after it was untangled from the cables of the barrier. It then moved over to the edge of the carrier deck and opened its giant claws to drop the plane overboard without the deck crew salvaging anything from the plane.

Now, the squadron was minus three planes, and I had been the first of several barrier crashes that would no doubt come before the cruise was over. That just verified the old Navy adage, that every carrier landing is a potential crash. Something can go wrong so easily, and it had just happened to me. After all, even the skipper had a barrier crash back on the Lexington when we were on that mock landing practice with the Marines going ashore on Maui.

I had not been injured in my mishap, so was able to take my second scheduled hop of the day, to the targets on Makin escorting our bombers. This turned out to be another uneventful strike for me, but after landing back aboard the *Enterprise*, we learned that Wayne Harrold had declared an emergency. The carrier had already been spotted for takeoff with our planes moved to the back of the carrier ready to fly off, and could not take him aboard immediately.

Why he had made a water landing on the port side of a battleship instead of back by the normal rescue destroyer, we will never know, for by the time the destroyer got up to the location of his water landing, nothing was floating. Although the destroyer stopped in that area for a while in hopes that they could discover him, their effort was futile, and we had lost another buddy.

The radio conversation did not indicate that he was personally injured, when he declared the emergency, but something drastic certainly must have happened. This became the topic for discussion at our meeting in the ready room that evening. The skipper cautioned us to make sure that we had the canopy locked open when ditching. It is difficult enough to get out of the plane after a water landing without having that canopy slammed shut from the sudden stoppage of the plane when it hit the waves. That would make it impossible to get out of your plane within the 30 seconds that we might have before it sinks below the surface. The second precaution was to make sure your shoulder straps were locked, so you don't split your forehead open or knock yourself unconscious on the gun sight during that sudden stoppage on landing, the same as your sudden stoppage when you catch the wire on a normal carrier landing.

It was Tarawa invasion D-Day plus 1, and our division was scheduled for two combat air patrols over our fleet. Both were uneventful, but the skipper's division that had the pre-dawn combat

November 1943

air patrol had garnered the squadron's second Japanese plane. It was a Betty (a twin engine bomber) that apparently had not dropped its bomb, or more likely it's torpedo, from the earlier nighttime attack against our task group, which had caused us to be at general quarters most of the night.

On D-Day plus 2 nothing exciting happened during our two scheduled combat air patrols except Mr. Eckhardt and myself were getting well experienced in catapult shots. We had been the first two off the flight deck during three different launches before the carrier hit the wind line for the rest of the planes in the launch to fly off.

Fleet Tankers

D-Day plus three. Our task group has a day of rest while we are alongside the *USS Lackawana*, a fleet tanker that will pump one million gallons of ships crude oil and half a million gallons of aviation gas over to the carrier. I really should have said the air group will have a day of rest, for the ships company (officers and men) will have demanding jobs keeping the carrier on course with the tanker for at least six hours while transferring all that petrol.

The tanker sets the course with the carrier along one side and a battleship on the other side, both jockeying to stay in position to receive its fuel before giving away to the cruisers. Then, time permitting, to the destroyers. If necessary, the destroyers could be topped off from a carrier or a battleship during normal fleet cruising.

That day was certainly a learning experience for me, watching our task group creep up to the refueling fleet shortly after sunrise. Our carrier slowly slipped into position next to the fleet tanker and both of them were rolling and tossing in the foul weather. The waves were pretty high and water swells at times were going over the side of the tanker and washing its deck. All of its seamen on deck had donned their life jackets and some of them were even tied with ropes to keep them from slipping overboard.

In foul weather, all this was necessary, because when the tankers arrived in the morning fully loaded, their main deck was usually only 8 to 10 feet above the water line. First, a small cord was shot from a rifle designed for that purpose across to the tanker. As the men aboard the tanker pull that cord across from the carrier, men on the carrier feed or tie on a little heavier rope. Then as men on the tanker pull that across, the men on the carrier feed on an even heavier cord. Finally an inch and a half hawser is tied to an 8 inch flexible hose that is then drawn from the tanker back to the carrier to be hooked up to the stand pipes. Different hoses were used for crude oil and for aviation gas, which would then be fed down to the storage chambers deep in the hold of the carrier.

The transferring hose would have some 30 to 40 feet extra laying on the carrier deck so that a crew of 10 to 15 men and a winch could keep the tubes taut at all times. As the two ships rolled to and fro, the men on the carrier would have to really pull fast and hard to keep the oil and gas lines from dipping down into the water. I don't think it really would affect the hose lines, but certainly would cause the pumps on the tanker to work extra hard with the dip and then having to pump the oil and gas upwards to the carrier's hangar deck. With all that going on, the carrier still has to maintain course and an equal distance from the tanker at all times.

D plus 4 found us back on station, with another task group going out approximately 200 miles east to meet the refueling group. We had several CAPs during the day but did not contact any Japanese planes. However, the carrier went to GQ (general quarters) just after the sun disappeared. Radar plot had picked up several groups of bogies approaching the task group. It was a rainy squally night, and we were under clouds apparently at the right time. The ship's gun crews that had been made ready to fire antiaircraft shells were ordered to hold their fire, thus not alerting the enemy planes to the fact that they were directly over our fleet. They passed on without ever making any semblance of an attack.

Thanksgiving Day, Nov. 25, 1943. Our division had two CAPs during the day, and then the fun started when the sun went down. The carrier again went to GQ. That meant that all doors and hatches between departments and on top of gangways "steep ladders" would have to be closed down tight to make the ship water tight, the smoking lamp was out, and all 20 and 40 mm guns had to be manned and ready to fire. Many bogies had appeared on the radar screen down in the carrier's CIC (combat intelligence center) room.

At first there were a few bogeys high above to the port side of the fleet. Between the many heavy clouds, we saw flares being dropped to float down silhouetting our ships on the horizon so that the Japanese Bettys could make their torpedo runs on the ships from the opposite side. All of a sudden one ship let loose with its antiaircraft battery and within a few seconds another ship let loose and before long every ship in the task force was firing.

What a display of power, with thousands of red and yellow tracers lighting up the sky. I can truthfully say that I have yet to this day seen a Fourth of July fireworks as brilliant as our fleet put up with all its 20 and 40 mm anti aircraft shells for quite a few minutes that night. The second carrier in our task group, the *USS Belleau Wood* had a narrow escape with a couple torpedoes barely missing its bow.

Butch O'Hare Night Fighting

Nov. 26 and the weather was still so bad that all flights were canceled during the day. But we had the same Tokyo express of Bettys that night, which annoyed Butch O'Hare to no end. He drummed up the idea of himself and a wing man flying for the firepower of the Hellcats guns with Cdr. Phillips in his TBF, which had the radar to locate the Bettys. Thus, carrier night fighting operation was originated.

They had some success in knocking down a couple of Japanese planes in between all the clouds and thunderheads, but our beloved air group Commander did not return. The speculation of his loss was that he was either hit by fire from a Betty that had joined their formation or that he was hit by one of the 50 caliber shells from the guns of the TBF's rear turret gunner.

However, we will never know. We missed Butch very much for he was a great leader and an inspiration to everyone who served under him. We liked him for his easy going manner, and he had a very likable personality. Later, he would be the namesake of O'Hare field on Chicago's northwest side.

Author noted in his log book the night "Butch" O'Hare was lost.

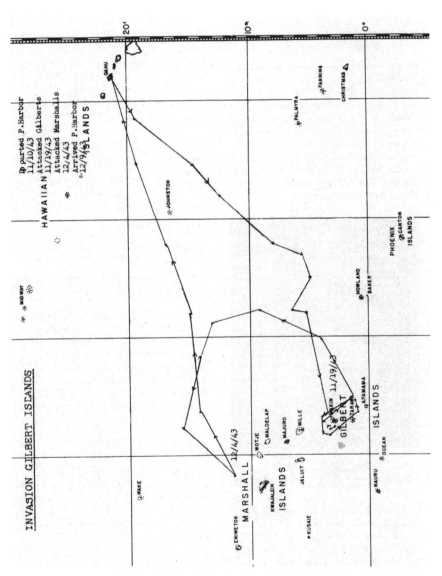

The Gilbert Islands Campaign

Clean up and back to Hawaii

That Gilbert Islands Operation was officially concluded on November 27th when our whole task group was rearranged, with the arrival of the *USS Essex,* with the flag of Admiral Montgomery aboard. We lost our task group commander, Admiral Radford, who was now aboard the *USS Saratoga* on its way back to Pearl Harbor.

The *Essex* and the *Saratoga* were part of the task group covering the Bougainville landing that had started on November 1st. It was now considered secure enough to allow that task group to come north and join our task group. The *Saratoga* was then detached and headed for Pearl Harbor, with Admiral Radford who had been the flag for our task group on the *Enterprise.*

Now the flag for our task group would be on the *Essex* with Admiral Montgomery making all decisions for the task group. The *Enterprise* and the *USS Belleau Wood* would be the other carriers included in the new task group. We also lost the battleships that had been with us as they returned to Pearl Harbor, but we had gained several heavy cruisers to replace them.

The *USS Princeton*, which had been with the *Essex*, was on her way to Pearl Harbor with the *Saratoga*, but before she left, three of its pilots flew Hellcats over as replacements for the 3 planes we had lost during the Gilbert Operation. I noted in my logbook, "We thought we would be refueling today but have not seen anything of the tanker fleet and we don't know when we will see them. It will have to be within the next day or two, for the orders now require us to hit the Marshall Islands on December 4th. It will probably be Kwajalein Island for a quick strike to do whatever damage we can and then to photograph the island for future landing site for our Marines."

Weather continued to be very foul and all flying was canceled during the next few days. On November 30th we lost 2 TBFs, one on take off; when the bow of the carrier dipped instead of rising, and the other on landing. It still had depth charges aboard that went off during the water landing, injuring the crew, but they all survived.

Without having to fly, we had been listening to much more radio, and had been amused by the beautiful music that "Tokyo Rose" had been playing. During the previous couple nights she had made the comment that Japanese planes had sunk the *Enterprise*, and then continued her radio program of the latest music. But we were still aboard and riding high.

We were cruising north during the last few days before D Day with battle plans indicating that we would hit Kwajalein. We were some 500 miles northeast and overnight would start a high-speed run toward the target for a quick hit-and-run strike. We were all eager and anxious to get a score on a Japanese plane. Half the squadron was quite disappointed when we learned the assignments for the next day. Only one strike of six divisions (24 planes) would be going against Ennylebegan and Ebeye (part of the Kwajalein atoll) land and seaplane bases. The rest of us would have one or two CAPs.

The skipper tried to appease us with the comment that Japanese planes would probably be following the strike groups back to our carrier, and we would have our chance then. The Admiral indicated we would probably have heavy action and be discovered by their search planes long before we would get to our launch point that was some 150 miles from the target. They actually got to the target and caught the Japanese garrison "with their pants down" for our bombers and torpedo planes hit various shipping targets with great success.

My division flew two CAPs that day and landed totally frustrated without a single vector out to investigate incoming Japanese planes during either flight. Yet it was only a half-hour after we landed that our task group came under attack by Japanese Bettys. For at least the next six hours, all during nighttime hours, we had a real Fourth of July fireworks display from our heavy cruisers and the destroyer screen. Especially when we could see the flaming destruction of a Japanese plane as it fell down to its watery grave after an AA hit.

My frustration was felt by all the other pilots that had flown

CAPs during the day, when we had the nightly recap of the day's results. Three more pilots got credit for Japanese Zeros - "Griff" Griffin, "Randy" Carlson, and "Shorty" (6' 2") LeForge were given the credits. Many more planes on the ground, mostly Bettys, were set on fire and most of the float Zeros in the harbor were left burning or sinking. "Red" Redmond did not return, and we were very concerned for his safety, although we later learned he had been picked up by a tin can (destroyer), and would be returned within a day.

After the recap of the day's activity most of us went up to the flight deck to watch the fireworks, but after getting tired of standing, we returned to the ready room to play several hands of bridge and to listen to our favorite broadcaster, "Tokyo Rose" who again announced that the United States carrier *Enterprise* had been sunk. We might have disappeared from the Kwajalein area for we had been on the "run" part of the "hit-and-run" all evening and were probably getting out of range of the Japanese Bettys that our screen of cruisers and destroyers had been firing at.

While the carrier was at GQ, we played bridge and listened to "Tokyo Rose" music. It was a good way to spend the time because we didn't feel like opening all the watertight doors to get down to our staterooms. Before calling it a night we heard "Tokyo Rose" announce again that among the other ships sunk, that the big "E" had gone to the bottom. Yet we were still riding high, although lurching and rolling in the very heavy, heavy seas.

Most of us slept in rather late after spending so much time the night before on the flight deck watching the fireworks and playing quite a bit of bridge while the carrier was at general quarters (when bulkhead doors and compartments are sealed to prevent fire and/or water damage from spreading throughout the ship).

I did have another CAP later that afternoon while our task group was heading for Pearl Harbor. We landed just at dusk again, but in time for a late dinner and then the squadron party in the ready room, the medical department furnishing ingredients to relax our nerves. And, you've never seen such a happy-go-lucky group of guys after imbibing that medicine (one ounce of brandy or one can of beer), it wasn't like being back in Atlantic City, partying every night at the Penn-Atlantic hotel, when one drink just got us started for the evening.

The next three days were just for leisure, playing bridge or acey-deucey along with some sun bathing on the flight deck, although we did take enough time for squadron pictures in the ready room and in front of a Hellcat on the flight deck. The photographer, however, had quite a time getting the photograph as there was a very strong 50-knot wind crossing over the flight deck that afternoon.

Our next flight was the usual fly off from the carrier when we were still about 100 miles from Pearl Harbor. We were launched at 0700, rendezvoused, and were headed for Barbers Point by 0730. Again, we would be land-based while the fleet was docked or anchored around Ford Island.

VF-2 on the flight deck of the USS Enterprise on December 7, 1943, on their way back to Pearl Harbor. Author on left end of middle row.

Goodbye, *Enterprise* - Hello, Hawaii

We soon learned we would not be going back on the Big "E" as the fighting squadron for Air Group 6. The skipper of VF-6 had apparently been satisfied with his pilots' conversion from the Wildcats to the Hellcat and he had trained the replacement pilots sufficiently well that he wanted to rejoin Air Group 6 on the *Enterprise* for this next engagement. I suppose VF-6 was behind it, when throwing a big party in the Barbers Point "O Club" to welcome VB-6 and VT-6 back. For now they were an air group of three squadrons again waiting to go back aboard the *Enterprise* for the next operation.

Our VF-2 was included in the party because, after all, we had been part of Air Group 6 during this last operation. The booze flowed freely with several toasts to our missing air group commander, Butch O'Hare. Even commander Phillips, the new air group commander had a good time, and pleased everyone present with a statement we would have the whole weekend off - NO FLYING!

I guess most of us woke up rather late the next morning with a reminder of the previous nights festivities. Headaches that took a little while to dissipate over several cups of coffee, but all the while giving us a chance to open up much of the mail that had finally caught up with us. Then a long-awaited shower, my kind, not the Navy shipboard kind of one minute saltwater soap down, with a one minute fresh water rinse off, but with a 15 to 20 minute warm water shower.

The Hawaiian miniature gauge railroad had a station on the far side of Barbers Point Naval Air Station. Many of us would meet there for the mid-morning scheduled run around Pearl Harbor and on into Honolulu. We enjoyed the afternoon on Waikiki Beach and dinner at the Moana Hotel's dining room where we might find some lady to dance with before we would have to leave to catch the mini train on its last run of the day back to Barbers Point.

On one of those days, H. R. Davis who we knew as "Stinky"

which was his squadron nickname, some how or another, garnered a Jeep by hook or crook from the motor pool for a welcome change in routine. I forget the exact number of us, but the Jeep was well overloaded by the time we left the base for a sightseeing jaunt around Oahu. We enjoyed the crooked road to the summit of Pali Road, where we were able to stop and enjoy the view before continuing on down the other side. We eventually wound up at the Moana Hotel again for a swim and sun bathing on Waikiki along with a few Mai Tais and a terrific leisurely Luau.

It had been such an enjoyable time that we had not noticed time to have passed or slipped away so fast before we got back to the Jeep. The sun had already set as we headed down Kalakaua Avenue to start our trip back to the base. We had not gone very far when a police siren sounded behind us. Stinky pulled over and we all tried to act as sober as we could.

Thank goodness the officer was quite congenial and had stopped us merely to warn us to dim the lights as Honolulu was under strict "blackout" conditions at night. That meant we would have to drive all the way without lights. If we were stopped again, the officer had warned us, we all could spend the night in the hoosegow. We started out again at a rather fast pace and the next thing we heard was "Have no fear, Stinky is here," coming from our driver. That became our battle cry as we wound our way out the Kamehameha Highway, around Hickam Field, and Pearl Harbor, then on to the Farrington Highway and finally to Barbers Point. Boy, what a night!

More Practice

We started flying again the next day on an Air Group Two coordinated attack with our bombing and torpedo two squadrons who had finally arrived in Hawaii and were based over at Kaneohe Marine Air Station on the East side of Oahu. We went to rendezvous with the rest of our air group and escorted them out to a ship towing a 200-foot sled on the end of a 1000-foot cable.

The bombers would drop 100-pound dummy bombs loaded with water which would make quite a splash when they landed, so they could see how accurate their dive bombing efforts were. The torpedo bombers were loaded also with the 100-pound dummy water bombs to make a simulated torpedo drop, but in that instance they would practice their skip bombing abilities, and our Hellcats were actually loaded with live 50-caliber ammo to give a more realistic attack by strafing that sled.

This was the first time all three squadrons of Air Group Two had ever worked together. This time was a total snafu, although an overcast weather condition gave us an excuse. The next day went a little better, although it was still a group grope. After we got back on base, the skipper called a meeting for all officers to inform us we would be transferring to Kaneohe to be with the rest of our Air Group Two, leaving Air Group 6 by itself at Barbers Point. He also told us that it didn't look like we would be having a carrier for the next operation, and we would remain on the island until the next carrier would come out from the states. But he assured us he was still diligently trying to get us aboard some carrier.

The next day was spent gathering all our gear again for another move, including a trip back to the big "E" for the rest of our squadron's tools and spare parts that would go direct over to Kaneohe.

It was just a short flight across the island to the Kaneohe Marine Air Station, where we found a super spacious BOQ and a beautiful officers' ward room (dining room) with background music and Philippine waiters that had been trained to the Nth degree serving delicious food.

The officers' club was also top-notch with a plentiful supply of hard booze. Even with all the rationing, the club had been able to buy the required amount of wine and champagne and get supplies of Scotch, straight whiskey, and bourbon. That night we were toasting anything and everything, for champagne was only five cents a drink and the bar manager was trying to reduce his inventory of that product. I guess we really tried to make up for lost time with such low prices and the knowledge that we wouldn't have to fly the following day.

An awful lot of coffee was consumed the next morning, and after lunch the skipper informed us that our executive officer Lt. John Eckhardt had received orders back to CASU One, and that a Lt. L. E. Doner would be joining us, along with three other Ensigns. Lt. Harris would be our new executive officer, and with all the changes I'd have to wait to see who my new division leader would be.

The skipper also passed out an all-leather money belt to each of us. He had received them in the mail, personally engraved in gold, with our individual names, from our beloved Mom Chung, with her warmest of Christmas greetings, and blessings for the New Year. The letter also informed us that she had finally received a tentative copy of our squadron insignia from a friend, an artist by the name of Walt Disney. It was to be a dragon ripping the Japanese flag to pieces. However, it still had to be submitted to the bureau of the Navy for official approval.

We all had quite a snicker when the skipper finally noted that Stinky Davis, Duffer Duff, and Red Banks had not come to the meeting. During lunch we had learned that Stinky had to go back to Honolulu to the Hall of Justice to pay a fine, or at least to explain to the judge their antics of the previous evening when they had garnered a Jeep for a nocturnal jaunt to Waikiki Beach.

While driving down Kalakaua Avenue he had passed a slow-moving car, to which Red Banks had given a ten finger (5 to each ear) salute to the driver of that slow-moving car. Unknowingly, it turned out to be a plain clothes traffic cop. They were lucky that the ticket was just for unbecoming action rather than the DUI that Stinky admitted it probably should have been, after all the champagne they had consumed. Especially, with a couple bottles of champagne still on the floor of the Jeep.

After the meeting a large amount of mail had finally caught up to us and was waiting at the registration desk. Everyone was busy for quite some time catching up on all the activities of family and loved ones. My roommate, Demi Lloyd, was rather disturbed and had a few choice words for whoever had censored the letter he had written to his wife while we were on the Enterprise.

If you remember, all mail had to be censored, usually on the evening before it would be transferred over to the tanker while the carrier was refueling. We were not allowed to censor our own letters, as all officers had to make sure there was no reference to the Air Group and the carrier it was aboard. If we used a return address of the Air Group, we could not even mention the name of the carrier we were on. Those in ship's Company could not mention the air group by name that was aboard their carrier. We were also not allowed to state what combat action we had been in, or headed for next, although that was usually not a problem because orders were normally sealed concerning the next operation until we were well on the way. Only the Admiral of the task group and the Captain of the carrier who had to set the course to the action knew our destination.

I couldn't believe that Demi would have violated any of those requirements when writing his wife, but he held up a letter she had returned to him in one of the envelopes he had just received. It looked like a fancy doily and there wasn't a paragraph that made any sense at all. We all had quite a laugh and figured the censor had to have been a young ship's officer making sure he was doing his job according to strict regulations.

Inclement weather rather restricted our flying for the next few days, so the skipper decided it was time for another squadron party while we had such beautiful accommodations there at Kaneohe. He appointed Happy Jack Holladay and Bill Blair to make the arrangements for Thursday, December 23, which would be our Christmas party in the station's O club. The skirt chasers went to work immediately and rounded up some

Twenty Navy nurses from the Marine base and also Army Air Corps nurses from the Kamehameha Army hospital. Some came in their dress uniforms while others really dolled up for the occasion by donning evening gowns, which they didn't have many occasions to wear while in service.

It was a grand evening, although many of the ladies had a hard time trying to finish their dinners when the music was so good and dancing was the order of the evening, especially with all the air group officers outnumbering the ladies two to one.

There wasn't much flying that next morning after such an enjoyable dinner dance, and the skipper secured flying shortly after lunch. However, he called an all pilots meeting to inform us that hopes for a carrier for the next operation was negative and the whole air group would be moving down to Hilo on the big island, and that we would be flying planes down on the 28th. All the non flying officers and the enlisted crew would board the shuttle boat for Hilo on the 27th. This news disheartened everyone, but the skipper wished us all a Merry Christmas and said he'd see us on the flight line with all our gear ready to fly on the 28th.

Discouraged, we headed back to BOQ to change out of our flight gear, to enjoy the rest of the afternoon before the Christmas eve dinner. But it wasn't long before By Johnson called to get a buddy to head for the beach at Waikiki, which would probably be the last chance to enjoy it for quite some time. He and Nol Harrigan were all set to go, and I joined them shortly. We headed for the main gate and after leaving the station we had to get our thumbs working for lack of any other mode of transportation. Several cars passed us by, for they were all well loaded.

All of a sudden a big Cadillac came along with the flags of an Admiral very well displayed on the front bumpers and our thumbs went down. But the caddy came to a stop and the voice from within boomed out "Come on boys, hop in. Are you heading for Waikiki?" After our affirmative answer, we again heard "Well, come on, hop in," and it turned out to be Admiral Arthur Radford, who had been our task group commander when we were both on the *Enterprise* at Makin and Tarawa. He had recognized us, and wanted to know all about the rest of our tour on the *Enterprise* after he had left. It was quite an enjoyable ride with a lively discussion all the way around the Southeast end of Oahu. He even instructed his driver to drop us off at the Moana Hotel where we were able to get rooms for Christmas Eve, and a place to change into our swimming trunks. Talking with the others in the hotel and on the beach at Waikiki, we heard "You will just LOVE Hilo."

This was Christmas Eve, and although we were dining with a good music background and excellent food, my thoughts were generally back at home. My father would have prepared the evening meal for mother, who had been bed ridden for three years already with the whole gauntlet of rheumatism, and both kinds of arthritis, which in those days was still virtually untreatable. Then he probably would go over to the church to meet a few of his parishioners to go on the traditional Christmas Eve rounds of singing carols to other invalids and shut ins from the church. I hoped he had been able to find another man to sing the bass parts of the various carols that I had sung back in school days when I had joined those out caroling.

No, Christmas would not be the same this year way out here with no chance of getting home to greet everyone. It wouldn't even be the same as last year at Corpus Christi, Texas, when many of us cadets were invited out to homes in or around Corpus to enjoy a leisurely turkey dinner prepared by the lady of the house. But we had a pleasurable day on the beach and swimming before back into the Moana for dinner and a few dances and then early to bed.

Christmas Day 1943 was a day of leisure starting with an extended long warm fresh water shower which was so much better than the Navy two minute salt water deal. Then we had a leisurely breakfast and spent most of the day on the beach swimming or sun bathing, then back into the hotel to have a quick shower and dress for dinner. Unfortunately, we had to enjoy our traditional turkey dinner without even one dance for the lack of females out for dinner. One more drink at the bar and then off to bed. Yes, this Christmas Day had been far different than any in the past.

We slept late on the 26th, even after such a leisurely Christmas Day, and took an elongated shower before lunch, after which we headed back to Kaneohe. It was a good thing we had headed back when we did for the weather was turning sour and the rain started almost as we entered the door of our BOQ. It rained, rained, and rained for the next couple days and our move to Hilo, at least for the pilots flying planes, was delayed a day because of the inclement weather.

It had been a total washout with rain, low ceilings and was in general unfit for flying anyplace, to say nothing of flying 200 miles down to a new base all in formation. Of course, the O club was calling, and all pilots just couldn't wait to hear the skipper declare the flight impossible for that afternoon, but to be on the flight line promptly at 0800 the next morning for he was under pressure to get the squadron moved.

He kept us all in the ready room waiting for a break in the clouds and finally he decided to let a division at a time take their chances dodging the thunderheads. The skipper had wanted all 36 planes to go together as we had flown from Quonset Point to Alameda, but there was no way, with such low ceilings and no navigational aids to assist if we could have gone on instruments to get on top of the weather.

So we were sent out to fly at 1000 feet if we could get that high, but told to stay under the clouds even for the trip down to Hilo. We were to stay well clear of Molokai and Maui, and well seaward of the big island 'til we determined we were getting close to Hilo. We had received a warning from the CAA when filling our flight plans that the 14,000 foot Mauna Kea would be completely obscured due to the inclement weather.

Most of us loaded our baggage and a case of booze in the small luggage compartment of the Hellcat. The scuttlebutt that we had heard about Hilo was that the O club had been closed due to some previous squadron getting too boisterous and shooting up the place, resulting in the base commander ordering the O club closed so there would be no future destructive parties. No wonder everybody had been telling us "You will love Hilo."

Thirty-five planes arrived before sundown, with the 36th to arrive in a day or two for it would need a complete engine change. Somehow or another, Dick Combs had nosed up on a taxiway heading out to the runway there at Kaneohe. The next day we were quite surprised to see our planes from VB-2 and VT-2 start arriving. Now we would be a complete Air Group again as we were for those few days at Kaneohe.

Weather improved somewhat, at least enough for us to get a

couple familiarization flights to see the area and then a flight around the whole island of Hawaii. We also had a couple of combined flights with our bombers before securing for the New Year's Eve celebrations. With the O club closed, we had to make our own party, which meant we picked a couple rooms in BOQ to celebrate in, and then broke out a bottle of our own hooch. In addition to a case of champagne from Demi Lloyd, who had helped the O club back in Kaneohe by purchasing several cases and having it hauled down by those that came down by the inter-island boat.

The O club manager was grateful for getting rid of the champagne and relieving the storage shed of several cases of bubbly. He made us a giveaway price of only $2.50 per case, for they had accumulated so much champagne with the required buy a case of champagne for every case of booze or Scotch that they wanted to order. No one really wanted to drink champagne, so they had cases and cases of it stacked up in the warehouse.

Yes, that O club manager was real happy to have Demi relieve him of so much champagne, and it certainly helped liven up our New Year's Eve celebration. Demi would have bubbly for a long, long time.

Hangovers and bad weather kept us from flying for the next several days. The squadron skipper called an all pilots meeting at which he informed us that he and Butch Voris would be flying up to Pearl Harbor. They wanted to see the Admiral with a special request that Fighting Two be assigned to some carrier for active combat or duty on an island where we could do some good.

He hated to have his squadron beached at Hilo with the next operation coming up in the very near future. And, before we were dismissed he read another letter from Mom Chung. If you remember Mom was the Chinese doctor in San Francisco that had "bastard sons" such as Bill Dean, Jimmy Doolittle, Admiral Halsey, Hap Arnold, Claire Chennault, Billy Mitchel, and others, and now the pilots of Fighting Two.

She wanted to make sure we all understood we were welcome, with an invitation to her home at 347 Masonic Street, San Francisco anytime we would be in or around the area. She was our "benefactor" and was still trying to get Walt Disney's design for our squadron insignia to be approved by the Navy department in the very near future.

Mom was well known in the area for her numerous contributions in the field of medicine, and her assistance to China's Air Force and the American Volunteer Group of Chennault's Flying Tigers in Burma. She was very instrumental in organizing the Women's Auxiliary Volunteer Enlistment Service, more commonly known as the U.S. Navy WAVES and in getting a bill through Congress to approve the WAVES as an established active part of the U.S. armed service.

The weather finally cleared enough on the 4th for us to take another familiarization flight to see more of the large island, and get reference points in case we would ever be caught in the usually bad weather of the island and its surroundings. On the 5th we flew a couple of short gunnery hops, firing our ammunition at a towed sleeve, which was towed back and dropped on our base at Hilo, all the pilots eagerly counting the holes that had their color paint that the 50-caliber bullets had been dipped in prior to the flight.

We had a couple of short gunnery hops on the 5th and then had a couple bags of mail to sort through when we got back to the barracks. Among the mail was a box for "Shorty" LeForge, which contained many new records for us to play on the record player. We had all chipped in to buy the records prior to leaving the states so we would have music aboard the carrier to relax with in between flights.

That was before we had known anything about "Tokyo Rose." The records were played mostly for daytime listening between flights. Then we found listing to the evening programs that "Tokyo Rose" presented and carried over the carrier's loud-speaker system took precedence over all of our records.

It was a welcome package that "Shorty" had received and most of us sent a thank you to Mrs. Leforge. The 5th was also a day that found four pilots receiving orders transferring them to Air Group 12, on the *USS Saratoga* for temporary "bat" duty. Jake

Nearing, Fox Norling, Mike McCloskey, and Al Scheele were the four selected for this training,

Foul weather precluded any flying on the 6th, but I had a real harrowing flight on the 7th, when we were scheduled for another gunnery hop. We were just short of the gunnery area when my windshield began to cloud over with oil, so I excused myself from the flight to head back to our Hilo base. I hoped I could get the plane back to the field before my oil tank ran dry.

It was a good thing we had already gained altitude before the oil appeared. Even though I set the engine at a lower power setting and cut my speed back to minimum, the oil leak kept getting worse and the oil pressure started down. I had to shut down completely just as the field came into view. I had a full load of ammunition still on board and I started to descend rather rapidly, just like a lead balloon.

The problem then became a flip of the coin, should I gamble on having enough altitude yet to make the field or should I hit the silk and let the plane do whatever it would, or do I prepare to make a water landing. Though I was losing altitude very rapidly, I gambled that I could make the field for a dead stick landing.

I called the tower to alert them of my problem and had to thank my lucky stars that the runway wasn't another hundred feet farther away. Even waiting almost too long to pump the wheels down, I barely made the very edge of the runway and rolled out to a stop.

The fire trucks and the meat wagon (ambulance) were ready and waiting for me. However, with the engine having been cut off, there had apparently been enough air over it for the oil to have cooled enough so it did not catch on fire as the plane slowed down.

I did, however, have to wait for the tow tractor to come out to pull me off the runway and on into CASU. There the mechanics started analyzing the problem to determine if they had to make a complete engine change or whether I had shut the engine off in time to save the engine cylinders and the plane itself.

The next few days kept CASU busy from various mishaps, while we were flying gunnery hops. Charlie Carroll had a belly landing. He said, "The landing gear apparently just didn't come down." John Banks clobbered up a plane when taking off with a sleeve for a gunnery hop. He also ruined a couple Hellcats from VF-36 that were waiting for takeoff instructions, during this mishap.

We also received word that Fox Norling, our quiet and affable buddy, who had been ordered to report for night fighter training, had been killed during one of those training flights. The destroyer escort had not been able to find him during the darkness of night, and an air search of the area the next morning could find nothing, either.

Chapter Six

"TAD" CRUISE

VF-2 pilots scattered as replacements
January to March 1944

"Temporary Additional Duty"

The skipper received a dispatch from ComAirPac on the 14th of January 1944. We all speculated that his trips to Pearl Harbor may have succeeded in getting us an assignment for duty in the upcoming operation. However, at the meeting he called on the 15th, our hopes suffered a letdown when he related his attempts to get the powers that be to move the squadron onto a carrier heading out for the next operation.

It was not the dispatch we had hoped for. However, he explained the dispatch ordered him to release seven of his now "combat experienced pilots" to go aboard the *USS Kalinin Bay*, a Kaiser flattop carrier to serve as replacement pilots and fly replacement planes to the larger carriers as needed during the next operation. Commander Dean put the order on a volunteer basis, to which he had more hands go up than needed. So he picked Bob Butler, Dick Combs, Duffer Duff, Stinky Davis, Red Redmond, Obie O'Brien, and myself. We were all excused to go back to the barracks to gather our stuff, because the transport plane would be arriving early in the morning to ferry us up to Pearl Harbor and then we would board the *Kalinin Bay*.

It was promised to all of us that we would be back with

Fighting Two at the end of this next operation. However, this hit the skipper with thoughts of such a reduction in squadron personnel that a get-together dinner in Hilo at Moto's Inn would help keep our comradeship together. Although the skipper did not offer to pay for the dinner, we found a regular steak dinner was only 50 cents and only 75 cents for a prime rib dinner, which we all found to be very delicious. Try having a prime rib dinner at those prices in today's world of inflation!

The R-5D kept us waiting, and waiting, but finally arrived on the 16th to take us up to Ford Island and the *Kalinin Bay*. But the *Kalinin Bay* was not expecting us until the 17th. So not to be outdone, we went back to BOQ, which was rather full. But the room clerk condescended to give the seven of us an Admiral suite room for the night.

The 17th produced quite a let-down from the Admiral's suite to cots on the hangar deck of this baby flattop while we were waiting for room assignments. We didn't wait around for long after the officer of the deck suggested we go over to the ferry that would take us to the mainland where we could catch the bus to Waikiki Beach and the Moana Hotel. But he had a specific warning for us. Be back aboard no later than 0600, for the gangplank could be pulled up any time after that to make ready for departure.

We had a very good time swimming and enjoying what probably would be our last good meal at the Moana for quite some time. We even had a few dances again. But the group thought we had probably better return to the carrier that night. No one knew exactly how long it would take to get back to the carrier or the bus to catch the ferry to Ford Island early in the morning prior to 0600.

Reading bus routes on their signboard was difficult at night especially when we did not know exactly which buses to take to get to the ferry. But we made it well before midnight and had to sleep on our cots. We were awakened rather early with the ship's crew making all kinds of noise hauling in the hawser lines that secured the carrier to the dock, and yes, we pulled out almost exactly at 0600, which was the departure time.

Out to sea again, with such a load of Hellcats and Corsairs that there would have to be some 25 to 30 of them catapulted before anything could possibly fly off the flight deck. Our battle station is our plane. Consequently we had lots of time for sun bathing and even target practice off the fantail. We hit quite a few clay birds with the rifles, but when we started using our pistols, we weren't quite so lucky with our shots.

The weather wasn't too good, so we soon found that the Kaiser job didn't pitch and roll near as much as I had thought it would. Plus the meals there on the *Kalinin Bay* were extra good, certainly much better than the K rations that friends of mine would be having in the trenches over in Europe. And we had clean white sheets to sleep on instead of muddy old ground in the foxhole.

The carrier air officer called a meeting of our "Little Rippers" to inform us that they had not been able to get the last Hellcat aboard. Therefore, he suggested we cut a deck of cards, with the lowest number to stay aboard without flying a replacement plane to a major carrier during this combat operation. I drew the duce of clubs, so you know who got the state room for the rest of the voyage and then would have to watch all the others fly off as replacement pilots and their planes when requested from other major carriers.

Monday the 24th saw all 18 Corsairs catapulted for their over-water jaunt to Funa Futi, and a couple hours later we were guided through the channel leading into Majuro lagoon, which had now become a fleet anchorage. This island had been the target of a quick fighter sweep just a couple months back. Now we weighed anchor amongst many other ships in the lagoon. Shortly after dropping anchor, the captain received a congratulatory message for "getting his ship through safely on the 22nd" when an intercepted message read, "sink *Kalinin Bay* at all costs." Fortunately, we had not been alerted to the danger and with the blessings of God that sub had not found us.

Since we were not required to be at a battle station, that left us with nothing to do but fish off the fantail or go ashore, or swim under the extended yard arm, which had Marine safety guards with loaded rifles to protect us from any sharks that might be swimming by. There were many LCIs (Landing Craft Infantry) going from one carrier to another, and we could hitch a ride on any one of them to get ashore for swimming on the beautiful coral sandy beach.

We found the beach to be an excellent sunning place, plus it usually had an extra attraction... a few Navy nurses from the hospital ship H-1 (Hospital-1). They had now become part of the usual landing force. The Marines would bring the seriously injured out to them after their corpsman had made whatever quick diagnoses or treatment of their wounds that they could.

Swimming became much more enjoyable when we could see women around, for it was one of the few times we ever saw a female once we left Pearl Harbor. I bumped into a few old buddies from cadet days and had a good time reminiscing about some of our training days.

We enjoyed the beach again on Wednesday, but when we arrived back to the carrier, we heard of the misfortunes of our Marines that had been catapulted off just a few days before. It seems they had run into very squally rainy weather on their way to Funa Futi and only one of them arrived. The rest, all 17 of them were lost at sea due to weather.

The big event at the end of the month, payday. That meant we had to pay our mess bill, although it was only $18 for the month, and then it was back to the beach. Meanwhile, the storekeepers of the ship were replenishing food and filling the storage lockers from barges bringing it over from the supply ships, which now brought the supplies direct to these forward areas rather than unloading them back at Pearl Harbor. Even crude oil for the carrier's engines was transferred from the tanker ships.

"Shellbacks" and "Polywogs"

We pulled anchor on Monday January 31, which was a day or two before the rest of the fleet would leave Majuro. I guess the Captain had a master plan of navigating over the equator during that extra day or two so that his shipboard crew could have their frivolous initiation. Probably half of his crew would be getting initiated from King Neptunus Rex of the Royal Court to summon all "thy lowly pollywogs" to fulfill all their penalties for being in such a lowly state, and then carry out the sentence they would have to complete before becoming a "Royal Shellback." That Shellback initiation has been a time-honored celebration for most of the ships of the Navy and for Navy personnel whenever they have crossed the equator.

On February 3rd, orders were received for one plane to fly over to the *CVL Cowpens*, which Dick Combs took. Then two planes were sent to the *CVL Monterey*, which Stinky Davis and Duffer Duff took. Orders were received on the fourth, for two planes to fly over to the old faithful "Big E". O'Bie and Redmond obliged, and then Butler went to the *CVL Belleau Wood*, leaving me all alone on the Kaiser flattop.

A few hours later, I saw the whole task group, every ship lining up in single file for entrance through the channel into the Majuro lagoon again, but swimming would be out for now because the wind and high waves kept all aboard. Even the supply barges carrying food and ammunition out to the various ships had a hard time navigating to the ship that they were supposed to go to because of the high waves.

Weather remained horrible for the next day, so it passed rather quietly, and I found myself reading in the library until late afternoon when the ships bull horn blurted out for me to report to the carrier's Air officer. He informed me that orders were being cut for me to report to the *USS Bunker Hill,* and he thought I should leave as soon as I could gather my gear together, as the *Kalinin Bay* had received orders to leave very early the next morning. The whale boat provided for my transfer didn't ride the waves very well and I was soaked to the bone when I climbed the gangplank to report aboard the *Bunker Hill.*

After climbing that ladder, as soaked and chilled as I was, I saluted the Ensign (flag) and gave my orders to the officer of the deck, who immediately gave me an assignment to a state room where I could change, dry off, and put dry clothes on. While doing so, I began to think, now, all seven of us "Little Rippers" were scattered throughout the fleet and I wondered when we would be getting back to good old Fighting Two.

The next thing I had to do was report down to sick bay, for the usual physical on joining a new squadron, Fighting 18. Just as I finished my physical, flight quarters sounded, and then the general quarters sounded for the carrier's radar had picked up a bogie some 80 miles away, but apparently only on a direct flight to one of their own Japanese held islands.

We enjoyed swimming again on those sandy beaches, weather permitting, during the next week while the barges filled with supplies from the AKS (supply ships) battled the waves and at times in pouring rain. On the 12th, we pulled anchor and started single file to exit out of the channel from the Majuro lagoon. We were several miles out to sea before the ships began separating into their assigned task groups, and this time we learned we were on our way to the island of Truk.

It was a strange island, for no one other than the Japanese had been on that island for at least a quarter of a century and our ACI officer's admitted any pictures they had would be at least 30 years old. There were no maps or photographs of the island indicating where our Marines could go ashore, nor would they be able to give us any specific targets on the island. Therefore, that became the primary purpose of this operation, to test the island's defenses and to get photographs for future use.

Destroyers came alongside, in turn for the usual fuel top-off before the fleet started its high-speed run into the target area on the 16th. Briefing for this operation was almost nonexistent. We had no area maps to put on our plotting boards to help in navigating to and from the target. The pilots returning from the target reported very heavy anti-aircraft fire with our bombing squadron losing three planes and crew, and had two more rear seat gunners come back dead in their seats. I imagine other carriers had about the same disastrous results.

We had just that one sweep over the island, and after it was over, the doctor issued a "sick call" for all those with pilot fatigue, and AV(S) with paralysis, which consisted of the usual one can of beer or the one ounce bottle of brandy. Take your choice. In short order we had a bunch of pilots that had relaxed to the point that they were really happy-go-lucky fellows. I believe Admiral Nimitz did everything he could to prevent our taking of Truk, with the information gained from photographs taken that day, which was why we eventually circumvented the Truk Island and went right on to Eniwetok and then Saipan.

I woke up on the 19th to see our carrier paralleling the AO (tanker, which I think it was the *USS Lackawana*) transferring up to one million gallons of ships crude oil and another 300,000 gallons of aviation 95 octane gasoline via the 8 inch hoses between ships. We pulled away after about five hours refueling and went to flight quarters to launch a CAP and then to receive a replacement plane from the "Big E," which would be heading back to Pearl Harbor. Lo and behold, it was Les Sipes who brought that plane aboard. He apparently was one from a second bunch of "volunteers" from VF-2 to serve as replacement pilots. Now we really had the squadron scattered around the fleet.

Saipan and Tinian

When I entered the fighter pilots ready room on Sunday February 20th, I found my name on the flight schedule for the day. This would be the first time I had flown since January 13th. It was for a CAP, and although the flight was not adventurous, my rear end really let me know I hadn't sat still in one spot for such a long time.

After that, I was scheduled every day to fly a CAP, all of which were uneventful with nothing happening during the hours I was in the air, with no vector out from the carrier's fighter director to investigate a bogey. The Japanese just never seemed to come out during my scheduled CAPs, only after dark, when the fireworks from most of our other ships on the perimeter screen of the task force really lit up the sky, with several Japanese Bettys going down in flames.

Our next operation was to give Guam, Saipan, and Tinian a going over on the 22nd. We found the black puffs of anti-aircraft shells quite accurate and very heavy over Guam, but not near as bad over Saipan and hardly anything when flying over Tinian. After the day's activity the task force set course for Majuro, and we entered the narrow channel leading into the lagoon to drop anchor on the 26th.

The next day I received orders to hop on one of the LCIs making the rounds between carriers, and depart when we reached the *CVL Belleau Wood.* It would not be going back to Pearl Harbor with us, but had several planes needing the 500-hour required CAA mechanical servicing. This was called the major overhaul and was done only in the big shops in Pearl Harbor or in Jacksonville, Florida.

I was to fly one of those "green duds" over to the *Bunker Hill* after having been catapulted from the *Belleau Wood.* It was a beautiful sunny day and my trip on the LCI was rather interesting, for we stopped at almost every carrier anchored in the lagoon before arriving at the *Belleau Wood.* I was a lot drier this trip than I had been when ordered to the *Bunker Hill* less than two weeks earlier.

I had a wonderful chicken dinner which was served to us pilots from other carriers that had been ordered to fly their "green duds" the next day to carriers heading back to Pearl after they got several miles out to sea. We also had reserved seats at the movie that night in the front row with the captain, executive officer, and air officer up on the flight deck where it was much cooler than it would have been on the hangar deck.

After the movie we all went back to the ready room where we had quite a chat with Butler and Harrigan from VF-2 and Phipps and Prejean from VF-8 and others we had known from Cadet days. However, we had to cut the reunion short for we had been told to be ready to go early in the morning. While having breakfast I was surprised to discover the portholes in the wardroom of the Cruiser hull carrier to be open so early in the day to allow fresh air in.

Flight quarters sounded about a half-hour after the *Bunker*

Hill had cleared the channel from the atoll. After starting that "green dud" I had to really give it a thumbs down. It just didn't turn up like it should for takeoff, especially to be catapulted, even though there was a fair amount of wind over the deck as the carriers swung while on anchor into the wind.

I was given another "green dud" or at least one that was approaching the 500-hour for major. In the excitement of changing to the other plane, I forgot to retrieve my overnight bag from that first plane and went off for the *Bunker Hill* without it.

We were heading for Pearl Harbor, and were now out of the direct combat area so we were able to dispense the usual CAP flights over the fleet that had been required in combat areas. Sam Silber, our squadron skipper, kind of closed his eyes to some of the booze parties that started after the evening dinner and movies were concluded, for he knew his air group would be relieved upon arriving at Pearl Harbor. The games of bridge and chess consumed most of the days while waiting to reach Pearl Harbor.

Flight quarters sounded as the carrier came close to the usual 100-mile fly off distance from Pearl. Planes would be flown from the carrier to land on a base and be available for the next squadron to use for training flights while the carrier was in port. I was not one of the pilots scheduled to fly, so I was able to watch our approach to Pearl, and we steamed for almost five hours more before clearing the entrance nets to the channel to Pearl Harbor.

Some of the fellows flying still enjoyed taking their chances of joining the anchor pool although in this case it was the docking pool, which I couldn't believe I was the lucky winner of all $36. The docking pool is determined on the exact second that the hawser from the carrier hits the docking pillars to secure the carrier to the dock while it is in port, or when dropping anchor in a lagoon. The anchor pool is won when the anchor hits the water on its way down to secure the ship.

Chapter Seven

"HORNET" (CV-12) CRUISE

VF-2 begins record-setting combat tour aboard the *Hornet*
March 30 thru June 10, 1944

March 30 & 31	Raid, Palau Islands; Peleliu, Eil Malk, Koror, Anguar, Urukthapel, Babelthuap, Malakal,
April 1	Raid, Woleai Island
April 21-24	Invasion, Hollandia, New Guinea - Wakde, Sawar, Sarmi Point
April 28-30	Raid, Truk Islands - Dublon, Param, Faleu, Fefan, Eten, Uman.
May 1	Raid, Ponape

VF-2 Reunited

I did not know where VF-2 would be after nearly two months, so I went over to the Pearl Harbor CASU. There I bumped into Vince Simms, who informed me that he had been giving field carrier landing practice to some of the new pilots of VF 2, and that they were now at Barbers Point. He agreed to fly me over to the Point to see the old gang and verify that I would be returning to VF-2. Then he flew me back to Ford Island for me to get my gear and to have Captain Silber sign orders for my return to VF-2. My temporary additional duty (TAD) was finally completed!! The orders were signed as of the 4th of March, instead of being signed on the 5th. When I made a comment to that effect, the officer reminded me that we had come back across the international dateline.

Our BOQ reunion that night was lively, and I learned that our air group would be going aboard the new *Hornet* (CV-12) on her arrival from the States, which should be about March 12th. In the interim, we flew practice gunnery hops and a few attempts at bombing targets, plus a few short field carrier-landing hops that were required of all pilots.

The *Hornet* arrived on schedule and on the 13th we flew out for an overnight shakedown and then back to Barbers Point for one more night on shore before the air group would fly back out to the carrier and head for Majuro. The ship had Captain Miles Browning as skipper and Admiral Jocko Clark and his staff as the Admiral in charge of our task group.

We started flying CAPs on March 16th, one division (four planes) over the carrier during all daylight hours. On the afternoon CAP of the 18th I was to be Tail-End-Charlie for the last division to fly that day. As I was joining up with the formation, I unfortunately witnessed a tragic accident.

I had been number 4 to launch, and as I was about to join up into formation I saw number 3 plane was too close to the number 2 plane. Lefty Carlson flying number 2 had already joined up on our division leader "Blood" Doner and "Cookie" Williams, who was No. 3, came up way too fast and apparently couldn't control his speed and distance from Lefty. His propeller went slicing through the tail of Lefty's plane, which immediately caused it to start somersaulting down from our altitude of roughly 1200 feet. With a closed hatch and somersaulting, Lefty must not have been able to hit the silk before he hit the water.

The engine on the number 3 plane had stopped with part of the tail wrapped around his propeller. The rest of the tail apparently binding "Cookie" in the cockpit, or even possibly with a broken windshield and glass all around with a closed hood, he was unable to get out to make a safe parachute jump before he also hit the water.

I added a lot of throttle to get up even with Blood Doner to let him know by Morse code that we had lost two planes. And for him to follow me down to the water to give whatever assistance we could give or at least circle the spot so the rescue Destroyer would know exactly where to look for survivors. We had to circle our way down to the spot were those two fully loaded planes with ammo, had dropped like lead balloons. It took a lot longer for us to get down to that spot and when we did, all we could find were just two oil slicks on the water.

I had played bridge with Lefty just that morning and would certainly miss his pleasant smile and disposition, for I had known Lefty since the squadron was organized way last summer. I had not gotten to know Cookie, for he had just joined the squadron as one of the replacement pilots while I was on temporary additional duty and I had only known him for less than two weeks.

I had hardly gotten out of my plane after landing when the bull horn sounded ordering me to Admiral Clark's quarters. He wanted to know everything I had seen as to how it happened and my speculation as to why he had joined up way too fast to control his speed and direction, for he had been on the bridge and witnessed the incident himself.

The rest of our voyage went without incident and we arrived at Majuro on the 20th for just an overnight stay in the lagoon. Bill Blair and Shack Shackford went ashore to get two new replacement planes and flew them out to the *Hornet* after we had left the island atoll on our way to Palau. Those two replacement planes brought us back up to our authorized complement of 36 planes.

We steamed southwest for five days, crossing the equator again before refueling on the 26th, with CAP flights from dawn until dusk. Perspiration pretty well soaked our flight suits during every hop because temperatures there on the equator were normally fairly warm. Showers were a necessary event for all pilots that had flown, but Capt. Browning came down on us for using more than 84,000 gallons that was manufactured each day and he set a pretty strict water policy for every one aboard.

He insisted we wet down for five seconds, take as long as you wanted to soap down, and then use no more than a five second rinse of desalted water, the Navy way when at sea. This didn't go over very well with most pilots for five seconds rinse off just doesn't clean our bodies after being so hot and sweaty on every flight. Our flight suits would hardly have time to dry out and I think most of them would stand in the corner by themselves.

We refueled the carrier on the 26th and then set course to the northwest for a high-speed run in to targets on Palau with high anticipation from all pilots to be the first one to get another Japanese plane. Briefings and target assignments started on the 28th as well as Capt. Browning ordering two divisions in the air as CAP all day long, now that we were getting closer to the target.

Commander Dean gave us another briefing on doing our best, and hoped we would all survive to return home with the air group when our tour of duty was completed in approximately six months. He reiterated that just flying alone is a dangerous activity, that operating from the carrier makes it even more dangerous, and being in combat is something else, with enemy antiaircraft shells coming up sometimes in box patterns and other times just tracing our flight patterns.

He also told of another possibility, the need for keen eyesight and making the first tally-ho, or missing it and giving the enemy plane an advantage on you. Combat is dangerous, attested to by the number of losses the Navy had already suffered. He also announced that we should give our plane a full check before taking it, for there had apparently been a doctor Jeckyll-Mr. Hyde aboard.

During the previous three nights, there had been two life rafts missing from the flight deck, a couple drums of oil emptied on the hangar deck, and evidence of some tampering with the planes. Beware! "If you see anything out of the ordinary, let the flight deck officer know. Good luck, and let's all go home together!" he said.

Hornet Strikes
Mar 29 to Apr 1, 1943

Our code name for this operation was IRON, with the skipper's division to be Iron-One and all divisions would follow in succession. Iron-Two, Iron-Three and so forth. We had hoped to get to Palau undetected, but on the 29th Capt. Browning ordered "condition one easy" (that meant the carrier was made watertight as much as possible, but not requiring the five-inch turrets nor the 20-mm or 40-mm guns to be manned). If we had gone to full general

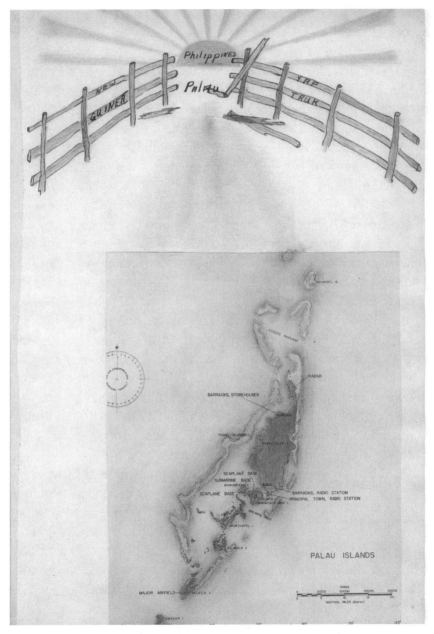

Palau Islands raid began March 30, 1944

quarters, those guns also would have been manned and ready for action. Shortly after lunch we got word that a CAP from another carrier in the task group had drawn blood. But our turn for a CAP was not until later that afternoon.

Our first activity came during the late afternoon CAP with a fighter director vectoring both "Iron-One" and "Iron-Two" out to investigate an incoming bogey. Iron-Two, which was Tex Harris, as flight leader, and Gabriel, Banks, and Elliott, gave a tally-ho when they spotted the bogey. Gabe got credit for a Japanese Betty. That was the sixth for our squadron, but it was our first credit aboard the Hornet.

My first flight on the 30th was into targets on Palau, then out to serve as CAP over the rescue submarine so that it could stay surfaced to pick up any pilot that was downed while over the target area. That is if they could make it back someplace close to that sub. The sub's usual station was about 5 miles at sea to avoid getting too close to enemy shore guns.

My second hop was over the target to drop a 500-pound bomb that had been loaded on my plane. Since we had not run into any aerial opposition, we could strafe the target while diving to release the bomb. I was able to set an AK (supply ship) on fire on my only flight on the 31st. Again, I didn't find a Japanese plane and got very envious when learning that Mike Wolf, Griff, and Stinky Davis had scored while flying a CAP that afternoon. That gave Fighting Two a total of nine planes to date.

The only problem was for my roommate, Demi Lloyd. He got mixed up in the afternoon's melee and got separated from our fliers. He finally joined a flight from the *Enterprise*. He broke away from that flight, which was going back on station, and landed on the *Bunker Hill*, which was landing planes at that time. Later when the *Bunker* launched planes again, he joined the launch and returned to the *Hornet* when it started recovering planes again. His return relieved tension of everyone in the ready room, for we had been thinking he had been lost at sea.

However, he made us all very angry when he related information about the *Bunker Hill* not being in general quarters but only

The author on the Hornet *waiting for takeoff signal.*

Target left burning after bomb runs.

for a very short time when CIC came on the loudspeaker stating that bogeys were incoming. We on the *Hornet* had been under general quarters for the last three days while we had been in combat. We were sweltering the whole time from heat generated in the carrier that had a poor air-conditioning system when made water tight under GQ conditions. And, that whole time we were eating K rations, while the *Bunker Hill* pilots ate in their normal wardroom with meals that had been prepared by the regular cooks.

On the first of April we flew strikes against the large airfield on Woleai as there seemed to be a lack of other military targets, which ended this operation. But Capt. Browning had us flying routine CAPs all the way back to Majuro to resupply for the next operation. We spent Easter while at anchorage there in the lagoon of Majuro Island along with about 60 other ships of the two task groups.

This time it was beautiful sunny weather and the water had no waves for it was as smooth as a baby's bottom. We were able to ride LCI's or whale boats between ships for basketball games and boxing matches in addition to the several trips into the sandy beaches. However, H-1, the hospital ship, was not anchored in the lagoon this time and there were no nurses swimming on the beach.

We knew we would be in anchorage for several days so we obtained cots to have something to sleep on. We could even stay ashore and swim whenever we wanted to. That first night soon taught us quite a lesson, for we had set our cots almost at the water's edge and gone to sleep after having consumed our share of beer.

We learned real fast that we had not considered the effect of tides. When I woke up to eliminate some of that beer my butt was soaking wet and my shoes, which I had put under my cot, were floating out in the lagoon. I had to wade out almost knee deep to retrieve them. We sure learned we could not assemble our cots that close to the water's edge. The CB's (construction battalion) had been there on the island working for several weeks already and didn't mind us coming over to their table for our eats while we stayed ashore.

Back to Combat & Setting Records

Our task group, including the *Hornet*, pulled out from anchor on April 13th, and we took our turn in exiting through the channel from the lagoon. Sometime during the process of leaving, word of a new ALNAV came in, which gave a promotion from Ensign to Lt.(JG) for 13 of us, and we darn near depleted ship service of all its (JG) insignia.

Two days out from anchorage, CAPs started again with "Bones" O'Neal having the first accident. His flaps came up on takeoff and without sufficient lift he wound up in the drink directly ahead of the carrier.

Those on the fo'c'sle watching the takeoffs happened to see the mishap and said they didn't think he even had the usual 25 seconds before the plane was pushed under from the force of the carrier spreading water as it plowed through the ocean waters. However "Bones" came bobbing up within a few seconds to be picked up by the rescue destroyer which was following the carrier for just such mishaps.

On the 18th our squadron set a new record for the *Hornet* with an average 19-second interval between planes for the takeoff that day. Later that day, a rear refueling party of Oilers and the strikers barely avoided collision. So close was the Oiler that those on the rear flight deck could hear the bull horn from the Oiler sound out "stand by for ram." Fortunately, the Oiler missed us but by a very few feet.

Battleships refueled half of the Destroyers from the screen and the rest came alongside the *Hornet* for their top-off refueling, and a treat for their crews. Ice cream always goes down good, but the Destroyers had no ability to make the ice cream for themselves. The carrier would always have a few gallon jugs of ice cream ready and waiting for the Destroyers when they would pull alongside.

That night we started the high-speed run in for Sawar, Wakde, and Sarmi Point on the 21st. But again, we did not find any Japanese planes in the air. We did, however, destroy many planes on the ground and left their runway with many bomb holes and the harbor with several ships either sunk or burning. The next day was virtually the same results, and then on the 24th, my roommate, Dan Carmichael, got his first, a twin-engine Japanese Betty while he was escorting a TBF on a search mission.

The whole fleet refueled on the 27th, with Truk scheduled for the 29th and 30th. While refueling, we also received mail for the first time since the 12th, and my roommate Demi Lloyd learned he had become the father of a bouncing baby girl. Earl Zaeske got the news he was now the father of a baby boy. Demi broke out the champagne and they both kept us supplied with cigars for the rest of the evening, although it was short lived with thoughts of the early strike going off a half-hour before dawn.

My alarm went off pretty darned early although GQ sounded shortly afterwards, which meant I would have one minute to dress and get up to the wardroom before the hatches were all buttoned down. This was Capt. Browning's decision again to be exactly as the book required. I grabbed what breakfast I could and then ran for the ladder to the hangar deck before the last hatch was closed that would have left me under the hangar deck. It would have required much effort to open that hatch from below, crawl through the center hatch, and close that hatch again before I could go on to the ready room.

I had to bring my plotting board up to date, and compute my navigation to the target before the order to man planes would come over the Teletype. Up on the flight deck, the plane captain would help me into the cockpit and then wait for the air officer's command to come over the bullhorn to "start engines." Then I would take my turn to be guided up to the rev-up point, although I would stop before reaching the point where Capt. Browning required us to be, 320 feet from the edge of the deck. From experience we had found that 320 feet was not really enough for our planes that had already been in combat to generate the necessary air speed for us to leave the flight deck without sagging almost to the waters edge on takeoff.

My division leader and his wingman would have been cata-

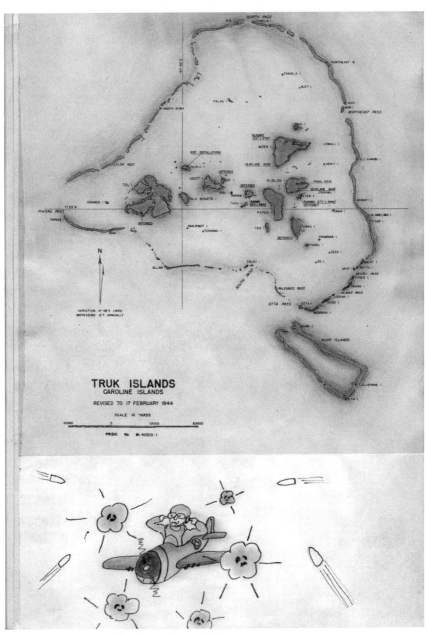

Truk Island Raid April 28-30, 1944

pulted as the carrier was swinging into the wind, and I would be the first to fly off, with my wingman following. Next, we would join up in formation and fly the usual 125 miles to the target that we were to hit just as the sun would come over the horizon.

We did not find any Japanese planes in the air, so we continued on to our assigned targets. Anti-aircraft fire was coming up with quite extreme intensity. One of our bombs got a direct hit on an ammo dump that produced three large explosions and helped reduce the amount of anti-aircraft coming up. The sea plane base was also hit and left burning profusely with a few smaller explosions.

I got back to the carrier, landed aboard, and had lunch before starting the whole procedure again, for a second strike that afternoon. Bombs had been loaded again and this time I was given credit for hitting a power plant. Then I had to figure my navigation back to the task group that we hoped would have moved east-southeast at the usual speed of 20 knots. This meant the carrier would be some 65 to 70 miles away from the point we had been launched from. I first plotted the carrier's movement, and then computed our flight heading back to the new point option, allowing for the effect of wind correction before coming up with a compass heading to fly back to the *Hornet*.

Relaxing in the ready room after dinner, we heard the ticker tape start up for a rare compliment from Capt. Browning. "WAVE-OFFS IN 44 LANDINGS OF FIGHTERS-NONE-WHICH IS REMARKABLE!" Then as the last CAP of the day landed, another ticker tape came over "THE FIGHTERS GOT ONE WAVE OFF THIS TIME TO KEEP THEM HUMAN STILL." So one wave off in 52 landings today meant not only perfect pilots, but a very efficient deck crew. The deck crew helped get the tail hooks disengaged and got the plane taxiing forward. At least one barrier up so that the LSO could give the next plane a "cut" after he had guided the pilot into correct position. All that with an average time of 20 seconds between landings.

Doc Stratton happened to be in the ready room when those messages had come down. He disappeared shortly thereafter, only to return in a few minutes with some, quote, "lemonade" to help us relax a little more fully. It was "lemonade" according to the Doc, but it tasted better. Capt. Browning didn't believe in a booze party aboard the carrier, as we had learned when we first came aboard.

Most of us had a case of spirits in addition to our personal gear in the small luggage compartment in the belly of the Hellcat we had flown aboard. Much to our surprise, we received an order from Capt. Browning to deliver all booze up to his quarters for "safekeeping." After the last pilot had complied with his order, we saw his aides destroying our cases or throwing our highly prized booze over the side and then watching them sink below the surface of that blue Pacific water. From then on I don't think anybody trusted Capt. Browning.

I was scheduled for two more strikes on May Day, 1944, to the island off Ponape. It seemed like it was the incendiary bullets in our belted ammunition that set a fire in one of the barracks buildings. Yet, overall, it was a rather dull target area with very little anti-aircraft coming up at us.

But back on the carrier, a 100 pound bomb that had hung up over target and had not released when it was supposed to have, came loose and bounced along the flight deck until it exploded. It had come loose when the new Curtis Helldiver landed on the carrier killing two flight deck crew and about 25 in the bombers crew ready room, which was located just below the flight deck explosion.

The fire was put out in short order, and the carrier's maintenance department accomplished the flight deck repairs rather expediently. We sure learned that truth of the often repeated statement "Each carrier landing is a potential accident, just waiting to happen." The very next plane to land, after the deck had been patched up, missed the landing wires and wound up in the safety barrier. That delayed the next few landings quite a while before the flight deck crew, who worked feverishly, struggled to untangle the barrier wire that had wound around the plane's propeller.

If that wasn't enough for one day, the very next plane, a fighter flown by Butch Voris, of all people, wound up in the barrier again. That made the third plane to be damaged within a relatively short space of just a few hours, although the rest of the day went without incident.

Resupply and Shellbacks and Pollywogs Again

May 2nd found us on our way to Kwajalein. This time, for resupply in the expansive lagoon there. We were not quite out of the combat area yet, so Adm. Clark had worked out a schedule for half the carriers to be free of CAP duty on the way for one day and then to alternate with the other carriers for CAP duty the next day.

This was because we had crossed the equator and had not had time for the "Shellbacks" to have issued the old long-standing Navy tradition of Subpoenas and Summons Extraordinary by The Ruler of the Raging Main and the Royal Court of King Neptunus Rex to us slimy "Pollywogs." My summons read "For individually causing mental agony and affecting the appetites of your squadron mates by neglecting to shave your upper lip." For that we had several different penalties to complete, one of them being to push a peanut up the flight deck by my nose for a distance of 20 feet and standing watch in only my shorts with a sheep herders staff for several hours at the edge of the flight deck.

A variation from the prescribed punishment meant an hour in the humiliating stockade with head and hands locked tight among other ridiculous sentences. Representatives of King Neptunus Rex made sure the penalty citations were complied to for each of us slimy "Pollywogs". Although I had gone through it all on the *Kalinin Bay*, my orders to the *Bunker Hill* had come before I got my certificate as a "Shellback." Butch Voris thought that since everybody else in the squadron would go through the initiation that I should join them too. This time I made sure I got my certificate of entry into the honorable society of Shellbacks.

All planes that could possibly be squeezed down on the hangar deck were moved to make as much room as possible on the flight deck for all the antics of induction to Shellback status. We all received our Shellback cards and I saved several pictures of

Subpoena and Summons Extraordinary

The Royal High Court of the Raging Main

Region of the South Seas }
Domain of Neptune Rex } ss.

To Whom May Come These Presents

Greetings and Beware

Whereas, The good ship ___Hornet (CV12)___, bound ___on war mission___ ___south and west___, is about to enter our domain; and whereas the aforesaid ship carries a large and loathsome cargo of landlubbers, beach-combers, guardo-rats, sea-lawyers, lounge-lizzards, parlor-dunnigans, plow-deserters, park-bench warmers, chicken-chasers, hay-tossers, four-flushers, cross-word puzzle bugs, dance-hall shieks, drug-store cowboys, asphalt arabs, and all other living creatures of the land, and last but not least, he-vamps, liberty-hounds, Market Street Commandos, masquerading as seamen, of which low scum you are a member, having never appeared before us; and

Whereas, THE ROYAL HIGH COURT of the RAGING MAIN will convene on board the good ship ___Hornet (CV12)___, on the ___3rd___ day of ___May___, 19 __44__, at Longitude **CENSORED** _8.9_, and whereas, an inspection of our Royal Roster shows that it is high time your sad and wandering nautical soul appears before **Our August Presence**; and

Be It Known, That we hereby summon and command you_____ ___Everett C. HARGREAVES___ now a **Lieutenant (junior grade)** U. S. Navy, to appear before the Royal High Court and Our August Presence on the aforesaid date at such time as may best suit OUR pleasure.

You will accept most heartily and with good grace the pains and penalties of the awful tortures that will be inflicted upon you to determine your fitness to be one of our Trusty Shellbacks and answer to the following charges:

CHARGE I:—In that you have hitherto wilfully and maliciously failed to show reverence and allegiance to our Royal Person, and are therein and thereby a vile landlubber and pollywog.

CHARGE II:—In that you caused mental agony and affected the appetites of your squadron mates by neglecting to shave your upper lip.

Disobey this Summons Under Pain of Our Swift and Terrible Displeasure. Our Vigilance is Ever Wakeful, Our Vengeance is Just and Sure.

Given under our hand and seal.

Neptunus Rex

Neptunus Rex

Davy Jones
Scribe

those antics. I also saved a list of the summons accusations for most of my squadron mates.

Getting Replacement Planes

After all the shenanigans of our Shellback initiation on our carrier and then on the other carriers in task group, we arrived at Kwajalein Atoll to go single file again through the channel into the lagoon where we dropped anchor early on May 4th.

Just to keep busy, I had volunteered to be flown by DC-3 from Kwajalein's detachment of CBs newly constructed runway over to Majuro. We were to fly replacement planes back to bring our complement back up to 36 planes. Not to waste time, the Admiral's barge was the first to be lowered into the water from the hangar deck storage place. We were almost immediately conveyed to shore, riding like kings, which is usually reserved for the Admiral's personal use only.

We made our way over to the runway and boarded the DC-3, which was strictly a cargo plane without seats or any plush conveniences of a regular passenger plane. We arrived at Majuro and were told the planes we were to get were not ready to go yet and that they would not be ready at least until the following day. They told us we could go over to supply to get a cot for the night and our meals would be served in the new Quonset hut they called the O'Club of Majuro. The CBs had really been busy since the last time we had been on the island. The beer and the swimming on that sandy beach was well appreciated before we actually got the planes to fly back to Kwajalein.

Our next operation was not scheduled until June, so after we got back from Majuro, we spent our days riding Higgins boats or LCIs to the beach for swimming and dinner-beer parties, or on rainy days, we participated in inter- carrier basketball games and boxing matches. Some of the latest movies were shown every evening on the hangar deck.

An incident that happened on the evening of May 15th

appeared to be the last straw for Capt. Browning. Most of the airdales of ships company that were not actually on watch usually enjoyed the movies, with the senior ranking officers in the first row and graduating back to the junior officers. Enlisted personnel always had the bleacher seats. The same movie would be shown the second night so those that had been on duty during the first showing would still have a chance to see the latest movies, which oftentimes were shown aboard ship before they even got to theaters back in the States.

That evening Admiral Clark and his staff decided they would like to see the movie also, and were seated in the very front row, with ranking ships officers sitting behind them and our officers from the squadrons ranked behind them. Anyway, a CO_2 bottle went off during the movie. Only those behind the bleachers that had set the CO_2 bottle off, knew what it was. The rest of the 2000 plus audience started a mad scramble forward to get away from whatever had created the noise.

Enlisted personnel came tumbling out of the bleachers and down into the officer's section. In that forward rush many officers got trampled on from the onward rush in the darkness of the hangar deck. It was several minutes before the movie projection operator was able to stop the movie and turn the lights on so people could see their way around the hangar deck. When the lights came on, we picked ourselves up, but sick bay got filled up in a hurry, for there were several broken legs and arms and many with deep cuts or scratches and blackened eyes.

Admiral Clark was unseated and bounced around a bit, but survived without serious injury. However, in the melee, an enlisted man was reported to have been seen going overboard, but with all attempts to rescue, he was never found. Of course, Capt. Browning got on the bullhorn to warn us we would never have another movie if such an occurrence ever happened again.

Hornet Change of Command

In retrospect Admiral Clark apparently went to work to have Capt. Browning removed as skipper of the ship. Even the Admiral didn't appreciate having the carrier at GQ every time we were even near a combat area. Admiral Clark had been a very successful commanding officer of the new *USS Yorktown* (CV-10) just prior to his being elevated to Admiral and bringing his flag aboard the new *Hornet* (CV-12).

Other things had happened as a result of Capt. Browning's by the book peacetime regulations that had disturbed Admiral Clark. So on June 1st we saw a number of changes. Capt. Browning was relieved of command and ordered back to Pearl Harbor. He was replaced by Capt. Sample. Our air group commander, Roy Johnson was transferred to the ships company to replace the previous air officer who had become the executive officer for the carrier. Commander Arnold, who had been skipper of the torpedo squadron, was elevated to become our new Air Group Commander, and Lt. Cdr. Ford from Torpedo 8 came aboard to be the new skipper of VT-2.

Capt. Sample coming aboard the Hornet *via Breech Bouy*

And, with all the changes, especially the change of command of the *Hornet*, we would have to stand the usual Navy full dress inspection for the new skipper coming aboard. Both Capt. Browning and Capt. Sample walked up and down each row of personnel inspecting our uniforms for proper attire. Capt. Browning then gave a short speech on his leaving the carrier, stating that he appreciated all the efforts from the crew. He had been in command of the *Hornet* from the day it was launched, all the way through its time in outfitting, shakedown cruise and its trip coming through the Panama Canal and into its first three months of combat.

Then Capt. Sample gave a short speech on accepting command of the carrier and what he hoped to do with the ship under his command. After all that transpired we learned that our skipper, Bill Dean had received a promotion to full commander. He didn't waste any time in getting down to ship service to get the silver leaves to replace the gold leaves he had been wearing for at least the last three years.

Top secret battle plans for the next operation apparently came in with the last mail delivered, without any mail leaving the carrier at the same time, just to make sure no letter could possibly include a statement of where we were to go next. Admiral Clark called all skippers and the CIC officers from all ships under his command to assemble aboard the *Hornet* to outline their proposed contributions to the next combat operation, which turned out to be the action taking us back to the Marianas Islands. Our new air group commander called a meeting on June 6 to inform all pilots of the information he had gathered from Admiral Clark's conference and provided us with our board maps for the Mariana's total area. Those maps would make our navigating much simpler when we put them under the surface of the hard chartboard.

Captain Sample decided he wanted to get the "feel" of his new carrier and its operation before we actually started out for the next combat tour. He ordered the ship to go on a two-day cruise at sea for him to observe his new command. This gave other pilots a chance to fly the replacement planes out to the carrier, the ones we had flown up from Majuro. The anchor was raised at 6 a.m. to get an early start, and then Charlie Harbert, who was flying one of the replacement planes, got confused and landed on the *USS Wasp*.

In his absence his squadron mates wrote an:
"Ode d'Harbert"
"Eenie, meenie, minie, mo,
To which carrier do I go?
It makes no difference where I land,
There'll be a crash crew near at hand."

Charlie did get back the next time we had planes landing. The exercise went pretty well for the rest of the day. But the second day had weather so bad that flights were all cancelled and Captain Sample headed back for our anchorage spot in Kwajalein Lagoon.

Some of the Admirals staff officers were sent down to our ready room to give us a lecture on late history and topography of Guam and Saipan. Then about noon we heard the anchor chain coming up and the carrier took its place in the line of ships filing out the channel of the lagoon on the 6th of June. We were served a delicious dinner that night while listening to the short wave radio that was broadcast over the carrier's intercom system.

We heard that American forces had invaded Europe with landings in France, so we were not the only ones on the move today. We were on our way again, to Guam rather than Truk as we had thought we probably would be. That was because we had already made sweeps over that island, which had been the usual procedure to get photographs for the powers that be. The photos and intelligence gained would then be used by the Admirals and everybody else to decide which or what beach would give the Marines the most advantage and the best spot to go ashore on their mission to recapture the islands. Maybe this operation would have some Japanese planes airborne, for most of us were chomping at the bit to get a chance to flame one, as nine of our buddies havdalready scored.

The whole ship seemed to be under a lot less tension, and

things started to move a lot easier and better. Although we had just that one day at sea under the new captain, he already seemed to have the respect of all aboard. Our task group headed Northwest, and on the 10th we pulled alongside the AO to replenish the carrier's crude oil and top off the aviation gasoline tanks. After that, we started our high-speed run into the combat area in hopes that we would get in undiscovered. We now were not only a task group, but the whole fleet of ships numbered more than any fleet had ever had together in all of history. The total heading for Guam and Saipan amounted to more than 500 ships, with more than 70,000 Marines aboard to go ashore on Saipan on the 12th, and the Army's 77th infantry still in Hawaii had been alerted for action in case they were called or needed.

Word was that were playing for keeps, as the Japanese fleet is supposed to be coming out (per coded messages our linguists had deciphered) for an engagement during this operation, although I believe they were expecting us to be heading for Truk, which our admirals had decided to bypass.

*VF-2 in May of 1944 after completing the Ponape raid.
Author is fifth from the left in the back row.*

Chapter Eight

RIGHT TIME - WRONG PLACE

June 11 to June 20, 1944

June 11-13   Raid, Mariana Islands - Guam, Rota
June 13   Raid , Japanese Convoy (350 miles)
June 15 & 16- Raid, Bonin-Kazan Islands - Iwo, Chichi, Haha
                 Jima
June 19 & 20 - Battle of Philippine Sea (Air battle west of
                 Guam. Air attack on Japanese carrier force)

VF-2 Sees Action

I was not even on the schedule for a single hop during the whole day of June 11th, but later that afternoon all hell broke loose. Tex Harris' division, which was flying CAP over the fleet, got three Japanese planes. The skipper's division and three more divisions, a total of 16 planes, were launched at 1300 hours and had a field day over Guam. When they came back, they were given credit for 23 Japanese planes.

Japanese anti-aircraft had hit Howard Duff at 15,000 feet as he started to make his strafing dive. It was reported that he had been able to make a water landing and was seen floating in his May West, but disappeared a few minutes later, from an apparent Japanese shore gun that had calculated the range very accurately. No trace was ever seen of him again after that.

It seemed impossible that our first loss in combat could have been the "Duffer" for him to have to have gone down, for he had such a likable personality and was always the life of the party with a happy-go-lucky manner, and never complaining. We sure missed the "Duffer."

The skippers 16 planes for the sweep over Guam took off at 1300 hours and he was to lead another 16 planes from the *Yorktown*, which all took off at the same time. A little bit later we received over the teletype in the ready room a message which read, "We got off that time in XXXXX minutes and the *Yorktown* took over six minutes longer."

Admiral Clark, appearing in his bright and lovely green pajamas was heard to remark, "I'll be damned if I know what ship that is. Sure can't be the *Yorktown*." Admiral Clark had been the first skipper of the new *Yorktown*. He had been in command of that carrier all the way from launching through outfitting, shakedown, down through the Panama Canal, and out to the Pacific, then continued as skipper for about six months of combat and had a remarkable history as skipper of the *USS Yorktown*.

The other carriers also scored heavily, and Cdr. Dean came back with four enemy planes. Mike Wolf and Tex Harris each had three and Danny Carmichael, Nol Harrigan, Davy Park, Van Van Haren, and Blood Doner all had two each, and single honors for one plane each went to Leroy Robinson, Butch Voris, Bob Grimes, Andy Skon, Les Sipes, and Charlie Carroll. A total of 26 for the day.

I was on the schedule for two strikes on June 12th. The strikes were to fly cover for our bombers and torpedo planes and protect them from any Japanese planes that might attack them. Again, in about the same place over Arota Point, Guam, and at about 13,000 feet, we lost my roommate, Demi Lloyd. Extremely accurate anti-aircraft shells in about the same exact spot that had picked off "Duffer" the day before.

That brings it pretty close to home when your roommate is taken down. It was especially unfortunate, for Demi had just learned that he was a new father of a baby girl that he had never seen. I certainly missed Demi for his dry humor and honesty and everything he did. Those that saw his plane hit said they didn't think he really knew what had hit him, and they don't believe he suffered at all, that his plane went straight in without ever making an attempt to pull out.

On the same flight and about the same place that Demi was hit, Red Brandt who was at 14,000 feet, got hit also. Red, fortunately, was able to bail out and landed in his parachute about a mile offshore. The rescue submarine on station that day was out five miles to avoid shelling from shore batteries, and was unable to surface. It did come in at scope depth only and the miracle of miracles! Red was able to lasso the conning tower and the submarine towed him a safe distance from shore so it could surface, and Red became a submarine sailor for quite a while.

Victoryless Carl

Life deals you all kinds of situations, and on my two strike flights escorting our bombers and torpedo planes I hadn't even seen a Japanese plane in the air on either mission. I became very envious when I got back to the carrier and learned that our CAP flights had scored again. Tex Harris and Griff Griffin had both been given credit for two planes. Frank Gabriel, Gene Redmond, Ross Robinson, Shorty LeForge, and Razor Blaydes, had gotten one each. On a separate flight, Red Banks and Mike Wolf had each gotten credit for shooting down a new twin engine Japanese night fighter. This total of 11 planes brought the squadron's total for the two days of combat to 37 Japanese planes downed, and I still haven't seen my first Japanese plane!

During the night our task group had backed off some 200 miles from the combat area to meet our resupply group for us to refuel. We were to fly several planes that were approaching the required 500 hour check over to a CVE that would be heading back to Pearl Harbor after refueling. Dick Combs was to fly one of those "duds" but had engine failure and had to make a water landing. A tin can heading back to Pearl Harbor with the supply ships and tankers picked Dick out of the "drink." We wondered when we would see Dick again, for he did not come back on the transfer by breeches buoy from that destroyer.

We were to fly a fighter sweep over Iwo Jima and Chichi Jima on the 15th to cut off any possible Japanese replacement planes that would be coming down from Japan to help repel our Marines going ashore on Saipan. The flight I was scheduled to be in went to Chichi Jima, but we did not see anything to shoot at in the air, so our bombs were dropped on targets on the island. However, the divisions that went to Iwo Jima came back victorious with 17 more Japanese planes shot out of the air. Barney Barnard was given credit for five, Charlie Carroll and Marv Noble were given credit for three each. By Johnson and Earl Zaeske got two each, Porky Connard and Conrad Elliott got credit for one each.

Both flights returning to the carrier found the weather already kicking up and in very heavy seas. Thirty-foot waves of gale proportions were tossing our flattops around like the bobbers at the end of a fishing line. We saw the tin cans on the perimeter of the task group pitching and yawing so much they were almost covered by mist and water as they pitched to and fro in the waves.

The carriers were rolling and pitching to the point that landings became very precarious. When you got a cut, you could look down to see only water, but then the carrier would roll back some for a landing usually on one side or the other of the flight deck. The LSO would have to signal us at times to add power to rise up enough to clear the fantail, or he would have to give us the high signal to compensate for the deck falling away from us as he gave us the "cut." All he could do was hope the pilots could adjust to the unusual position we would be caught in before floating up the deck to catch a barrier, which created many problems and several crashes.

By day's end on the 15th, three-quarters of the original pilots that had left the States together had scored. Three had become aces (5 Japanese planes shot down) already. So our skipper, Bill Dean, made an edict that all pilots not even having seen a Japanese plane yet, would be scheduled on every hop when airborne enemy planes would be expected. He wanted every pilot to have a chance to score with out any one pilot getting a lopsided bunch of kills and others without any kills to their credit. He evidenced his theory by showing us he had already scheduled himself for tomorrow on the CAP flights, which the junior officers normally received, and turned the lead division over to others for the fighter sweeps.

Weather was still bad on the 16th although we did get to fly a sweep to Iwo Jima, but again my usual luck prevailed, for there were no Japanese planes in the air. Weather remained lousy on the 17th as we were heading south, for the Admiral had received word that units of the Japanese fleet had left their ports for a rendezvous to hit our fleet.

On the 18th, I had a long 380-mile search with a 50 mile cross leg and return to the carrier, but had no luck in seeing any of a potential Japanese fleet. All we saw was nothing but water and more water below us during the whole search. Other pilots flew similar search flights at about a 30-degree difference in compass headings, also without luck in finding units of that Japanese fleet.

Bob Shackford though, shot down a twin float, single-engine Japanese search plane about 200 miles from our own fleet on his search pattern. This was a cruiser-based plane, so it was evident their fleet couldn't be too far away.

That evening we received a message of confidence from Admiral Nimitz that read "YOU AND YOUR MEN HAVE THE CONFIDENCE OF THE UNITED STATES NAVAL SERVICE AND THAT OF THE COUNTRY ON THIS EVE OF A POSSIBLE FLEET ACTION - WE COUNT ON YOU TO EMERGE COMPLETELY VICTORIOUS. NIMITZ." Our task group therefore steamed WSW all night at 22 knots to close on the approaching Japanese fleet.

The early searches on June 19th were also unproductive, but by mid morning our CAP was vectored out to investigate a bogie. Both Tex Harris and Tex Vineyard scored, for what started to be a very busy day.

Carl Misses the Action

(Also known as the Mariana's Turkey Shoot)

While they were returning, the carrier's fighter director had picked up a rather large bogey approaching, still about 100 miles away, so skipper Dean's division and Butch Voris' division were launched to investigate. Very shortly after they were launched, my division was launched on the day's schedule, along with our bombers and torpedo planes, which we were to escort to targets on Guam.

We found the antiaircraft fire quite a bit lighter this trip than we had found back on the 11th and 12th. Our bombers had no trouble laying their eggs on the airfield and other targets that had been assigned to them. We made our strafing runs on targets that had been assigned as the most likely source of all the antiaircraft fire that had come up to us on previous flights, and dropped our bombs on the nests of machine gun pill boxes near the air airfield.

I guess we were a little early for all the action was happening out west of the fleet. The Japanese planes had not had time to fly the additional hundred miles on into their airfield on Guam. They were supposed to refuel and rearm and then hit our fleet again on their way back to their carriers.

We had had no aerial opposition on the way in to our targets nor even over Agana Town where the antiaircraft had been so heavy before. And none during the whole time we were over the target area, nor on our return flight to the *Hornet*. When we arrived we found the deck spotted forward as the skippers and Butch Voris' flights had just landed.

Back in the fighter ready room for debriefing produced information of the success of their two flights. Twelve more Japanese planes were added to the early CAP results. All those pilots seem to have the same comment that they had been up against the Japanese first team for they all had a fight on their hands. In that dogfight, Capt. Dean and Leroy Robinson were each given credit for two planes. Dan Carmichael had credit for three planes, Davy Park, Nol Harrigan, Butch Voris, Mike Wolf, and Bob

Grimes were given credit for one each.

The flight deck crews had their hands full feverishly refueling and rearming the fighter planes, as the fighter director was already picking up another large group of bogeys coming in, still a long distance away. In addition to refueling and rearming all planes that had been parked forward after landing, they had to be respotted to the rear before eight fighters on the next flight could be launched. They did get off in time to gain enough altitude to meet the incoming enemy flight and after another dogfight, came back to land with nine more Japanese planes to add to our total. Credit for those nine went to Doherty, Van Haren, and Gene Redmond with two each. Obie O'Brien, Earl Zaeske, and Randy Carlson each got credit for a single.

The second strike group on the schedule for the day took off with escorting fighters and had a field day this time, over Orote Airfield on Guam. Even "hard luck" Bill Blair who had lost his belly tank back on the flight to Iwo Jima, forcing him to return to the carrier and missing the dogfight that resulted over Iwo when others in his flight all scored in the ensuing dog fight.

This time it was something for everyone included on the flight, with Bill finally getting his first and even a second Japanese plane. Griff Griffin, Andy Skon, and Charlie Carroll also received credit for two planes. Jack Vaughn received a credit for three planes and Marv Noble, Porky Connard, and Kenny Lake had credit for one each. However, Porky amazingly got back to the carrier with one wing shredded from 20-mm holes, and Charlie Carroll's leg was somewhat banged up from a 20-mm shell that had exploded in his cockpit. Kenny Lake's return was also a miraculous event with one more tribute to Grumman, for his plane was completely full of holes from engine to tail and was tossed over the side after he landed. A bullet had passed through the cowling, grazed the headrest and went on out the other side. Kenny was lucky he wasn't resting at that time. I guess I should have been scheduled on the second strike group rather than the first group.

The last strike of the day was led by Russ Reiserer of VF-76, which was a division of the new night fighter squadron which was assigned to the *Hornet*. They had specially built planes with a large radar bulb on the right wing of their Hellcats. Adm. Clark did not want to take any unnecessary chance of damage to those four new radar bulb equipped Hellcats. He had therefore stored them on the hangar deck, although they were ready to fly they had not been flown in nearly a month. Nor had the pilots had any time in the air.

Jocko was anxious to get the four pilots into the air so they wouldn't forget how to fly planes during a daytime flight without damage to those specially built planes. He had ordered our skipper to schedule the night fighter pilots on some of our VF-2 schedules and in our VF-2 planes. Because of that requirement our skipper had scheduled the night fighter pilots as one of two divisions to escort our dive bombers and torpedo planes on the third strike of the day. They bumped into a swarm of Japanese dive bombers that somehow or other had escaped disaster over our task groups and had flown on to Guam to refuel per their battle plans. They apparently were to hit our fleet on the way back to their carriers, but Russ spoiled their plans. He shot down five, and Spider Webb did even better. He got into the landing circle with the dive bombers and flamed six for sure and probably two more. Dungan got two and Levering a single.

At the end of the day when totals were counted, our flights that had tally-hoed enemy planes, 51 plus Japanese would not be returning to their carriers. Later, we learned that the tally from all pilots from the three task groups went to 385, plus many probable planes on that one day of action. It would later be known as the "Mariana's Turkey Shoot."

Although our squadron, VF-2, was lucky with all its pilots returning, word from the Admiral was not so good. Squadrons from other carriers lost an average of one pilot for each 11 enemy planes shot down. Maybe this had really been my lucky day in that I had not been in the right place at the right time with the guts to pull the trigger on some of those Japanese planes. But I sure was envious of the 28 buddies that had scored at least one victory during the day. I was left as one of the small handful of pilots still a virgin in the squadron.

I had a long talk with skipper Bill Dean, who was very sympathetic and encouraging in his comments. Your day will come. Just be ready and don't lose your nerve, for there has been a couple pilots come back without a single victory on flights that have scored very heavily. He then assured me that he would see that our division was on every flight where enemy action would be expected. He said he wanted to keep all pilots totals about as equal as possible.

Light Up the Carriers

Our anticipation of getting the enemy fleet on June 20 had us scheduled for several 380-mile searches, with a 50-mile cross leg. The first one being launched at 0530 and the usual CAP to be ready to be vectored out to intercept any bogey that might appear on the fighter director's screen. All efforts, however, were negative until late in the afternoon when a garbled message of a contact was received. This message indicated the Japanese fleet to be only 205 miles distant, and we were told to be ready to launch as soon as possible.

Sometime during the day, though, we received a communication from the Task Force 58 commander, Vice Admiral Mitscher expressing his appreciation for a job well done, which Fighting Two shared in a large way. The message read: "THE AVIATORS AND GUN SHIPS OF THIS TASK FORCE HAVE DONE A JOB TODAY WHICH WILL MAKE THEIR COUNTRY PROUD OF THEM X THEIR SKILLFUL DEFENSE OF THIS TASK FORCE ENABLED THE FORCE TO ESCAPE VICIOUS WELL COORDINATED AIRCRAFT ATTACK CARRIED OUT WITH DETERMINATION X MITSCHER."

On one of the long searches in the morning, which proved negative so far as surface contacts were concerned, Earl Zaeske shot down a torpedo bomber, and Gene Redmond and Van Haren each got a float plane. At 1330 a second search was launched, led by Charlie Harbert. Long before he had returned, our ticker tape sounded an alert, and all aircraft, including fighters were armed with bombs, except the TBFs that were to carry "fish" for the first time and the bombers carried 1000 pounders. Reports of the sightings came in fast and furiously, but they were more voluminous than accurate, for what was reported to be 205 miles proved to be more than 300 miles. Because it was so late in the day, Capt. Dean's forebodings were expressed in the somber act of checking his waterproof flashlight that we normally carried along with our Mae West.

I was one of a dozen pilots that had been relaxing in Ready One when that original message came through that the Japanese Fleet was only 205 miles to the west. Even though it was getting late in the day, we got to work bringing our plotting boards up to date with all the latest codes and started figuring our navigation to the point that the enemy fleet had been reported. We were all ready to go when Adm. Pete Mitscher gave the word that we should launch a deck load and head for that Japanese fleet. Air Group Two launched 12 fighters to escort 12 dive bombers and 9 torpedo planes. Our fighters had even been loaded with 500 pound bombs for maximum striking power, since this was the first time a Japanese carrier fleet had come out since October 26, 1942. If we ran into any enemy fighters, we could always jettison the bombs to be a little more maneuverable should there be a dogfight.

Our air group commander, Lt. Cmdr. Arnold was to be in charge of the whole task group's contribution of planes from all of the carriers, with Bill Dean to supervise the activities of our own Air Group Two's contingent. There was a feeling of jubilation and misgiving as we left the ready room for the flight deck to get into the planes assigned. It was somewhat after 1600 when we were actually launched and headed west.

We realized it would be almost dark when we returned and I think most of us were very conscious of our gas supply, for I know I leaned out my mixture as much as I could, without falling behind the flight formation. We flew to the reported position of the original sighting, but there was no enemy fleet there.

We heard skipper Dean talking on the radio to Cmdr. Arnold

trying to decide what the best course of action would be, whether we should turn around and head back to our fleet or go on a little farther west. The decision was made to continue looking for the Japanese fleet, which had been the order of the day. We knew Admiral Mitscher would not be happy if we turned around without making an extra effort to sink that enemy fleet, especially after we had destroyed so many of its planes the previous day.

We passed the 300-mile mark on our plotting boards and finally sighted the Japanese fleet just as the sun was about to set. Air groups from the other carriers had separated in an effort to lengthen our search line, and they stumbled onto a second Japanese task group, which launched a few fighters to combat the attack. But our planes found no aerial opposition - just 5-inch antiaircraft shells bursting all around us, for it got to be very heavy as we approached the pushover point.

As I remember it, Bill Dean took his division in first to lead the attack on a large carrier, and got a direct hit. Some of the bombers that followed his attack got more hits on the large Shokaku carrier, which was left gutted and in flames. Having gone in first, the skipper was then low in order to provide coverage for the dive bombers, and especially our torpedo bombers after they had dropped their torpedoes and were low and slow, which is where the Japanese planes would be waiting to attack them.

As we were flying to get into position for our dives, we heard on the radio that another part of our larger task group of planes that had extended the search line, had discovered another part of the fleet about fifteen miles away. It was the second unit of the three different units that had been reported earlier. Each unit had a couple carriers, an oil tanker and several cruisers with many destroyers on the perimeters. Plus, they had run into a small hand-ful of Japanese planes protecting it.

When I finally got in position to commence my own dive, I had all switches on. I think that dive was about the longest I ever made. If not from the time from 12,000 foot altitude, then certain-ly in the time I spent watching my own tracers going down and try-ing to distinguish them from all the flak that was coming up at me.

It seemed like the point of release for the bomb I was carrying would never arrive, even though I had the guns going in short bursts all the way down.

What a difference in daylight, for it had been still sunlight up above, but now at the lower recovery altitude the sun had already set and darkness of night had set in. Joining up in formation again was a problem until we got a fair distance away from the Japanese fleet. We were not to put our running lights on until we got well outside the range of the Japanese guns that would be firing at any lights in the sky.

Rendezvous was most difficult even after we got far enough away to turn our running lights on. Planes stayed in the formation they had joined even though in some cases they were planes from other carriers. The weather was bad with clouds that restricted visibility and you didn't want to get separated on a night like this to be flying by yourself.

There was no air traffic controller with radar that would help guide you back during that deep, black cloudy and endless ocean or warn us of near misses - just your sharp eye looking for another set of running lights to join up with. Bond up, regardless of what the tail feather is on the plane you had joined with just as long as it was another fighter. There was no moon to help light the way and no lights from cities reflecting off the clouds to help us navigate as there would have been back in the states. There was also no railroad tracks or highways with cars with headlights and taillights that would help you judge distance or give you a direction to the next city.

We just simply had to face the shear darkness of flying on instruments in and around the clouds. It certainly was a precarious and very scary flight back to our carriers and as time went on you kept watching your gas tank indicator, and lean the carburetor mixture back just a little bit more as long as the cylinder head temperature did not rise above normal readings.

When we got about halfway back according to our plotting boards and navigation, we began to hear calls of "going down" or "out of gas" coming from our dive bombers for they had the least amount of gas to begin with. They had only 320 gallons total capacity for the plane. The torpedo bombers had 360 gallons capacity, while our Hellcats with our belly tanks had a total of 400 gallons.

After hearing some of those calls of going down, I began to think of the instructions we had received when standing night fighter duty in combat areas. "If launched before midnight, bail out when you get low on fuel, for the Admiral won't chance putting the fleet into the wind long enough to land you aboard and give the Japanese Bettys or submarines their chance at the carrier or other ships in the task force."

And, "If launched after midnight, try to conserve gas so we can bring you aboard as soon after sunup as we can after respotting the deck for landings." But as we flew along towards the carrier in that pitch darkness, and amongst the clouds, I began to think certainly they won't stick to those instructions with so many planes in the air - not only from our *Hornet* but from all the other carriers in the task group.

Very few of our pilots had ever made a night landing on a carrier even back in the states where the ships probably had the blue deck lights on, and the landing signal officers well lighted. Only the more senior officers that had been in the Navy prior to the war would have had any experience at night landings. Out here though, the carriers would most likely not even show the dim blue deck lights that could be seen only from an airplane as it was approaching from just the right position in the groove.

There would only be a black light showing on the "skeleton suit" that the LSO would probably have to haul out from storage, so we could at least see any instructions he might have to signal in assisting us in the final groove to make our carrier landing. And the pattern for our landing would have to be made with only the visual aid of the florescent wake from the carrier's propellers as they churned through the water.

It's strange, the thoughts that go through your mind, besides those associated with trying to mentally prepare for a landing especially at night. As we flew on and on in that pitch darkness, I began

to question the navigation of the lead pilot of the group that I was
flying with, for it seemed like we should have found our carriers
quite some time ago. However, checking my watch indicated we
still had more than a half hour to go before we should be sighting
the wakes of the task group below us.

That is, if we had a leader that had plotted the navigation
right. I was indicating a few degrees different in my own personal
navigation in returning to point option for the moving carrier, for it
would now be some 120 miles, hopefully, closer than when we had
taken off for the flight. All navigation had to be plotted in the dark
murky glow of the red lens flashlight, which was used to help preserve night vision. As I thought about possible navigation errors, I
leaned the carburetor mixture just a wee bit more, as long as the
cylinder head temperature stayed just under the red unacceptable
limit.

The florescent wakes of the carrier fleet below was finally
spotted and permission for first landings went to the very few
remaining torpedo and dive bomber planes. But in their despera-
tion to get aboard the carrier for lack of fuel and in their haste to
land on a deck that was not well lighted, they landed aboard even
when they had not received a cut and weren't really in position to
make the landing. Instead of picking out a destroyer and making a
water landing just ahead of it so that destroyer could pick them up
in short order, they took a cut anyway knowing they were so low
on gas that they probably could not make another full carrier landing pattern. Most of them lacked experience at night landings and,
because the LSO was trying to help them, he may have given a cut
when he should not have, for it was reported that one plane landed
on top of another before they both hit the barrier mid ship flight
deck. Other planes bounced or their tail hooks didn't catch a wire
and several of them floated on into the barrier creating lengthy
delays in landing the rest of us.

With so many crashes happening, Admiral Mitscher gave the
word to "**Turn the lights on!**" this being the first time a ship in
combat had ever turned lights on at night. However, it did help
reduce the number of accidents with the deck lights making it a lit-

tle bit easier to judge distance for landings after the LSO had given a cut.

I had made one carrier approach but got a wave off because the plane ahead of me had hit the barrier. I still had a little more gas than other planes reporting, in so I climbed back up to 3,000 feet to be out of the way for any pilot low on gas to get aboard. I circled for quite a few minutes, at least until I could see the deck was clear and no other planes with navigation lights in the landing traffic circle. I let down and made a standard pattern with wheels and flaps down and reduced my speed to the usual 72 knots, and "hung on the prop" for my cross wind leg of the landing pattern, and picked up the LSO as I turned in for final.

I got a Roger all the way in to get a cut and landed without incident on the number four wire. Then with a blast on the throttle to get the plane moving forward I spotted a taxi director who indicated that I should look for the next taxi director up the flight deck. He would give me the sign to hit the knob to fold my wings after I had crossed the last barrier. Then he would give me the sign to pick up the next taxi director that would direct me to the final taxi director for parking. They parked me about fifty feet forward of the number five barrier, the last one that was still usable after all the crashes.

I was climbing out of the cockpit when my plane captain dropped everything and jumped down off the front of the wing onto the starboard wheel and then ran in front of the next couple planes. I was perplexed at his action for I had not glanced back as he had. I now saw the reason for him getting out of the way in such a hurry. He had seen another Hellcat that had just landed but had not caught a landing wire and was barreling up the deck heading straight for me.

I had been reaching back into the cockpit to pull my plotting board out of its container and for the next few seconds my heart was in my mouth. I had no place to go because the wings were already folded leaving the usual exit to the rear of the wing and down to the deck, which would have put me closer to that approaching plane, and that I did not need. Fortunately, the number five barrier had slowed the Hellcat somewhat, but not enough to stop it. However, it did jerk the Hellcat to the port enough to avoid hitting me by inches. It did however hit and clipped a plane in the next row to my port, which probably forced it a little more to the left until it slid over the side of the deck and landed on top of the forward port quad 40-mm antiaircraft gun mount.

The flight deck crew rushed over to the plane with the fire-fighters bringing their fire extinguishers to throw foam on the engine of the plane before it could really spread fire all over. A couple of the flight deck crew got the "Big Boy crane" to secure the plane's tail so it would not fall over the side taking the dazed pilot and those trying to help him out with it. However, once he was out of the cockpit, the flight deck crew untied the ropes from the "Big Boy" and with very little effort pushed the plane on over the side and into the ocean. Unfortunately, no one thought of getting the camera and film from the plane before it went over the side, so all pictures of our action that night had been lost.

The pilot of that plane turned out to be our newly promoted air group commander, Jack Arnold, who had previously been skip-per of the dive bomber squadron and had hardly any time in the Hellcat which he was flying that night. He had had very few carri-er landings in the plane even in daylight. I guess I was saved by a fortunate roll of the ship coupled with the number five barrier jerk-ing Commander Arnold's Hellcat to the port.

In all that, Commander Arnold was shaken up, but he could-n't have been any more frightened than I was when watching his plane with that still whirling propeller, coming straight for me when I had no place to go. But I survived and stumbled on down to the fighter ready room. The air group flight surgeon had the ingredi-ents for "sick call" already set up for us to relax on while we tried to learn more about the rest of our buddies who had not landed yet on the Hornet.

Only six of the eleven of us that had made the trip were in the ready room. As time dragged on with no other landings being made we realized that five of our buddies were out there some-where. On the other hand we had several pilots from other carriers sitting in the ready room with us so we had hopes that our missing buddies were similarly on some other carrier.

It was a glum, somber ship, but as we finally relaxed a bit more, word came in that two of our pilots were on the *Yorktown* and one was on another carrier.   Much later, word came in that a destroyer had picked up the fourth pilot. Finally we learned the last one had been plucked out of the water by personnel from a cruiser. It was well after midnight before we could really relax, knowing that all of us were safe, although, we would certainly need some replacement planes.

About that time my plane captain made a special trip to the ready room to inform me that I had been real lucky in having enough gas to even make a landing, to say nothing of being able to taxi forward in time for the next plane to land. He had put 400 gallons of gas in the plane while refueling, which is the rated capacity of gas for the Hellcat.

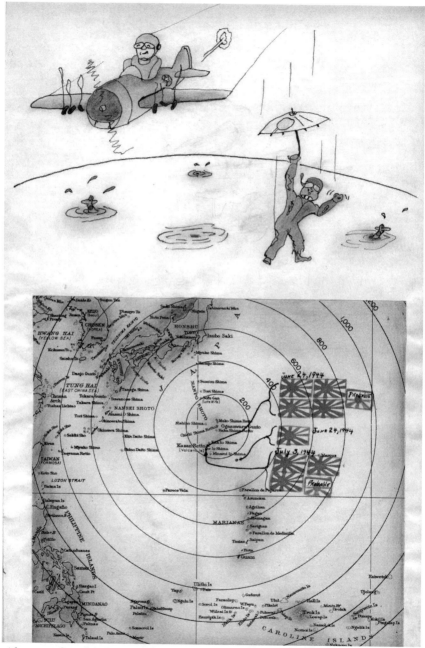

After months of not seeing even one enemy aircraft while his squadron mates were racking up victories, the author finally encountered the enemy and became an ace in a day. The next time he encountered them, he got three more.

Chapter Nine

A VICTORY AT LAST

June 21 to August 28 1944

June 23   Raid, Marianas, Pagan Island
June 24   Raid, Bonin-Kazan Islands - Iwo Jima
   June 24 Lt.(jg) Hargreaves becomes an ace-in-a-day
July 3&4   Raid, Bonin-Kazan Islands - Iwo, Chichi Jima
   July 3 Hargreaves adds three more to his total
July 6   Raid, Invasion Mariana Islands - Guam, Rota
July 25-28 Raid, Yap Islands, Lesser Carolines - Yap, Sorol,
                 Fais, Ulithi
Aug. 4&5 Raid, Bonin-Kazan Islands - Iwo, Chichi, Haha,
                 Muko Jima

We got to sleep in late that next morning but pilots that had not flown the previous attack flight were launched at 0630 in an effort to do more damage to the fleeing Japanese fleet. However, remnants of that enemy fleet had apparently turned directly west and at a higher speed than normal to escape further damage. The flight searched for a while before the decision was made to return without expending their lethal loads, and they landed aboard the carriers with all the armament they had been loaded with.

In the meantime Bill Blair's division was launched in an effort to locate flyers that might still be afloat after some 12 to 14 hours treading water. That is, if they had been able to get out of their planes before they went under, after they had run out of gas and made a water landing in the darkness of night. That division did find seven crews and reported back to Admiral Clark who then issued orders to have planes from the cruisers (float planes) dispatched to pick them up.

All participants received a hearty "Well done" from Admiral Clark. One of the pilots rescued reported seeing large explosions and fires aboard the *Shokaku* and confirmed its sinking. He also reported seeing a second large carrier burning and listing to one side.

That afternoon we suffered the loss of another pilot, Ensign Charlie Dobbins, who crashed during his approach for landing as he returned from patrol. He was picked up immediately by the rescue destroyer, but died shortly afterwards. The skipper, sometime during the day, had put a message of gratitude on the blackboard for all of us to see:

THE MISSION WAS OF THE UTMOST IMPORTANCE X ENEMY SEA POWER HAS BEEN BROKEN X OUR SITUATION WAS VERY CRITICAL X THE HAPPIEST MOMENT OF MY LIFE WHEN I LEARNED EVERYONE WAS SAFE X THE CAPTAIN.

June 22nd was a day of relaxation and sunbathing while the Hornet was alongside the tanker for refueling. But we had a funeral service for Dobbins on the flight deck that morning prior to his being buried at sea. Dobby was a quiet and unassuming fellow, conscious and fearless in the air taking many dangerous missions. We would miss his cheerful disposition.

Back in the ready room we found several messages on the teletype:

THE JAPANESE NAVY HAS DEMONSTRATED IT IS NOT READY TO ACCEPT ACTION WITH OURS X ENEMY AIR ATTACKS ON THE 19TH WERE CHECKED AND MAXIMUM DAMAGE INFLICTED ON ENEMY AIR STRENGTH X OUR OWN LOSSES WERE TRIFLING X THIS WAS ACCOMPLISHED BY THE SPLENDED WORK OF OUR FIGHTER PILOTS, SHIP A/A, SKILLFUL MANUEVERING OF FLEET UNITS.

ON THE 20TH THE HEAVY DAMAGE WAS INFLICTED ON THE ENEMY FLEET IN AIR ATTACKS EXECUTED BY OUR AIR GROUPS WITH SKILL AND BRAVERY, AT MORE THAN EXTREME RANGE X OUR AIRCRAFT LOSSES WERE REGRETTABLY LARGE DUE TO LONG RANGE AND NIGHT LANDINGS X OUR COUNTRY OWES OUR CARRIER

AIR GROUPS A DEBT OF GRATITUDE X THEY BORE THE BRUNT OF THE ENGAGEMENT AFTER EIGHT DAYS OF COMBAT IN THE MARIANAS X WELL DONE TO ALL HANDS X CINCPAC X

And: CINCPAC SALUTES THE CARRIER TASK GROUPS FOR THEIR DEFEAT OF THE JAP FLEET ON JUNE 19-20 X THOSE BRAVE AIRMEN WHO MADE THE SUPREME SACRIFICE WILL LIVE LONG IN THE MEMORY OF THE NATION X WE DEEPLY MOURN THEIR LOSS X

Action started again on the 23rd, when I was scheduled on a strike for the island of Pagan. Our fighters were loaded again with 500-pound bombs, which we dropped on the airfield when we found no planes in the air. We also made several strafing runs and hit many planes on the ground, leaving many of them on fire and exploding. When we got back to the carrier and landed aboard the *Hornet,* we learned that our task group 58.1 and task group 58.4 commanded by Admiral Harrill were to start for Eniwetok for supplies needed while the other task groups stayed to protect our Marines on their invasion of Saipan.

Admiral Clark, though, must have had quite a premonition of Japanese planes being sent down from Japan and staging on Iwo Jima, for he took the responsibility of suggesting a slight detour to Eniwetok via Iwo Jima. However, Admiral Harrill would not go along with Jocko, and headed directly to Eniwetok as ordered. Jocko must have had Admiral Mitscher's approval though, for we started our detour at an increased speed so we would be fairly close to Iwo for an early morning fighter sweep over Iwo. And, what a day it turned out to be!

Day Started with Four Victories (June 24th)

I was scheduled on that sweep as the skipper had said I would be whenever it could be expected to find Japanese planes in the air. We had four divisions (16 planes) scheduled for the sweep and were loaded with bombs to do some damage even if we didn't find many Japanese planes airborne. My anticipation for getting a victory was extremely high, for I didn't want to be left as one of the few pilots in the squadron without a victory, which we had been trained for as fighter pilots. I had not been much of a letter writer during the cruise so far, but that evening I tried to compose a letter home to my folks, and to my girlfriend just in case something happened to me.

Admiral Clark increased the speed of our task group from the normal 20 knots for cruising to some 25 knots all night long, so as to get the task group within launching distance for us in the morning. Although we were still some 250 miles from Iwo, 16 of us were launched and eagerly headed for Iwo. However, one plane developed mechanical problems within a short distance and immediately turned back to the carrier leaving 15 of us in full anticipation and hoping to finally see a few Japanese airborne. Many of us on this flight were like me, anticipating our first skirmish to prove our abilities and with the nerve to squeeze the trigger if the opportunity presented itself. A couple pilots that had been on previous flights acknowledged their lack of effort while others in the flight had come back with a pretty good score of kills during the skirmish they had been in.

Anticipation was so great that I made sure my guns were charged and the gun camera switch on long before we first noticed a small speck in the distant sky when we were still some 65 miles from Iwo. That speck grew larger and larger and we were soon able to recognize it to be many planes in close formation just slightly lower than us. We "tally-hoed" the enemy, and our flight leader, Bob Butler came on the radio reminding everyone to have their guns charged, and switches on. Then he commented "I guess we'd better drop the bombs," because it began to look like we were going to be horribly outnumbered and in a fight for our lives.

Even though we had no target for the bombs, they were too heavy to keep on our planes and allow us to maneuver should we get into a dogfight that was now evidently about to occur in a few short minutes. He also told the division leaders to spread out a bit, and forget the thatch weave as it wouldn't help much with the apparent number of planes coming against us. Pick your target and help each other as much as possible, but it's everyone for himself. We came in high hopes to score, so let's get in there and do it!

We had gained some altitude after spotting that blip on the horizon and watching it grow to the large group of planes and even after our tally-ho, they were still under us. As I remember it, it looked like they were trying to fly under us and then all of a sudden gain their altitude for their attack after they had crossed under us so they could come at us from the rear. The whole flight consisted of Zeros, which we had identified them to be.

The Zero was a very maneuverable plane and was so much lighter than the Hellcats because they were without armor plate protection for the pilots and they had no self sealing gas tanks. That gave them a very maneuverable plane that from statistics could out-climb, out-dive, out-turn us, and could fly faster than we could.

We will never know what their theory of attack was in this instance for as they flew under us, all we had to do was roll over and we all made high side runs on their flight before they had a chance to gain any altitude. It came down to our first division leader making a run, taking their lead plane and his other three pilots took the next three enemy planes. They had stayed in formation, so that made it easy to pick a target.

My division leader took another section of Japanese planes and I took his wingman, making a high side run from the right. I was so anxious to squeeze that trigger, but I held off, as we were taught don't waste bullets. So I waited until I was probably less than 300 feet from the all yellow plane with the red meatballs on its wings before I squeezed the trigger for a short burst. My guns were aimed at the inboard section of its wing next to the pilot's cockpit.

I must have had the correct estimated lead for the relative speeds of our two planes. I don't think I hit the pilot, but I certainly got the gas tanks, which gave me an almost unbelievable huge ball of fire that I couldn't avoid. Even yanking back and to the starboard on the control stick, I still flew through the flames and it really disturbed me, wondering if some metal part of that exploding plane might have hit my Hellcat. I had actually been that close before firing my first burst from the 50-caliber guns.

However, there wasn't much time to worry about the possibility of damage to my plane, for it was still performing well. There wasn't even time for me to gloat over my first "Meatball" since I had waited so long for it to happen. There was still work to do and as I looked around I saw another yellow plane with a large red circle on its wings just below me, to my left. It was crossing to my right, and on the tail of one of my buddies. I don't think he even saw me in his efforts to get at the Hellcat. All I had to do was drop my nose and throttle back just a trifle to be in a pretty good position for another high side run from the right, just as I had done on the first plane.

To stay with him I had to add just a trifle throttle again for I was probably only 200 feet from him to begin with and traveling maybe just a little bit slower without that added throttle. All I had to do was check my gun site for proper lead before squeezing the trigger again. The result was another ball of flame too close to avoid. Number 2!!!! And, again I hoped no metal from its explosion hit my Cat.

By this time, there was no formation of flight order on either side. It was as Bob had said, every one for himself in a ferocious dogfight. Looking around I saw another Zero crossing some 300 feet below me with a blue Hellcat getting in position to shoot at it, but by the same token there was another Zero getting lined up to shoot at the Hellcat. I added throttle, did a split-ess and got to the Zero before it did any damage to the Hellcat. At least the Hellcat appeared to be okay and still generally chasing that Zero he was after when I squeezed the trigger on the Zero that had been after him, and had the third ball of flame to fly through. Number 3!

There was no time to try to figure out who I had helped, for glancing around, I saw another Zero all by itself but some 400 feet above me and a good thousand feet almost straight ahead. I had to pour on the coal to come up to it from the under side for a straight-on shot at it. After two bursts from my guns, all I got was a stream of gas trailing from that Zero. Another squeeze on the trigger still didn't get a ball of fire. By this time I was getting way too close and had to veer away to avoid a mid-air collision and to avoid having to fly directly through the falling ball of flame should it have exploded while I was virtually under it.

I had had to reduce my throttle setting after having gone full power to catch up to it, but had popped my flaps in order to slow down, and of course chopped my throttle quite a bit when I was finally under that plane. Now that I had veered to the right, I could raise my flaps and add throttle again to stay with it at its speed.

I am sure I could have had that plane with its gas streaming back, but as I glanced around I saw another Hellcat in trouble with a Zero on its tail. It didn't take long to make up my mind to go help another buddy rather than stick with the streaming gas for my fourth meat ball. But making a 150 degree turn to the left and pushing throttle again put me in a pretty good position for a high port side run on this Zero. Then by reducing throttle to slow down after catching up to it, I was again concentrating on the Zero rather than figuring out who I would be trying to help.

When I got to within 300 feet of that Zero, I squeezed the trigger and got a beautiful stream of gas again but the pilot apparently realized he was in trouble for he tried to dive off to the right that would have my bullets going over his head. But I stuck with him and the second burst from my three 50-caliber guns did the trick. The plane became my fourth ball of fire and started its vertical descent to the ocean below.

By this time I was at only 15,000 feet having lost some 5000 feet of altitude in all my high side runs and also kind of off to the side of most of the action. Although glancing around I couldn't see much more around me as the only yellow planes were apparently on their way back to Iwo Jima being probably two miles ahead of me with no Hellcats in chase. Everything else seemed to be dark blue, which meant they were our planes, and I could see at least 18 to 20 balls of flame on their descent to the blue waters below.

It seemed like we had cleared the sky of yellow meatballs in something like 10 minutes. If there was any Zeros left, they had made themselves scarce by heading back to their base. It wasn't but a minute more before I heard the radio squawk out, "Let's head for home, join up on the way." We were really scattered over a large area from the dogfight we had just been in. I was elated with the success of finally getting a meatball and joining most of the rest of my squadron mates in finally attaining the success which we had been trained to do. Perseverance really does pay off, doesn't it.

That is the results of what I remember, but after I reviewed the Aircraft Action Report recently declassified, I find several discrepancies. These may be the result of Tom Morrissey's (our ACI officer) getting the notes from his debriefing mixed up from all the pilots that had been on the flight in interrupted sequences, as we were in and out of General Quarters several times during the debriefing.

After all the interruptions, it is understandable that my version of memory versus the official Aircraft Action Report differs. And, without anyone that I know of left to dispute or corroborate the discrepancy the official version will have to stand as is. The report says that we had an altitude of only 12,000 feet to begin the dog fight. I approached my first plane from 6 o'clock above and it burst into flame after a short burst from my 50 caliber guns. The second plane was caught from 7 o'clock below while recovering altitude from the first plane. Now here is the big discrepancy. I sure don't remember having a pilot bail out on me, especially when we understood that Japanese planes had no parachutes. All I remember was the four balls of fire and another one leaking so much gas that he never could have made it back to his base.

The third Zeke gave me quite a tussle and was not able to pull out of his last maneuver before hitting the water and exploding. I was trying to regain the altitude I had lost on number three when attacked by a Zeke which hit my starboard wing knocking out the three guns on that side. But I don't remember losing any guns on the port side, when the official says I was down to one gun in getting my fourth Zeke, which was the plane streaming gas profusely and never would have made it back to its field on Iwo Jima. I had left this fourth plane to go after a Zeke when I saw it on the tail of a buddy. All I had to do was head down a bit to get a high side run from 5 o'clock to get my 5th Zeke on this flight, I thought. Here again, all I remember is another ball of fire, not a Japanese pilot bailing out.

The problems of debriefing were many and I like to think my memory was more accurate than the often-interrupted ACI officer listening to several pilots give their reports. He took the position of not allowing anyone to review his work. Therefore, any corrections that might have been made never got made, and of course my memory remains much better than the uncorroborated record.

(Getting back to my narrative)

Bob Butler who had lead of our flight, set a slow cruise speed so stragglers would be able to catch up. Within minutes we had quite a collection of Hellcats that even included a few from the *USS Yorktown*. However, they soon left to join their own group, leaving just fourteen with *Hornet* tail feathers.

Bob flew for just a few more minutes and then started a 360 degree turn in hopes that the 15th plane would have been able to catch up. However, the 15th did not appear even as we completed the circle and headed for home again.

We were to be in radio silence after leaving the target (so enemy radio directional finders would not be able to pick up our route back to our carriers). Bob did use the radio, though, to tell everyone to get sorted in proper divisional order so he could determine who was missing. It was Conrad Elliott, who no one had seen

Author records "Five victories in a day" in his log book June 24, 1944.

after the first flurry of the dogfight, but we had hoped he might have had engine trouble and headed back to the carrier all by himself or for whatever reason.

While the rest of us had no idea as to the total enemy kills our group would be given credit for, we in each division used our hands by Morse code between pilots (the open palm for a dash, and a closed fist for a dot) to at least get some idea of the success we had had.

Then as we flew onward, it became evident that several planes were damaged. Stinkey Davis was coming back with, in the words of our ACI officer, a plane that "resembled the top side of a salt shaker" from the 20-mm shell that had exploded in his cockpit. And I found that my plane had been hit, for my hydraulic system would not safety my guns. At least I could not hear the usual thump from the bolts when they should go back to the safety position.

While this meant that one of my buddies had probably saved my life by getting an enemy fighter off my tail. I had not seen any bullets going by me, but as I had not been forced to make evasive maneuvers I probably had been a good target for some Japanese pilot until one of my buddies did the same for me as I had done for a couple of them.

The question then arose as to would I have any hydraulics to get the wheels down and the flaps down for landing aboard the carrier. Wheels, I could use the backup system for hand pumping them down, but I would have to go in at a little faster speed if I could not get the help from the flaps for my slower landing speed.

The fourteen of us got aboard without incident, but I had to make doubly sure my finger did not hit the trigger, as my guns were still hot. I certainly didn't want to be spraying 50-caliber bullets up the carrier deck as By Johnson had done just a few weeks ago.

Number 5 - Ace in a Day, no less

Tom Morrissey, our ACI officer, as usual had to debrief us individually about our fight, and accomplishments, but was interrupted several times when the ship's General Quarters sounded.

The carrier's fighter director had vectored both the 10,000 and 20,000 foot CAPs out to verify several bogies to be friend or foe, planes that had not made the correct recognition turns around the two destroyers out on picket (some 40 miles away from the carriers). Planes returning from a mission would know the proper recognition turns for the day.

The Japanese had guessed fairly well as to a general heading needed to find our task group and when the word "foe" came back from the CAP leader a warning for GQ was sounded. All hatches between compartments were closed, making the carrier watertight, gas lines were virtually closed except for actual need in refueling planes, and the armory department was also restricted. The ship's complement manned their guns and non-flying aviators had time to take shelter should the carrier actually come under attack.

After several interruptions, Tom was able to finish the debriefing when GQ secure sounded for the "nth" time and he came up with a total of 37 victories for our 14 pilots from the fighter sweep over Iwo Jima. I got credit for only four meatballs and a probable for the gas streamer. Stinky Davis, Bob Shackford, and Tex Vineyard each had four also. Bob Butler, John Banks, Blood Doner, and Roy O'Neal each had three. Kenny Lake, Randy Carlson, Razor Blaydes, and Ross Robinson each had two. Lat Latimer got one, and it was everyone's guess as to whether Conrad Elliott had taken down any Japanese planes before he was lost, for he was still missing with no word from other carriers that he might have landed on one of them. We would miss that Texas twang, guitar player with all his yodeling and entertainment that he provided on evenings when we had no movie to watch.

The CAPs that had been vectored out by CIC (combat intelligence center) to investigate the bogeys found the whole flight to be enemy and tied into them for a second dogfight for the day. This group of enemy planes was mostly torpedo planes with only a small escort of Zero fighters. They were apparently on their way to damage our fleet, with our two larger carriers as their most likely prime targets.

After those two divisions had landed and had been debriefed, the flight was given credit for another 18 Japanese planes. John Deere and Paul Doherty each with three, Griff Griffin, Russ Reiserer, Leroy Robinson, Frank Gabriel, Les Sipes and Shorty LeForge each with two. This brought the total to 55 for the day

Our task force had been steaming southeast all day by at least 25 knots in an effort to arrive at Eniwetok anchorage shortly after Admiral Harrill's task force did. We would have gotten some 225 miles farther away from Iwo than we had been at the time of our launch for the predawn fighter sweep that morning.

After lunch and all the debriefings, a few of us were relaxing in the ready room with a hot game of Acey Ducey in progress. When the squawk box screamed out "Fighters, SCRAMBLE," which meant grab plotting boards and flight gear, and head for the plane as fast as you can get up to the flight deck.

The CIC fighter director had picked up another unidentified blip on his radar board. It appeared to be much too large a blip for the one division normally flying CAP over the fleet and he thought he had better get more fighters up there to help. Some ten to twelve of us grabbed our flight suits, Mae Wests, and plotting boards and headed for the flight deck to occupy the first plane in the takeoff spot that didn't already have a pilot in it.

We barely had time to gain enough altitude to help our CAP buddies that had already engaged the flight of Japanese planes. By this time they were in sight of our task group and all hands on the ships of our fleet could witness the ensuing dogfight, which this time had many Zeros escorting the torpedo bombers.

We had taken off in such a hurry that we really did not have a usual division formation climbing up to help our Combat Air Patrol, that was already in a dogfight, so it was about like this morning, everyone for himself for it's either him or me. The plane I picked for a target gave me quite a tussle with some pretty tight turns mixed with a couple high-speed dives and climbs trying to get him in my gun sight with enough lead. I finally got him in my sights with enough lead and close enough so I wouldn't be just

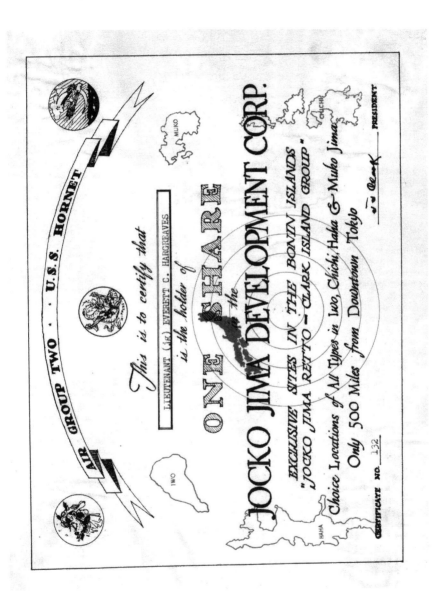

wasting bullets. We were way down from the rest of the combat-
ants, but he couldn't go much lower without flying into the water.
We had pulled some pretty heavy "Gs" in all that maneuvering on
the way down, but I finally got that ball of flame again and started
looking around. All I saw was numerous balls of flame descending
to the water from those that had met their maker at a much higher
altitude.

The Hellcats were starting to form up in divisional arrangement to go back over our fleet for a good rousing zoom of the
Hornet's flight deck. We had shot all the Japanese planes down, for
our CIC officer said he had no blips on the screen leaving the area.
After landing and I had been spotted forward, my plane captain
described the action to me - that it was a bunch of vapor trails and
falling balls of fire. Quite a sight that he couldn't believe if he had
not seen it for himself, he uttered.

Morrissey just couldn't wait for the debriefing. When it all
came together Tex Harris and By Johnson each got two torpedo
planes. Marv Noble and Ross Robinson each got singles, but Ross
also scored a Japanese Zero. Butch Voris got two Zeros and eight
of us got a single Zero, Barney Barnard, Razor Blaydes, Bob
Grimes, Frank Gabriel, Kenny Lake, Shack Shackford, Jack
Vaughn, and myself. This totalled 17, and along with the previous
55, gave VF-2 a total of 72 for the day, a new U.S. Navy record for
a carrier squadron. But the best of it was, we had kept that many
planes from their staging at Iwo Jima for flights on down to Saipan
to attack our Marines in their effort to take the island of Saipan.
Seventy-two Japanese planes for the day now brought the VF-2
Squadron accumulated total to 192, also a new Navy record, and
when that last meatball that I got on this flight became official, it
made my fifth for the day to become an "ace in a day."

The Plane Captain
The Unsung Hero of Naval Aviation

A plane captain was an enlisted fellow that had been

assigned to do a specific plane any time it was on the flight deck. Each of the fighter planes had a plane captain when it was moved, from the time the plane landed until the time it took off. After the pilot landed, the plane captain would guide the pilot to a forward parking spot and help get the wings folded on the way. He would then help the pilot out of his parachute harness and out of the cockpit.

Anytime the plane was moved by the tractor, or by a half a dozen men, if there was no tractor available, the plane captain had to be in the cockpit to operate the brakes. It was a precaution to keep the plane from rolling into other planes. After all the planes had landed, each plane would have to be respotted, that is, moved, from its forward parking spot to the rear flight deck ready for the next takeoff. The plane captain was responsible for getting the plane refueled and making sure that it was fully armed - that each container box for the six guns was filled with a full load of 400 rounds of 50-caliber ammunition.

If the ship were caught in foul weather, the plane captain would help the flight deck crews in lashing each plane to the deck. Just as would have been done on a field on land during rough weather, except on land you don't have to worry about the earth rolling as the flight deck of a carrier would do when battling very heavy seas.

The plane captain was always there to assist the pilot assigned for the next hop to get into the cockpit. He would get him strapped into his parachute harness and assist with whatever else he might have needed before flight deck officer would give the command to stand clear to start engines. He was the one that would have to remove the chalks and start the plane rolling up to position for takeoff. It was his responsibility to make sure the wings were spread and locked in place before pointing to his head and moving his hand forward to indicate he was passing taxi instructions up to the yellow shirt.

The flight deck taxi director, who was identified by the yellow shirt he wore, was responsible for bringing the pilot up to the takeoff spot. When the plane was in position, the yellow shirt would give the signal to stomp on the brakes and hold until he would get the all clear from the flight deck officer to rev up to full power. The yellow shirt would then listen, along with the pilot, to make sure the engine was not missing and was giving the necessary power for takeoff. When the pilot and the plane were ready the yellow shirt would drop his hand from above his head and point down the flight deck to the bow for the pilot to release his brakes and start his takeoff roll.

When I left the debriefing room and was on the way down to the mess hall for a sandwich, I noticed the plane captain from the plane I had just come back in, sitting there waiting for me. He wanted to tell me that his examination of the plane revealed both tail elevators to have been buckled and he had to move it down to the hangar deck for the mechanics to get the necessary repair work done on it. I guess I had really pulled a lot of "G's" sticking with that Zero, and I was lucky to have been able to make it back aboard safely, but that Zero I had just shot down was number 5 for the day. What an innovation to become an "ace in a day" after looking but never seeing a Japanese plane in over eight months of combat, not seeing even one!

The Photo Shoot

The 25th was a day of leisure and sun bathing as I was not scheduled for any of the CAPs normally launched while in combat areas. But on the 26th, I experienced something really new. A breeches buoy ride across from the *Hornet* to a destroyer that had pulled alongside the port aft quarter of the carrier.

The line that I had to ride from the *Hornet* over to the destroyer was first obtained by firing a leaded weight thin line by shot gun across the bow of the destroyer and then increasing the size of the line until it got to be a one inch hawser. The line was then mounted into a block and tackle so the slack could be kept taut by about 20 seamen on the carrier deck as the two ships rolled apart and came back together again. That was so I would remain probably about 30 feet above water, rather than being dunked when the roll of the ships would give slack to the line. It sure was a new experience for me.

I was on the destroyer riding all the waves for about an hour after it left the *Hornet,* while it maneuvered its way over to the *Belleau Wood*, which was a cruiser hull carrier. The *Belleau Wood*, which had been out for more than the usual six months tour of duty, was returning to Pearl Harbor and would not need its full complement of planes. At Pearl Harbor they could get more planes, supply the rest of the carrier's needs, and have a change of air groups.

I was catapulted from the *Belleau Wood* and had to fly around by myself over our task group for a while before I could land on the *Hornet* along with the last CAP of the day. This would save having to turn the whole fleet into the wind for me and then do it again a little later for the CAP to come down.

We were pretty well out of the combat area by the dawn of the 27th, the deck had been respotted, and a Hellcat was moved out and its wings spread for a squadron photo. A Lieutenant Commander Kerlee, official staff photographer, had been sent over to the *Hornet* to get our squadron picture for the Navy Public Relations office. We had quite a bit of fun while Kerlee was arranging the group to his liking and balancing the picture.

Of course Adm. Clark (commander of our task group) and Captain Sample (skipper of the *Hornet*) and all pilots of VF-2 were to be in the photograph. First, Kerlee tried to arrange us by height from one side to the other, but he didn't like that, and he didn't have a lens that would take such a wide picture. Six or seven men on the tail end had to come to the center and kneel on the deck, but he didn't like that either. He moved the camera closer to get more of our facial expressions, but the group on the port wing was too numerous so he wanted two of us to leave the wing and get up on the propeller. He didn't like that arrangement either for the third blade of the propeller was straight up.

He then made the group standing by the propeller move away so the prop could be turned for the third blade to be straight down. Then he wanted two of us to be up on the top two blades of the propeller. But there was still an unbalance on the port wing, so he wanted a third man to get up on the propeller. I was told to sit on the hub of the propeller with the other two balanced on the second and third blades of the prop. Tex Vineyard and Frank Gabriel were behind me on the other two blades.

With all the rearrangements, I wound up sitting on the prop hub in the photograph that was finally taken at the preference of the photographer. He was satisfied, and I ultimately learned that the Navy reproduced the photograph to nearly full life size. It was placed on the right hand sidewall of the entrance to Radio City Music Hall in New York City as part of a Navy recruiting exhibit featuring the Navy's top squadron. Its theme was "Join the Navy Air Corps."

We dropped anchor in Eniwetok lagoon on the 27th after that picture had been taken and everyone got to the beach for a beer party on the 28th. It seemed like Charlie Arnolt of United Press was just waiting to corral some of us that had just become aces, for he spent almost the whole day with just our group, and most of the afternoon with By Johnson and myself, getting our stories.

It was almost two weeks later when we received our next batch of mail with letters from all over the country with clippings and articles, and pictures of us from our hometown papers and many national or large city papers giving the people back home proof that we were winning the war. The next day Charlie came aboard the *Hornet*, along with Joe Rosenthal of the Associated Press, to take our individual pictures. They worked all day interviewing Adm. Clark, Captain Sample, Bill Dean, and many of the other pilots, for what we would eventually find out would be articles in LIFE and TIME magazines, as well as all the newspaper articles.

More Action at Iwo Jima

Several of us were ordered to go ashore on the 30th to fly replacement planes from the pool of planes on the Eniwetok airstrip

"Fighting Two" on the USS Hornet (CV-12) 6-27-44, - Center on propeller: *Tex Vineyard, Connie Hargreaves, Gabe Gabriel **Viewing to left wing:** Standing - Dan Carmichael, Dave Park, Obie O'Brien, Bill Blair. Sitting on wing - Shorty LeForge, Gene Redmond, Van Van Haren, Spider Webb, Lattie Latimer, Barney Barnard. **Viewing to right wing:** Standing - Shack Shackford Sitting/Kneeling - Jack Vaughan, Dick Combs, Red Doherty; Zes Zaeske, Ross Robinson, Charlie Dobbins, Les Sipes, Stinky Davis **Front Row Standing:** Kenny Lake, By Johnson, Randy Carlson, John Banks, Griff Griffin, Mike Wolf, Tex Harris, Bill Dean (Skipper), RAdm. Jocko Clark (flag for our Task Group), Capt. Sample (Capt. Of the USS Hornet), Butch Voris, (later to skipper the Blue Angels), Bob Butler, Al Scheele, Charlie Harbert, Blood Doner, Razor Blaydes, Andy Skon, Marv Noble, Conner Connard, Nol Harrigan, Charlie Carroll.*

out to our *Hornet* when she pulled anchor and cleared the lagoon. We were now on our way back to "Iwo Jima" for a third trip to that island. July 4th was our "D" day but Jocko apparently became suspicious of a couple reported Japanese search planes shot down by our CAP and launched a fighter sweep mid afternoon on the third from about 300 miles off Iwo. Japanese Zeros had gained only about 15,000 feet of altitude and we were well above them to make our initial runs, so I guessed they really had not been forewarned and we had surprised them after all, for they had to scramble to even gain much altitude to engage us.

A Zero that was somewhat under me provided a nice high side run from the left as my first target. My guns had already been charged and the switch turned on as I drew closer to the Zero. I identified that there was a red so-called meatball on its wings before squeezing the trigger. It flamed at first, but then exploded with never a chance of avoiding that ball of flame. Emerging, I saw another yellow plane with red suns painted on the wings and fuselage crossing in front of me, just a trifle lower, so that making another port high side run made it about as easy as possible to have the fiery explosion for number 2.

Then I spent probably two to three minutes looking around to see what assistance I could give maybe to a buddy, before I spotted another Zero fairly well away from all the action. I had to push the throttle almost to the stop in order to catch up to my next target. Once I got close enough, I had to throttle back and pop the flaps in order to slow down enough to his now twisting, turning antics. I did get him in my gun site with the proper lead and a short burst from the guns, and had my third ball of flame in front of me. I really had an easy first two targets, but that third one really gave me quite a tussle, and I think he was the best pilot I had ever run into in my short history of finally seeing Japanese planes.

Again it had been everyone for himself in that dogfight, for in each and every dogfight it is either him or me. When you survive you're lucky. When the action was all over and we started on a heading back to the carrier, we had two planes missing. As we flew on course back to the carrier it was determined that Bob Butler and Roy O'Neal had flown our missing planes. No one had seen Bob or Roy after the first skirmish. You just don't have time to keep track of everybody when you're looking for your next victim and you have to keep track of your own tail. In a dogfight that isn't the easiest thing to do when there are Japanese planes all around that are just itching to get a shot at you.

After we got back to the Hornet, our ACI officer totaled our score after debriefing all pilots that had been on the flight. He counted 33 kills for us, and there could possibly be more if Bob and Roy had gotten any before they were lost. They have not returned to the carrier yet and no one knew what might have happened to them. The score broken down included Bill Dean, Blood Doner, Red Banks, Cunningham, and myself each getting credit for three. Then Danny Carmichael, Bill Blair, By Johnson, Butch Voris, and Andy Skon each getting credit for two, and a single credit went to Lat Latimer, Razor Blaydes, Davy Park, Spit Spitler, and Mike Wolf.

I missed Bob Butler very much, for we had often been partners or opponents in a good game of bridge. He had been with Fighting Two since the early days of our organization in Atlantic City. We thought a lot of him for his genial manner and thoughtfulness concerning everybody. I had not gotten to know Roy O'Neal very well, for he had been with the squadron a much shorter time, although he seemed like a nice fellow and had occasionally joined a bridge game in the ready room. He joined us at Hilo while I was on temporary additional duty on the *Bunker Hill*.

Our Fourth of July fireworks went off per schedule. Our fighters were loaded with bombs, to be jettisoned if we should run into aerial opposition while escorting our bombers. Our targets were Chichi Jima and Haha Jima where we found a number of ships. They were mostly supply freighters, and by the end of our flight they would be on the bottom, making future navigation around the harbor almost impossible. The only air action during the whole day was a four-engine Japanese Emily on search. It was shot down by one of our new pilots, Howard Stockert, who had received orders to our squadron just as we were leaving Eniwetok.

We lost two planes to antiaircraft although both Bill Blair and Bob Shackford were rescued by destroyers and they would be learning something of life aboard a "can" for a few days until they got transferred back to the *Hornet*.

That evening we enjoyed a couple large delicious cakes that Captain Sample's pastry maker had baked, to be sent down to the officers mess, as a well-decorated celebration of the 6000th landing made on the *Hornet* during today's activity.

Guam Survivor Rescued

After enjoying those scrumptious cakes that Captain Sample had sent down to the officers mess, the whole task group headed out of the combat area heading for point option where we would meet the refueling task group in the morning. We understood that even the crew had enjoyed specially made cakes to celebrate that six thousandth landing.

After refueling we headed south, back down for Guam as we were to hit the Orote Airfield and Agana Town on the island of Guam, on the 6th. However, with news that had come over the ticker tape, we began to wonder if we would be going back to Saipan to help our Marines retake that island. It seems several thousand fanatical, sake-loaded Japanese that had been trapped in

July		1944		VF-2		CV-12	
Duration of Flight	Character of Flight	Pilot		PASSENGERS		REMARKS	
3.9	RSP ESCORT	Self		CATAPULT #10	Cl #85		
4.0	SWEEP	"	Iwo Jima	3 Zeks	Cl #86		
3.5	STRIKE	"			Cl #87		Bonins
3.9	RSP	"			Cl #88		
3.3	CAP	"			Cl #89		
2.7	STRIKE	"			Cl #90	Agana Town	Guam
2.0	STRIKE	"			Cl #91		"

Author adds three more victories to his log book on July 3, 1944.

the northeastern part of Saipan had made an unexpected attack using sharpened sticks and anything sharp. They were even picking up rocks and different things because they were out of guns and ammunition. But we had rushed in the Army reserves that had been sent in to relieve the Marines when they thought the island had been completely taken.

My division had targets around Agana Town where we dropped our bombs and strafed some objects that seemed or appeared to be machine-gun nests. The antiaircraft guns were quiet, and we had little trouble finding our targets. I guess I spent the eighth doing hobbies, for sometime around then we would get expended 40-mm shells before they were tossed overboard. We would cut them off at about four inches from the bottom and then put them on a metal bandsaw, so we could make a second cut but leaving enough metal to fold over to hold a cigar or a cigarette.

I would also coat those 40-mm shells with wax and then scratch through the wax with writing reading *USS Enterprise* and *USS Hornet*. Then I'd use an acid over where I had scratched my writings. After drying it off, I'd then heat the shell so the wax would come off, and I had a beautiful memento.

I also had started a wood carving out of teakwood, which was large enough to carve a picture of the *Hornet* in the waves and still hold a clock. I had been able to scrounge and unscrew the clock from its location on the dashboard of one of the planes before it was pushed over the side. The plane had so many holes from shells that had hit it on one of the combat sorties and would have required major maintenance with all its problems.

My division was scheduled for a strike on July ninth even though it was Sunday. We were loaded with bombs again and found targets on Guam. I was not on the flight scheduled for July 10th, and was, as usual, curious when a destroyer pulled up to the carrier's port rear side. This time it was to transfer a seaman over to the *Hornet*.

It was to become a miracle, for it turned out to be the transfer of one RMM 1/c C.R. Tweed, with an incredible story. He had survived the Japanese occupation of Guam by hiding in the hills for well over 2 1/2 years, aided only by an occasional handout from a friendly Chamorros native who would sneak up with a little food for him. The native even passed Japanese guards on the way.

His story: When the Japanese took Guam back in early '42, he was able to get up into the hills along with four or five other Americans, but one by one they were discovered and killed. When Tweed saw planes that were not the usual Japanese variety, he found a secluded spot to send a Morse code message that was picked up by one of the flyers over Guam. That message was relayed back to a destroyer that had been stationed off Guam for rescue purposes.

Fortunately, the skipper of the *USS McCall*, Lt. Cmdr. J. B. Carroll, dispatched a motor launch with armed guards to investigate. Tweed's remaining little piece of broken mirror used to reflect the sun's rays guided the motor launch into a spot where he could get down to without the Japanese capturing him. He swam out to the launch, which returned him to the McCall, which in turn brought him out to the Admiral of our task group, Jocko Clark.

Jocko's interrogation of Tweed led to his message to Admiral Nimitz in Pearl Harbor who returned a message to get Tweed to Pearl Harbor as quickly as possible, for he was sending a plane to Asleto Airfield on Saipan to expedite the return. After Jocko heard his story, he immediately and on the spot gave Tweed a promotion to chief and sent him down to ship service to get his new uniform. After he was fitted, Jocko ordered him to go as a passenger in a TBF in lieu of the usual gunner, and for two fighters to escort the TBF as there was still fighting on Saipan.

Griff Griffin and I happened to be the only pilots in the ready room, after landing from that earlier strike escorting bombers and finding targets on Guam. All other pilots had secured to their staterooms or to the mess for lunch, leaving Griff and myself as the "volunteers" to escort Tweed on the first leg of his journey home to the States. We covered the 150 miles to Saipan and landed on the short runway of Asleto Airfield where our Seabees had been able to fill in the craters our bombs had dug just a week before.

The Seabees were feverishly working to extend the runway

for the larger transport plane coming from Pearl Harbor for Tweed. We noticed several Zero's somewhat damaged by our strafing, of even just a week before, but still recognizable as Zeros. With a camera that Griff had brought, I took his picture in the cockpit of a Zero, and he took my picture sitting in the cockpit of a Zero. All the time we were there on the ground we heard gunfire from snipers still within audible distance of the field. We didn't waste any time in leaving for our return to the *Hornet* after saying goodbye to Tweed and trusting the Sea Bees to take care of him until that plane from Pearl arrived.

Back to CAP Duty

On the 11th I had an early flight and carried a bomb to drop for it was mounted on the plane in addition to the requirement of using the plane for its designated purpose, for it had three cameras mounted on the underside of the plane. The cameras were mounted, one vertical, one right, and one left for oblique pictures. The very sensitive cameras could take vertical pictures and also oblique pictures from even 10,000 feet and show details as accurately as if I was taking your picture from just 10 to 12 feet away with a regular camera. The lenses on those cameras were pretty good even back in those days.

For the next few days, I was scheduled for the usual CAPs. Then I flew a strike into Guam to drop more bombs on Orote Point, the shore area where our Marines would be making their landings in the near future. The invasion had been moved up to the 21st from the scheduled 25th. By this time we had no aerial opposition, just the ever present antiaircraft that luckily just put a few holes in our planes without actually downing any of us.

On the 19th, however, being one of three pilots checked out in the operation of our squadron's photo plane, I was scheduled for a special photo mission. I was assigned to fly a one-mile path along Orote Point at 1000 feet offshore and at a 45-degree angle to the shoreline. That would show our Marines leaving the troop ships

The author in captured Japanese Zero on Asleto airfield, Saipan.

what they would see from the LCI's as they were going in to the
shoreline they would be landing on.

After making the photo run I then had to reverse course and
come back over the same mile at 1000 feet for a 45 degree angle
from the on shore position to show what our Marines would be facing and going against during their landing. The 1000 foot altitude
was so that pictures would be at a given scale to enable very accurate deciphering as to the size of guns and placements of revetments
there on the shores of Guam.

After landing back aboard the *Hornet*, my plane captain
came down to the ready room to inform me he had counted 108
holes in the plane from small arms bullets that very easily would
carry that 1000 foot distance. Of course that would've been really
only 54 holes as the bullets would've gone in one side and then out
the other side, probably. Fortunately, none of those shots crippled
me or my plane and the trusty old Grumman Hellcat had brought
me home once again.

The squadron was assigned to make six strikes carrying
bombs on the 20th, which was Guam's D-Day -1. I flew twice that
day and had another photo hop on the 21st to cover the Marines
actual landing.

There was no aerial opposition, which could have made
quite a difference to our Marines landing on Guam. Without that

aerial opposition, our task group was able to head north to Saipan in hopes that we could get a restock of bombs after dropping so many on Guam. We would need them to hit Yap and Ulithi on the 25th through the 28th when I would be flying a strike mission escorting our bombers all four of those days and would fly the photo plane on the 28th to get evidence of the destruction we had accomplished. We had caught an estimated 40 Japanese planes on the airfield, which had not taken to the air over Yap. Again the only thing we had was that ever present antiaircraft to fly through over the islands.

I had a CAP flight on the 29th and then retired to do some of my handicrafts as the fleet headed north to a point west of Guam to meet our refueling oil tankers. We then found out we were not scheduled to go directly to Eniwetok, but to take another trip up to Iwo Jima to make sure Japanese planes were not being shuttled down to give our Marines on both Saipan and Guam a hard time. We were scheduled to fly a fighter sweep over Iwo Jima on August 4th and then to borrow a phrase from Admiral Mitscher's operational plan we were to;

"GET THE PLANES,
  GET THE SHIPS,
FINISH THE BONINS,
HEAD FOR THE BARN, (Eniwetok)."

I did fly the fighter sweep over Iwo Jima on the fourth of August, but this trip was not like previous ventures to Iwo Jima. We had no aerial resistance and the few planes on the ground did not even taxi out, so we strafed them and left most of them burning. Then we dropped our bombs on specific targets.

On the fifth I was scheduled for a 350-mile search, which would put me up within 120 miles of Tokyo, the closest anybody had really been to that city for a long, long time. Kenny Lake and myself were to escort a TBF on the search. Even though the weather was none too good, with a few squalls, we were launched anyway.

We had finished the first leg and the second cross leg,

uneventfully and started back on the third leg returning us to the carrier when we discovered a small Japanese destroyer. I led Kenny on a few strafing runs and the destroyer started smoking. We had to leave the smoking destroyer and get back on course back to our carrier. Since we still had some 300 miles to go before we found our carrier, we could not waste too much of our gas or ammunition in case we found something to fire at on the way.

After about five minutes, we saw a Japanese Emily to our right below us and went after it. As we circled to our right, it continued on course making it an easy target for us both to make a high side firing run on it from the right. Then I reversed course to make a second run, firing on its nose. As we approached each other, it burst into flames, then it dropped to the water below. We had seen gas streaming behind it after that first run.

We have no idea who was on that Emily, for it is a large plane and could have been carrying many passengers, or it could have been carrying a bunch of freight back to Japan. It also could have been carrying Japanese higher command personnel returning to their homeland. But we probably will never know, and it was such a shame for they were less than 200 miles from Tokyo and home.

When we got back on course I noticed the wave caps and mist from them to be blowing almost 180 degrees, or opposite from what they had been on that first and second leg of the search. This would make quite a difference in navigation, for the wind was fairly strong that day. It was only a guess, or estimate, of how long we had been blown off course in a wind from a direction opposite from what our navigation had originally been computed.

I made a couple estimates and recalculated our heading back to the *Hornet* that also would have been affected by the change of wind direction. My estimates must have been about as accurate as they could have been, for we arrived right on the nose of our task group. After landing, and in the usual debriefing, the ACI officer suggested I give the total plane credit to Kenny, for he needed just one more to become an ace. I already had attained that status and rather than splitting credit for the Emily, Kenny became an ace with my compliments.

We were then scheduled to head back to Eniwetok to restock everything: armaments, food, and crude oil along with aviation fuel. However, once again Jocko detoured us to Iwo Jima as we passed, just to make sure that Japanese were not using Iwo as a staging area for sending planes down to Guam making the Marines landing on Guam more difficult.

Change of Command

Later that afternoon we learned that Dick Combs had shot down another Japanese plane, which brought our present score to 228. Then our cruisers and some of the destroyers were detached to go after the remains of the Japanese AK's and destroyers that our bombers could not get to in the afternoon strike. The bad fall weather limited the ability of our bombers to chase after that Japanese task group.

At dinner that evening the Captain's steward brought down another large cake appropriately decorated to celebrate the 8000th landing on the *Hornet*. With that news it seemed like some of the air group members that had been chanting "The ol' front door by August 4" were now chanting "The ol' front gate by November 8." Our fighter squadron had been in actual combat for seven months already, whereas the Navy's normal policy was a tour of duty for six months in combat before relief and a trip homeward.

Now, we weve officially informed that we would be a part of the Palau invasion with D-day set for September 15th. Then we would make a trip to Davao, Mindanao, and Manila all in the Philippine Islands, before we could even begin to expect our replacement air group to take over. At least we would have the next two to three weeks of relaxation on the beach at Eniwetok or we would be able to spend time on our hobbies without the pressure of waiting for the bull horn announcing flight quarters. When that happens you have to drop everything you are doing and head for the ready room to get your plotting board brought up to date with our latest codes and navigational aids.

Captain Sample had ordered on August 7th a special banquet dinner for all aboard to celebrate his promotion to Admiral, and he and a special guest that came down to eat with us in the wardroom. It was Captain Doyle, who would become the new skipper of the *Hornet*. As a special welcome aboard for a new Captain, the stewards were allowed to break out all the delicacies, choice steaks, and even ice cream to go with the cake.

This was very welcome after being served dehydrated potatoes, dehydrated milk, and Spam for the last 10 days. The carriers refrigeration storage for foods had been based on prewar stays at sea for at the most a couple of weeks, and we had been out for over a month. Then the stewards had to do it all over again for those who had been at duty stations during the first serving, while those that had eaten would go on duty stations.

Captain Sample would be leaving us for his new command as soon as we dropped anchor in the lagoon at Eniwetok, and we would be getting supplies to replace our delicacies we had enjoyed that mealtime. Later that evening Captain Sample with Captain Doyle and Admiral Clark came down to the ready room to look at the gun camera films that had been taken over Guam and Iwo Jima during the past four to five weeks.

The flight deck on August 8th saw us all decked out in clean khakis and ties for the first time in a longtime, to stand a Captain's inspection for the change of command ceremony. Captain Sample delivered a short farewell speech thanking all hands for such a successful tour of combat. He then introduced Captain Doyle to everybody standing at attention, who spoke for a few minutes accepting command of the carrier that already now held most of the Navy's records.

Adm. Jocko Clark was then introduced and expressed his gratitude to all hands aboard for their diligence to duty for such a successful cruise of combat during the last couple months. He then proceeded to present awards. Andy Skon received a Navy Cross (prized above all others by men of the Navy) for his heroism in accompanying Butch O'Hare on his last flight that was actually the first night fighter operation ever conducted from a carrier. Captain

Dean and several others received DFCs (Distinguished Flying Cross), and others received Air Medals and Purple Hearts before we were excused. That evening Captain (now Admiral) Sample came down to the officers mess for dinner, for he wanted to let Captain Doyle experience his first dinner undisturbed in his own quarters, and we ate like kings again.

We dropped anchor about noon on the 9th for what was supposed to have been a two to three-week period of resupply for the ship and rest and relaxation for the air department. The first barge to come alongside the carrier was the mail, with some 90 bags of it. We wasted little time in opening it. Much of the mail was from our homes and loved ones, with many of my squadron mates producing clippings that lauded the conquests and even included pictures of By Johnson and myself. They were apparently from that day on Kwajalein when Charlie Arnolt of United Press had cornered By and myself at a beer party on the beach in late June. The clippings were from all over the country and in major newspapers including from Honolulu, San Francisco, Chicago, New York, and even the Grumman Hellcat plant news itself.

We had one of the latest movies every night and beach parties every day or we were on the circuit for the championship basketball round robin teams between all carriers. We did pretty well, winning all games from the other carriers. All of that was mixed in with our handicrafts, and works of art. However, our stay in the lagoon got cut short, for our new ship's skipper wanted some experience operating the carrier before he was thrust into actual combat.

He wanted to go out for an overnight cruise and wanted to see for himself, for he didn't believe our fighter squadron had usually gotten launched at the rate of four planes per minute takeoff speed and a 19 second interval for landing. We accomplished that for him to prove the records correct. Not only once, we did it a second time. The bomber and torpedo squadrons also showed him their proficiencies. Then it was back into the Eniwetok lagoon for more barges to tie up along side with supplies to be hoisted aboard by the cranes on the hangar deck.

While half the ship's company personnel were busy unloading the barges and storing all the goods in their compartments deep in the hold of the carrier, the other half was granted shore leave. There were beer parties and many of the group were always sure to be swimming on that beautiful sandy beach and guzzling more than their share of beer. At the end of the day we all had to return to our ships, for there were no accommodations yet, there on Eniwetok.

After a whole day of partying we had to wait on the pier for our Higgins boats to take us back to the carrier, and things got a little boisterous and a bit out of hand when several fellows were pushed off the pier and into the water. And, it just happened that Admiral "Whiskey" Jack McCain was also on the pier waiting for his Admiral's barge when somehow or other he also got pushed.

When we realized who had just gone into the water, most of us rushed to lend assistance in pulling him out. Of course, we were all very apologetic, for we didn't know just what he would be doing in retaliation. Under the circumstances I guess he could have made things quite difficult for us.

However, he was a pretty good Joe and seemed to have a pretty good time laughing it off with the rest of us while waiting for transportation back to our carriers. When we got back, we found more mail had come aboard with a whole new stack waiting for each of us, which included the skipper's letter from Mom Chung, which he posted for all of us to see.

It included a clipping from the San Francisco News:

"Mom's Boys Deliver" lauded the accomplishments of my squadron as members of her "Bastard Sons Club." It included her postscript "Bill Dean and his men are the finest examples of my sons. They are the grandest men in all the world. Please, come home soon for the Rippers party - am so proud of you all. Love, Mom."

And another clipping enclosed was from the Oakland Tribune:

"Wild Bill's Air Heroes"

Admiral Nimitz, bringing up to date the destruction of Japanese war craft by Carrier Air Group Two of the Pacific Fleet, reports that the group destroyed or damaged 19

Japanese war ships, including two large carriers, a heavy cruiser, and two destroyers in two weeks of furious activity from June 11 to 24. The same pilots also destroyed 200 enemy planes in that period. Since June 24 the Air Group commanded by "Wild Bill" Dean of Coronado, California, has shot down 33 more Japanese planes in aerial combat, bringing to more than 200 the bag of Nip planes in combat. This, Admiral Nimitz says, is "an all-time record for naval warfare." Our hats are off to "Wild Bills" gallant boys.

We had kind of hoped that we would be relieved here at Eniwetok, for we had been on the *Hornet* for six months already and had been a fighting squadron already on the Enterprise for two months last year. Several of us also had a month of TAD (temporary additional duty), making us nine-month veterans, when the Navy's usual procedure was to rotate air groups each six months to avoid pilot stresses and fatigue.

On Aug. 25th we received the long awaited news, at last: a dispatch to the effect that our relief would be Air Group 11 and it was en route to Manus Island in the Admiralties! It also stated they would arrive by September 24th so this operation would be our last operation. And then it was announced the movie for that night would be "Lady in the Dark" starring Ginger Rogers.

August 26th was a day for celebration. Vice Adm. Mitscher came aboard for the honor of presenting medals and awards. He had been a former skipper of the old *Hornet* (CV- 8) and wanted to make the presentations, which he had already approved, as a day of reborn glory, for the name of *HORNET*.

In his comments he stated, "I am proud to return to the *Hornet* on this occasion. When I served on the old *Hornet* she was the greatest ship in the Fleet. I now return to an even greater one." Then from the makeshift platform with bunting covering the railings, he presented the Navy Cross to Admiral Clark, Commander Arnold, Commander Dean, Barney Bernard, and Spider Webb. A Silver Star and DFC to Tex Vineyard, a Silver Star, DFC, and Air Medal to Dan Carmichael, and a Silver Star and two DFC's to me.

Then we had a rather long listing of 37 pilots being presented DFC's and/or Air Medals, or both.

August 28 had our new task group Commander, Admiral McCain, calling a meeting of all ship captains, ACI officers, and squadron commanders for a staff meeting about the *USS Wasp*. Later in the day we had several new pilots reporting to the squadron. They had not been in their previous squadrons long enough to return to Pearl Harbor with their air groups and the carriers which were going back for maintenance and resupply there.

Chapter Ten

FIGHTING TWO
HEROES' WELCOME

August 29 thru October 1944

VF-2's Last Combat Operation

The anchor chain came up early on the morning of August 29th and we were off again, for our last combat operation. It was now official, this time to invade Palau and fly fighter sweeps and strikes against the Philippine Islands.

We would also be celebrating the *Hornet's* first year since its launching. What an illustrious year it had been. Its record short time for outfitting after launching, its shakedown cruise to Guantanamo Bay, its trip through the Panama Canal to the west coast, and now six months of record-setting air group action in combat. For that, all personnel aboard were served a special dinner that night in celebration of that one-year anniversary.

Weather was so bad for the next few days that even the usual CAP flights were canceled, giving us time to finish up some of our handicraft projects that we had started several months ago. I had a few ashtrays made from 40-mm shell casings, and then my scrapbook covers made of mahogany slats and brass metal hinges for the opening cover. I also had my teakwood carving of the *Hornet* with clock, which I think all of them will become relics, if I should live so long. We also had started to hand tool our leather squadron insignia for our flight jackets after we had received a picture of it from Mom Chung. We were allowed to work in the workshops only during normal business hours (8-5) each day.

At night we had many hours of bridge, chess, or acey-duecy. We also had the ACI officer lecturing us on how to survive in the jungles of the Philippine Islands and how to recognize inhabitants of the different Islands. The Negrito, or the Tagalog, or the Moros, and what to say when paraded before the Dato. We also discussed "keeping your head, if downed," or "when confronted by a head-hunter, don't lose face." Then one pilot commented, "The trouble is, you load yourself down with a machete and all this gear till you weigh a ton - then you go in off the bow on takeoff and sink like a rock for your Mae West won't hold you up with all the extra weight - or you don't carry it and find yourself forced down in the jungle! You just can't win."

I had a combat air patrol on the fifth, and then nothing on the sixth. So we had lots of time available to play many hands of bridge. Randy Carlson had been my partner for most of the afternoon and then my opponent that evening. He didn't want to leave the game when he was on a winning streak. As I remember, we had to blow the whistle at midnight for he was scheduled on the first fighter sweeps in the morning.

On the seventh, reveille was at 0330 with three strikes scheduled for the day. One against Anguar and Ngesibus Islands. Randy was on that early flight, and I was dumbfounded when seeing a division come back with only three planes from that pre dawn flight against Palau. That missing plane turned out to be piloted by my often time bridge partner, who was reported to have gone down in a strafing run and never pulled out, going straight on in.

We will never know whether it was a mechanical problem, or a lucky hit by a small arms bullet or an antiaircraft shell. It sure put a somber feeling in all of us that had chummed around with

Randy for his ability, devotion to duty, and record of service, He was admired by all. He was one of the first in the squadron to get a Japanese Zero, when he shot one off "Griff's" tail in the early days over Kwajalein.

I certainly missed Randy, for he and I got along so well playing bridge together, and I don't know how many pennies we had won from opponents when we played for a penny a point. It must have been many dollars as Randy and I seemed to be able to guess very well what was in our corresponding hands after our cock-eyed bidding had been completed. However, I was scheduled to fly a photo hop later in the day to get pictures of specific targets and also take anything of interest that I felt might help determine where our Marines could go ashore with the least amount of resistance. So I could not spend a lot of time grieving over Randy's loss.

I also had a flight on the eighth when the task group was beginning to move west to be somewhat closer for the next day's targets on Mindanao, which was on the western side of the Philippines. On the ninth, it was still an extra long flight to targets on Mindanao Island, which we also hit on the 10th before retreating out to meet the tanker fleet to refuel.

Those flights were over land, and we began to understand why we had had lectures on survival in the jungle. It was the first time we had flown over land for such a long distance - 400 miles one way. One of the pilots made a comment, "Don't those engines sound bad over land." Capt. Doyle had ordered the wardroom stewards to fix a luscious turkey dinner with all the fixings as a thank you for those long distance flights. And after dinner, of course, Dr. Stratton had sick call in the ready room for us on the eve of refueling. He still called it "lemonade" but this time we had a choice of two cans of beer or two little one ounce bottles of brandy. Most of us had seen the refueling process so often that we opted to work on our handicrafts, or finish our leather squadron insignia that we could have sowed onto our flight jackets.

After a fast run in during the night we were just off the Visayan group of Islands. The weather was none too good, and was quite squally, but the first fighter sweep was launched anyway on the 12th. The first report we heard over the radio was "Many rats over Negroes." Charlie Harbert's flight got credit for 9 planes, with singles going to Charlie, Bernard McLaughlin, and Tom Tillar, with a pair to Beetle Berrey, and Spit Spitler got credit for four. Then on another escort flight led by Commander Arnold six pilots came back with singles. Credits went to the Commander, Razor Blaydes, By Johnson, Earl Zaeske, Van Van Haren, and Barney Barnard. But again, on the flights I was on, we found no aerial opposition. At dinner that evening we enjoyed a couple delicious cakes again from the Captain's steward to celebrate the 9000th landing on the *Hornet*.

That evening at the squadron's review of the days activities, it was revealed that Ensign T.C. Tillar, one of the pilots reporting in to the squadron just as we left Eniwetok on August 28th, did not return from the strike. When the story had been patched together, it became evident that McLaughlin and Frank O'Brien chased Zeros off Tillar's tail, but they had already hit an oil line and Tillar started losing oil and power, and was forced to make a water landing just off Leyte Island. McLaughlin and O'Brien saw that he had been able to get out of the plane, and inflated his rubber life raft and had started paddling towards the shore, but they had to leave when their gas supplies started dwindling. We did not know whether he was in the hands of Japanese or with friendly natives, so our fears for his safety were on edge.

On the 13th, Andy Skon and Les Sipes were allowed to escort a cruiser floatplane to the spot where Tillar had been forced down. They did not find him there at first, but after a short search they saw the red arch of the fire works from a Very pistol from a small island close by, which they had flown over. The floatplane was able to land near the shore and made a successful rescue, and all returned to the cruiser with Tillar staying overnight on the cruiser. When he returned to the carrier the next day, he had quite a story to tell as Fighting Two's "Ambassador of Good Will," which could be abbreviated, but his own story, as told on his return is so packed full of thrilling experiences that it would be a shame to let it fade into oblivion in the dusty corners of the library of congress.

Ens. Thomas C. Tillar's story

"We were assigned a target on Cebu and were escorting the TBFs and SB2CS. We were high cover at 17,000 feet. The bombers had completed about half of their runs and still were bombing the field. Our division leader, Lt. McLaughlin, led us down in a strafing attack on Opon Field, Mactan Island. The last two planes in the formation, Lt.(jg) C. P. Spitler's and mine passed them on the way down. At 4,000 feet Spitler spotted two Zekes and we started after them. Then I was jumped - tracers went by the cockpit and I looked back and saw a Zeke on my tail, riding me down at very close range. I turned left under him and continued diving - McLaughlin chased one of the two. He turned left and I chopped throttle. He over-ran me and I got in behind him - we then were at about 1,000 feet. He leveled off and headed south, I after him. I was overtaking him in level flight indicating 210 to 220 knots. He apparently was aware of this, and when I was within 2000-foot range he went into a wing-over to the left. I turned inside him and followed him around in the turn, firing at five second intervals. One half his wing and part of his tail came off. By that time we were going straight down to the water from 2,000 feet. I pulled out about 100 feet off the water and saw him splash - he did not bailout or burn, he just crashed.

"I then was at 100 feet, indicating about 250 knots, and two Zekes made a formation run on me from my starboard bow. They were shooting at me from head-on. I turned into them and fired at them as they went by. I smoked one but do not know what happened to them. I applied full power and climbed to 9,000 feet without difficulty. My windshield started to cloud up due to an oil film as I got up there. I flew around with Stockert for about 10 minutes. I noticed my oil pressure was down to 40 and dropping gradually. I cut down the power immediately - the plane was not overheating. I called Stockert and told him I thought I would have to make an emergency landing. I flew about 15 more minutes in formation,

even joining them in a strafing run because I did not dare lose them. We headed home and I asked Stockert to lead me to the rescue point as I had no forward vision. We headed toward this point from 5,000 feet; my speed dropped off to 110 knots. I was losing altitude all the time and when I increased throttle my oil pressure dropped off. Charlie Harbert called me and told me to try and get over Leyte and if not to make a water landing. I was at about 1500 feet then and my prop went into low pitch. When it did so my plane began to overheat - I had only 15 pounds of pressure. I knew I would have to make a water landing. I jettisoned belly tank and hatch. I had difficulty getting the hatch off because I was indicating only 100 knots. I finally pushed it off using both hands. I tightened my shoulder straps, lowered my tail hook and flaps - which came down easily-, and prepared to land. I felt the tail hook drag the water just as the engine cut out. The plane made an easy landing. I got out easily with all my gear strapped to me. The plane remained surfaced for approximately 20 seconds, during which time I was in the water in my Mae West. After the plane sank I unbuckled my gear and got out the rubber boat. The sea was calm. Just before I opened the boat I pulled one of my dye markers. There were friendly planes - Skon and Sipes - flying over me all the while until I was safely in the boat. I kept my chute, which I held in one hand while climbing into the boat. This added somewhat to the ordinary difficulty of climbing in. I previously had tried to climb into the boat with the back pack and chute on me but was unable to do so. I then bailed water out of the boat.

"After I was in the boat I determined that I was about 10 miles west of Amogotada Point, Leyte. I decided to stay away from the beach and wait for them to come back for me. I knew that they knew where I was and felt that eventually I would be picked up. I was about 600 yards north of a little hilly, volcanic island with a 100 foot shelf dropping down to the sea - later identified as Apid Island. I was drifting away from it very slowly and had no intention of going into it. My first thought was that this island, with its scrub trees above its gray shelf rock was deserted. There were to the north of me some fishing boats. I had seen these before I went *down but decided they probably were friendly. They stayed where they were and did not seem to be aware of my presence.*

"After I was out there about an hour - in which time I had drifted only about 200 yards - I noticed several outrigger canoes coming from the north side of Apid Island. There were three at first, and, as they came half way out, three more followed them. An elderly man and a boy were in the leading canoe and a single man in each of the others. They seemed suspicious of me and I was even more so of them. They stopped about 20 yards from me. They were jabbering away in a foreign tongue which I presumed to be Filipino - first among themselves and then directly to me. I was unable to understand. All this time I had my revolver in my lap as I was unable to determine whether they were native or Jap, friendly or unfriendly. I made a lot of motions to them, none of which were of an unfriendly character. They gained confidence and came within ten to 15 feet of my boat. When they got that close, the young boy - about 15 - in the canoe with the leader - a man of about 50 - stood staring at me while the old fellow talked. I decided to curry their favor by offering them razor blades which I kept in my emergency belt kit for that purpose - I later learned that cigars were highly acceptable. I opened up a razor blade and offered it to the young fellow and he showed it to the old man, and the others tangled up their out-riggers getting close enough to study it. They passed it around, continuing to talk among themselves and occasionally to me. They evidently decided to take me ashore as they motioned to me to get into the largest canoe. They threw me a line with which to tie my raft to one of the canoes. I spent my trip to the shore bailing water as the canoe leaked badly. I had decided that they were friendly and had no hesitancy in going with them. My only concern was to make them understand me. I would look at them with a dumb look when they addressed me and they laughed. Half way back to the beach a formation of our planes approached from the east. They started to row like mad and I could make out the word 'Japanese' as they pointed toward the planes. I made hand signals to the old man indicating they were friendly planes - they seemed to understand. We went almost right under the shelf of the island and

around to the south side where there was a beach. There was a native village and many people - about 200 - were waiting for us. The whole population had turned out. They were scantily clothed - those with anything wore a tough type of cloth that resembled burlap. The men were about five feet four inches tall, of dark yellow complexion, with almond shaped Filipino type of eyes, and straight, black hair.

"I waded ashore in two feet of water and a boy who looked to be about 18 - actually 26 - met me at the beach and said. 'Hello, Sir,' and shook hands. He could speak broken English, mixed with Filipino. He engaged me in conversation. From then on I used him as my interpreter. I told him I was an American flyer. They did not know what 'Navy' meant or what 'aircraft carrier' meant. I told them the planes were American. They could see and detect the approach of planes long before I could. They kept asking the questions, 'Who are your companions?' and 'Where are they?' I kept telling them 'aircraft carrier,' which I think they failed to understand. I told them my companions were those fliers 'up there' and I think they understood this. They brought all my gear ashore and put it in a big open shed which the Americans had left there a long time ago. The shed had 'Apid Water Tank' written on it in English, but the water tank was gone. There was a good concrete foundation remaining. I handed out some more razor blades, then I opened my chute which was soaked and covered with dye marker. The chief's wife felt the texture of the silk and mumbled something. She told the interpreter she would like to hang it up and dry it out and the chief indicated a desire for it. He told me through the interpreter that they did not have much clothing. I immediately gave it to the chief's wife. She took it to the house and hung it up to dry. The chief's house was made out of board with thatched roof - probably taken from the water tank - while the other huts were completely thatched affairs on four inch wooden poles. Their floors were made of split bamboo. One of the men cut his finger with one of the razor blades and winced in pain. I took out my first aid kit and wrapped it up for him. They appreciated this immensely. They seemed curious about the rest of my gear so I opened my back and

seat packs to show them their contents and held the mirror in front of the chief's wife - she turned away and laughed.

"The boy - who could speak broken English - told me to wait, and he came back in five minutes with his identification papers to show that he was a member of the Philippine Army. They gave his name as 'Sosa' and rank of Pfc. He told me that he had been in Cebu and had escaped about a year-and-a-half ago. I gathered that he had been a prisoner. He then asked me if I had eaten. I said, 'No,' and he sent someone to bring me food. One of the women brought back three raw eggs and gave me them. I ate them although they almost gagged me - I guess because I thought I would offend them by refusing. They hung all my gear on a line between two trees. They then took me to the chief's house and we sat down on bamboo seats, the interpreter sitting next to me. I asked him all the questions I could. He told me they had had no contact whatso-ever with the Japs - that the natives in the area had no personal hatred for but were unfriendly toward the Jap - partly because of what they had heard and partly because they knew their supplies had been cut off from the time the Japs came. I asked him whether the Japs were around and he said there were none on any of the small islands. He further stated that a seaplane went over their vil-lage every two or three days pointing westward. During our con-versation a carrier strike came over from the east. They heard it long before I did - everyone started jabbering and then suddenly became quiet. It was at this moment that I heard the planes for the first time. We went down to the beach and I tried to signal the for-mation. The planes were between 8,000 and 9,000 feet. I used my mirror but apparently it was ineffectual. After the strike had passed over we heard the bombing of Cebu.

"We went back to the chief's cabin and were sitting there, they staring at me during a lull in conversation. They asked me if I liked fish and, when I said I did, brought out two fish about eight inches long which were highly colored in purple, red, and pink hues. These were hot, recently cooked, entrails and all. I broke one and gave half to the interpreter and we each ate some. He ate the head and tail as well but I just the fillet. At the same time they

brought me a big plate of rice which was very dry and garnished with two fried eggs served on top of it. I ate about half of this. They then brought me four more raw eggs and insisted I eat them. I did although I nearly gagged. We then heard another plane and went to the beach. I could barely see it, but it was very apparent to them. It disappeared to the north. We came back to the chief's home and the interpreter said he was going to take me somewhere but not to be afraid. (The warning was unnecessary as I was completely at ease by this time.) We walked about one-half mile to the other end of the island. A large group of people were gathered around a shed, and, when I looked in, I found it contained my belly tank, in perfect condition except for a slight dent in one side - it had been dropped from 2,000 feet. It still contained about ten gallons of gas. The natives thought it was a bomb, and I opened the cap and showed the interpreter its true nature. He seemed to understand what it was after smelling the gas. Then we went back to the chief's cabin, and I opened my back pack and took out the emergency rations. I gave out the chewing gum, vitamin tablets, and candy. One of the natives who had not spoken a word of English, exclaimed, 'Sweet!' I gave the interpreter the rest of the razor blades which pleased him immensely. I also gave him the rubber sail in the life raft, my sea anchor, and bailing bucket. About this time the strike that had passed over was returning and again I tried to contact it with a mirror but failed. The next planes we heard were a couple of F6s, which came over and circled at 3,000 feet - Skon and Sipes. I used the mirror again - they came down close. Then I shot a .38 tracer right in front of them. They must have seen it because they joined up and came down still closer. I then ran back to the chief's cabin and got the Very pistol out of my seat pack. I fired a Very shell which they saw.

"Just after I fired the Very pistol an outrigger came over from a little island to the south. The interpreter recognized its occupant and said he was a Lieutenant in the Filipino Army. This man was a Filipino, about five feet, five inches in height. He was better fed and was fairly well dressed in civilian clothes - pink sport shirt and trousers. I think they sent over for him. I was given to

*understand that he made regular trips to and from Apid. He intro-
duced himself in pretty good English - he did not mix Filipino with
his English and I was able to understand him. I told him I was an
Ensign - a pilot from an aircraft carrier. He asked how many carriers we had out there and I said a great many. He seemed quite
pleased with this. He told me - in answer to my question - that there
were no Japs on Leyte. He inquired as to how many bombs we had
dropped on Negros and Cebu. I told him over 300 on Cebu and as
many more on Negros that morning. He repeated it to the natives
and all were greatly impressed, repeating several times in amazement the words '300,' throwing up their hands and jabbering. He
represented the guerrilla forces and told me they were badly in
need of arms and medical supplies.*

*"Just then I saw the SOC coming in from the south. I ran
and got my back pack and helmet. Skon and Sipes directed the SOC
over to me. I fired another .38 tracer at the SOC, which he did not
see. He flew over the island once without sighting me - then he flew
back around the island, and when he returned I fired a Very shell
which he saw. The plane landed and taxied within 75 yards of the
beach and I paddled out to it in my rubber raft."*

*Less than an hour after he was back aboard, Tillar was
preparing to return to the vicinity of his rescue. Chief Reese, our
parachute rigger, had an especially prepared pilot chute rig with a
box of cigars for our newfound friends - and carefully tucked away
under the canvas container was the following note:*

*"Teniente Sosa,
Muchas gracias y par usted estos cigarros.
Hasta la vista,
Ens. Tillar."*

Weather remained very squally and uncertain on the 13th,
but it was launch planes anyway, and Skipper Dean led a flight up
to southern Luzon. We found no action there but dropped our
bombs on specific targets. On the way back to the carrier the skipper detoured leading the flight down to Northern Negroes Island
where he spotted a single Zero some 4000 feet below him and he

made short order of disposing it. But of course there wasn't enough for me to score on just that single plane.

Then on the second strike flight, Bill Blair, John Banks, Barney Barnard, By Johnson, and Kenny Lake each got a single Japanese plane. A little later on the third strike group of the day to Cebu, Evald Holmgaard got one more, and I had taken various pictures for posterity from the photo plane I was scheduled to fly.

Later that evening we got a ticker tape from Admiral McCain which read:

"AS REPORTED YOUR AIR GROUPS ARE GOOD IN ACTION AND, OF EQUAL IMPORTANCE, IN RECONNAISSANCE" X McCAIN.

Then later that evening we received a dispatch from the cruiser concerning Tillar's rescue:

"NATIVES STATE THERE ARE NO JAPS ON LEYTE BOSOL APID OR SMALL ISLANDS IN THE AREA X NATIVES VERY FRIENDLY X TILLAR TAKEN ASHORE BY NATIVES X LOCATED HIM WITH ASSISTANCE OF FIGHTERS WHO HAD SEEN HIM GO DOWN AND CARTRIDGE FIRED FROM ISLAND X RESCUE PILOTS WERE LT.(jg) ALCOCK USNR AND ENS. SPINELLI USN X THEIR SECOND SUCCESSFUL MISSION TOGETHER."

On the 14th our task group dropped down to the Davao Gulf area in the search for a reported convoy, which was successful. Griff's division led a strafing attack on a large destroyer and their efforts quieted the antiaircraft so that our bombers were able to sink that destroyer in a relative few minutes. However, his plane was pretty well shot up from the antiaircraft fire.

On the 15th our task group had dropped down still farther south to the Halmahera area in the Dutch East Indies. We were to standby while McArthur's forces invaded Morotai, off Halmahera's northern tip. "Gabe" Gabriel's division was the only one fruitful. They knocked down a Japanese bomber that was out snooping us.

There was not much air activity over Morotai on the 16th when I had a CAP flight. However "Butch" Voris' division was vectored down to Halmahera on a mission of mercy. He was to try and find another fighter pilot from the *USS Wasp* that had landed in the water off Lolobata Airfield. He managed to find the pilot and dropped a life raft to him but he apparently was too weak or injured to control the course as the wind was drifting him towards the beach after he was able to crawl into the raft. The Japanese were firing at him from their slit trenches on shore. Voris strafed them continuously despite intense return fire.

When their gas started running low they were relieved by a division of fighters from the *Wasp* who took over strafing the Japanese trench trying to stop them from hitting the life raft of the downed pilot. His rescue seemed out of the question but it was later learned that he survived to tell the story of a thrilling rescue by plane and a PT boat.

A Mr. Eyerman of LIFE magazine and Bill Gray of TIME magazine came aboard on the 17th to get the story of Fighting Two's record-setting flights aboard the *Hornet*. The two had all day for interviews and picture taking while the task group had backed off the immediate combat area for a day of refueling. They talked to everyone, the Admiral and his staff, the Hornet's skipper and his staff, Bill Dean and most all of our pilots in their effort to get a story. Even pilots that were still hoping to become aces. (The story would eventually be published in the October 23rd, 1944 issues of both LIFE and TIME magazines.)

We had an unfortunate accident that morning, which never should have happened. It happened during the usual engine "pull through" that was done each morning to keep oil from accumulating in the bottom cylinders. It was the plane captain's duty to pull the prop through whether the plane would fly that day or not. Somehow or other the switch had been left in or bumped to the "on" position. When the prop was pulled through, the engine sputtered enough to kick over. The plane captain was ever so lucky in just having a broken arm. It could have been much, much worse, especially if the engine had really started.

Return to the Philippines

The fleet steamed north during the night and the next day. While on our way to Manila, a George Jones from the United Press was transferred via breeches buoy and joined the new correspondence club aboard the carrier. All three of them now worked incessantly trying to corral as many of us as they could get between flights scheduled for the next day, the 18th. Most of us would be flying maybe most of the day on one of the most important jaunts in history.

We sat in briefings taking notes of target assignments, rendezvous locations, with alternates for "just in case," or for weather that possibly could continue to be squally and unfavorable. This would be our last combat, hopefully. Down deep in our hearts, we were thinking of the atrocities reported from the area we would be over for the first time since Corregidor. The death march from Bataan to Fort O'Donnell, the prisoner of war camps that we should try to find, and avoid.

But my mail should present a beautiful sight.

The usual 2200 evening prayer that Chaplain McMahan gave over the ship's loudspeaker very beautifully expressed the sentiments of the ship and squadron on the eve of one of the most daring raids of the war:

"GRANT, O LORD, THAT THE MEN OF THIS SHIP MAY BE BRAVE IN BATTLE, PATIENT IN HARDSHIP, AND COURAGEOUS UNDER ATTACK. INTO THY HANDS WE COMMEND ESPECIALLY OUR AIRMEN WHO TOMORROW WILL AVENGE OUR NATION'S HONOR AND RESTORE HOPE TO AN ENSLAVED PEOPLE. MAY THEIR MISSION BE CROWNED WITH VICTORY, AND DO THOU GRANT THEM, EVERY ONE A SAFE RETURN. THROUGH CHRIST OUR LORD. AMEN."

All during the night of the 20th/21st we were closing on

Luzon at 22 knots with the seas having kicked up and this morning we were on the edge of a typhoon. There were squalls all around us - the skies were black, angry, and with intermittent downpours. Reveille 0500, with flight quarters sounding 30 minutes later, and my division would be launched predawn, for us to take station on the combat air patrol even when the carrier had been pitching and rolling most of the night. The time for us to get our plotting boards up to date with point option and other necessary information was cut short when the ticker tape read "pilots man your planes." Then we headed up through the flight deck and I stumbled around in the pitch darkness of the flight deck to find the plane I was assigned to.

My plane captain helped me get into the harness, hitched me up to the seat pack parachute, and my shoulder straps buckled on around me. In a couple minutes I heard the flight deck loudspeaker belch out "stand by to start engines," then it would be "stand clear of propellers," and then "start engines." In pitch darkness I had to start checking my gauges and engine settings, cylinder head temperature, guns switch "control off" so I wouldn't have 50 calibers firing up the deck when I got the signal from the taxi director to spread my wings. The taxi director could tell if the wings had "thumped" into place and locked, before he got me into takeoff position. Then he would give me a signal to rev up my engine to full power and a quick recheck of all gauges again. If everything checked out okay, I'd give the signal that I was ready to go, with a forward nod of my head. Then it was a short wait for the launch master to give the signal that the deck was clear for takeoff. All this while it was still pitch black out.

Then the signal for full power and the GO with him extending his right arm forward to the bow of the carrier. Immediately after releasing brakes, I had to hit the switch for flaps to get me more lift as I left the carrier's deck and then get the wheels up as soon as possible so I could decrease drag on the plane to help build airspeed. If I understood correctly, this was to be my next-to-last flight from the *Hornet*.

About an hour into the flight, we got a vector out for a snooper, apparently on a search mission. John Banks and I both made high side runs from behind and we had another Japanese fireball dropping to the 10 to 12 foot waves of the ocean below. Although it actually exploded on my third burst of fire, our ACI officer suggested we share it, for each of us already had eight victories.

While we were still on CAP our first strike group heading for Manila was launched, and Capt. Doyle turned the Manila radio broadcast on the ship's loudspeaker system for all aboard to hear. It was the sounds of Tokyo Rose and her American music, which we had so often enjoyed, the popular tunes of the early '40s. The music even continued after the second radio which the Captain tuned to and broadcast over the ship's loudspeaker system intermittently indicated that action had already begun.

Those still aboard the *Hornet* related that it was several minutes after the start of action before the Manila radio was interrupted with, "This is an air raid, this is an air raid, take shelter -- all people hearing this, notify all people in your neighborhood." They said it was delivered in English at first, although with a Filipino accent. Then a Japanese voice came on, and in hysterical gibbering in their language, for a few minutes, then back to the music of Tokyo Rose before the message was repeated in both English and in Japanese.

Our score for that first strike was another ten Japanese planes to increase our squadron total. Andy Skon and Marvin Noble got two each, Tex Harris, Frank Gabriel, Gene Redmond, Beetle Berrey, Evald Holmgaard, and Les Sipes each getting a single. They had been escorting the bombers and torpedo planes, which returned with close to 50,000 tons of shipping laying on the bottom of Manila Bay Harbor. The second and third strikes of the day proved unsuccessful for anything in the air for our fighters. But our bombers and torpedo planes just added thousands of tons of shipping to their earlier success, and I flew one of our photo planes to take pictures of the destruction on the last strike of the day.

The first strike on the 22nd was productive for our bombers and torpedo planes only. Charlie Harbert and the Gene Redmond each got a Zero on the second strike. Tex Vineyard and Spider

Webb each got a Judy while on the third strike of the day, during which our task force was starting to head south for action on the 24th against Coron. It would be a 330 mile one-way flight where we supposedly would find a lot of shipping and who knows what else. Our bombers and torpedo planes had another field day, for they found shipping in abundance. However, there were no Japanese planes that came up to meet us. The second strike of the day diverted to Panay where we did find many supply ships which we strafed in an effort to cut down the antiaircraft fire for our bombers and torpedo planes. However, one of the newest pilots in the squadron, having joined VF-2 on the last day before we left Eniwetok for this operation, was hit by some of that antiaircraft.

Ensign Frank O'Brien became our seventh casualty during our total tour of duty. Frank had been with us for less than one month and had flown his share of combat flights with competence and aggressiveness. In his devotion to duty he paid the supreme price. We cherish the memory of Frank for what he was - a hero of Fighting Two.

Unfortunate as this was, we wound up our combat action with far fewer casualties than most all other squadrons suffered. Our safety record in combat was almost unbelievable when you compare the overall Navy average of one pilot lost for each 19 planes shot down compared to our loss of one pilot to 89.5 Japanese planes shot down. Now our fourth loss to antiaircraft shells, although we did have others that were able to bail out and were saved by either submarines or destroyers during our nearly 10 months of combat duty. My last combat flight was on the 25th, a combat air patrol over the fleet as we started leaving the combat area heading southeast for Manus Island where Air Group 11 would relieve us of duty on the *Hornet*.

Time to Head Home

Nol Harrigan was the last VF-2 pilot to land aboard the *Hornet*, coming in from our combat air patrol just as darkness fell

over the task group. I had landed just before him and we had barely made it to the fighter ready room when the ticker tape printed
out:

"I WATCHED THE LAST LANDINGS WHICH WERE AS
USUAL SMART X YOUR GROUP HAD A FIGHTING REPU-
TATION AND MORE THAN MAINTAINED IT WITH ME X
GLAD TO HAVE SERVED WITH AIR GROUP TWO X WISH
THEM LUCK LADIES AND THE GOOD TIME THEY HAVE
EARNED X ADMIRAL MCCAIN"

We spent the 26th and 27th finishing whatever handicrafts
we had not completed down in the leather shop, the metal shop, and
the wood shop, and gathering our possessions, for the carrier was

*Author made this from Teak wood and salvaged
Hellcat clock before it went over the side.*

due in Manus Island in the Admiralties the next day. I can't say we
were wined, but we certainly were dined in style that evening.
Capt. Doyle had ordered a special menu with a very specially printed menu (which were unique to say the least) with a choice of
turkey or ham and all the trimmings with ice cream and cake for
desert.

Both Capt. Doyle and Admiral Clark joined us that evening
(leaving their usual private mess tables) to be a part of the celebration. Both were introduced and gave a short message of farewell,
and when I got up to our fighter ready room for a last night of
bridge, although without my usual partner as I still missed Randy

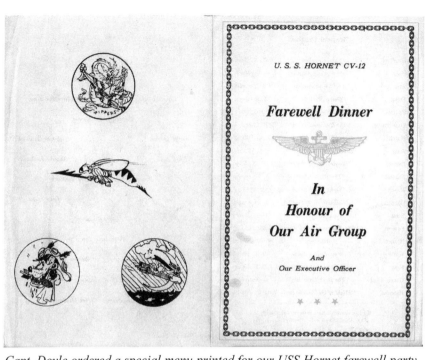

Capt. Doyle ordered a special menu printed for our USS Hornet farewell party.

Musical Program

Overture	"San Francisco"	W. A. Dean
Song	"Just Fueling Around"	C. H. Duerfeldt
Aria	"Aria to an Airdale"	R. L. Johnson
Polka	"Going My Way?"	A. K. Doyle
Foxtrot	"The Jocko Jima Jive"	J. J. Clark
Tone Poem	"The Burdened Beast"	G. B. Campbell
March	"Sky Forward March"	A. G. Pelling
Song	"Somewhere I'll Find You"	R. L. Riserer
Dance	"Boogie Woogie Bogey"	H. N. Riise
Foxtrot	"The Ripper Rag"	L. E. Harris
March	"The Flying Tin Fish March"	L. M. Ford
Concerto	"Concerto in F6Flat"	J. D. Arnold
Song	"Too Sleepy People"	C. A. Myers
Foxtrot	"The Mooring Board Blues"	E. E. Fickling
Minuet	"Rosemary"	W. E. Gaillard
Waltz	"Serenade to a Snipe"	J. T. Hazen
Song	"Mares Eat Oats"	D. B. Hilton
Dance	"The Heat Rash Rag"	O. Schneider
Rhumba	"Flight of the Bumble Bee"	V. H. C. Eberlin

Music by the Ship's Band under the direction of
Chief "Royal Baby" Deardorf

Menu

Hors D'oeuvres Woleai

Celerie Ulithi   Olives Iwo Jima

Pomplemousse Manila

Soupe Saipan   Entree Eniwetok

Boeuf Rota   Asperge Hollandia

Pommes Ponape   Sauce Shellback

Beurre Bonin   Pain Palau

Glace Guam

Patisserie Yap

Fromage Truk   Raisins Sarmi

Cafe Kwajalein

Cigarettes Davao   Cigars Mindanao

Vice-Admiral Mitscher present awards to Hornet crew on August 26, 1944.
The author received the Silver Star and two DFCs.

so much, we read a message already typed on the ticker tape machine:

"ON LEAVING THE HORNET MY HEARTIEST CONGRATULATIONS AND ADMIRATION TO THE SHIP AND AIR GROUP TWO FOR AN OUTSTANDING RECORD OF BATTLE DAMAGE TO THE ENEMY X AS A RESULT OF YOUR SUPERIOR AND SUPERB PERFORMANCE TOKIO ROSE HAS BEEN FORCED TO CHANGE HER TUNE X GOD BE WITH YOU ALL AND GOOD LUCK X ADMIRAL CLARK"

As we approached Manus Island, general quarters sounded which was strange to us, for when we had entered Majuro, or Kwajalein or Eniwetok lagoons we had never gone to GQ to enter any of those channels. However, we supposed Capt. Doyle didn't have the latest sea charts and wasn't going to take any chance of not having the carrier water tight if he wasn't quite sure at low tide of there being a sandbar to ground the carrier on.

We dropped anchor about noon on the 28th, and saw Admiral Clark and his staff leave immediately, for an apparent flight back to Pearl Harbor. Our transportation to quarters assigned for us would have to wait until the following morning when two LCI's would arrive to take us about 35 miles to Ponam. The water in the bay was horribly rough and very choppy and most of us got totally soaked during the trip to a temporary home which we found out was just a quantum hop to the swimming beach and "all club." We had a good time swimming and we could buy 10 chips at the all club for 50 cents, which made any kind of drink you can think of to order from the bartender for a total cost of five cents - a bit different than the $3.50 to four dollars at today's price. Isn't inflation wonderful.

We spent the next ten days waiting for any kind of ship going back towards Pearl Harbor and we spent the days swimming and the evenings drinking. Someone had a friend who had a PT boat, which took them out fishing, but without much luck. They said it was because they didn't have the right bait! Although most of us did not go fishing, we were able to pick up "cats eyes" on the beach a little ways down from where we were staying. From those "cats eyes" we could make beautiful necklaces.

Time passes so slowly when you are waiting, waiting for word that a ship in the harbor is heading back to Pearl Harbor or better yet, to the States. It wasn't until October 6th that a CVE had been detoured to Manus to pick us up for a ride to Pearl Harbor. Of course we had another 35-mile ride back to the harbor in those same LCI's. This time, though, we arrived at the destination without being totally soaked as we had been on the first trip.

We left anchorage there on Manus early on the seventh. And we were FINALLY on our way home. Then we found out the carrier could not make it all the way to Pearl Harbor without stopping at Majuro for more fuel. So we had an overnight stop on the 11th before we were finally headed for Pearl Harbor, where we arrived on the 18th. Again, they had no immediate transportation lined up for us and so the BOQ on Ford Island became our home for the next five days waiting and waiting.

Mom Chung's Welcome Home Party

When you are waiting for something special to happen, that special event takes so long to happen. Each day waiting for our final transportation home seemed to be a week long, although we did have a good time back on Waikiki Beach swimming and enjoying food prepared by somebody other than the Navy cooks.

Each day we reported in at 0800 for news, hoping that the skipper had found some transportation available to finally get us to San Francisco. But, each day he gave us a negative answer until the 22nd, when the skipper finally announced he had been able to get priority for the whole squadron on a big Matson liner that had been converted to a troop ship status. So we still had one more day to enjoy the beach and then make it back to BOQ for a very early alarm and be set for getting out to the Matson liner. When we were going aboard, I think every one of us, all in unison, were singing "San Francisco, HERE WE COME."

Dr. Margaret "Mom" Chung

Our quarters were far from luxurious, but we were finally on our way home, riding along with probably between 5,000 and 6,000 Army and Marine veterans from their battles at Saipan and Guam, for most likely their first leave in over two years' time. Our bunks were stacked triple high and we had to make a choice of our preference for early, mid, or late servings in the officers mess for the whole voyage. But, we were on our way home, and no one really complained.

The ship did have a calisthenics time schedule that we could join if we so desired. At times that was a lot better than just standing at the railing trying to count the flying fish like we had done so often while aboard the carriers in between flights. That often led to a dispute, though, as to which fish had flown the farthest distance, especially when we had a quarter riding on the farthest distance. The fish would not generally come up together and then it was a judgment call as to how far the last fish had flown in comparison to the first flight, which might have been five or six seconds earlier. We had no measuring instruments to be totally accurate about the actual distances.

As we passed under the Golden Gate Bridge, everyone was thinking of the year and two weeks earlier when we had passed under it going the opposite direction in that heavy blustery rain storm we had gotten into just after leaving the coastline. As we came back, the Golden Gate was again shrouded in thick fog, but the Matson liner eased into the pier 7 where our adopted "Mom" had the band playing our favorite songs. Behind a table, she had somehow or other been able to get mounted a big sign "WEL-COME HOME, FIGHTING TWO."

She even had that large table set up with a large pile of small containers of fresh milk, and many varieties of apples and the best of all, some home-made cookies. They were all handed out by several very attractive waitresses, and those items were what most of us had missed the most while aboard carriers in combat. They went down so good.

Mom even had buses arriving in a short time to take us to the St. Francis Hotel, for she did not have room for all of us in her home. After disposing of our luggage, the buses were back to take us on out to her home, which we found to be well decorated for FIGHTING TWO's welcome home.

We were wined and dined like we were all kings. Even though scotch was apparently hard to come by during the war, she had instructed her bartenders to place a sign above the bar saying: "Please do not ask for scotch, it's saved for FIGHTING TWO, the NAVY'S No. 1 SQUADRON." That evening it really flowed pretty well, but only after we had our fill of stuffed pork chops or roasted turkey with all the trimmings.

Later, she gathered us in the ballroom for her official welcome home speech. She listed the reasons she was so proud of us. We had the lowest number of pilots lost in aerial combat, with an average kill ratio per pilot of 1 to 89 as compared to the Navy overall average of 1 to 19. The most number of planes shot down, in total, and in one day. We had 30 aces and five pilots that just missed the coveted title by one plane. We also had four "aces in a day." We had the most planes destroyed on the ground and the most enemy shipping tonage sunk for a fighter squadron in one tour of duty.

Then she presented our skipper with a beautifully engraved silver bowl, before introducing the entertainment for the night which consisted of several Hollywood stars, with Dennis Day singing many of his Irish airs for us. Then to end the evening she invited us all to make her home our headquarters while waiting for orders. That was not just for the next few days, but for any time we would be any place close to San Francisco, for she wanted to hear from us, as one of her "Bastard Sons."

The next night Mom had arranged front row tickets for the opening performance of "Winged Victory" at the theater, and then on out to Charlie Low's "Forbidden City" night club for more gracious wining and dining. The next day we had a bus ride to City Hall where Mom had arranged for Mayor Lapham to present the keys to the city of San Francisco and a small silk American flag to each of us. The program was wrapped up with a very touching speech for all in the audience to hear, in which Mom pointed out the successes of the Pacific Fleet and more particularly of FIGHTING TWO. It has been kind of an inspiration to me for most of my life, and certainly deserves space in my book:

Dr. Margaret Chung, affectionately known as "Mom" Chung, gave this message, which can be found in the "Odyssey of Fighting Two":

My Beloved Son, 631,
Commander William Dean, and
Men of FIGHTING TWO:

Ever since you offered me 16 Jap planes for a Christmas present last year and promised me 200 enemy planes for a Christmas present this year, I've carried each one of you deep in my heart. Innumerable times during each day I've bragged about you and shouted your praises in no uncertain terms. When the good

*news would flash over the radio of carrier based operations strik-
ing deeper and deeper into enemy territory, I knew you would be
leading the fight, and mingled with my pardonable exultation over
what I knew was your achievement would be a clutching anxiety
over your welfare and a continuous supplication to Almighty God
for your safety. Wherever you flew, my prayers followed you, and
my love winged its way to each one of you. Today, I give my humble and grateful thanks to God that in His gracious wisdom and
infinite mercy He has spared you and brought you home safely to
the America we all love.*

*You have more than made good your promise to me - you've
given me the most wonderful Christmas present possible, 506 Jap
planes destroyed and 50,000 tons of enemy shipping sunk. By your
fearless accomplishment you have shortened the war, saved innumerable lives and ships, hastened the day of victory, covered yourselves with immortality and America with glory. No wonder I burst
with pride when I think of you or speak of you. No wonder I love
each one of you.*

*There are no words in any language which can adequately
express my gratitude for your magnificent defense of decency and
democracy. I know I express the sentiments and gratitude of the
entire nation, which looks up to you and acclaims you the heroes
that you really are. As your proud and adoring Mom, may I exercise my prerogative and give you a little motherly advice?
Remember - wherever you go - whatever you do - wherever you
may be - to the whole world, YOU are the heroes of FIGHTING
TWO - the most outstanding squadron in the U.S. Navy. You have
hung up an unbeatable record, you have written one of history's
most brilliant pages, and you are and will be the idols and inspiration of America's millions. Please conduct yourselves as befits
members of the famous FIGHTING TWO. Remember your lives
are no longer your own - you dedicated your lives to America and
you did a superb job. Young America will look up to you of FIGHT-
ING TWO and pattern their lives and ambition. Now that you really are heroes, don't let your public down.*

I like your singleness of purpose, I admire your courage,

your skill, your utter disregard for danger and personal safety. I like your modesty and your humility. It is men like you who made America great - You Are America.

I wish that I were wealthy that I might shower extravagant gifts on you today, but of money I have none. But you of FIGHT-ING TWO have bestowed on me the greatest treasure of all - loyalty and friendship - and your friendship makes me the richest woman in the world. There are many things in this world which mean more to me than money or the material things it will buy - one of those things is the privilege of being an American. I was born on the soil, drank the water, and breathed the air that is America. I was educated on the taxes of free men whose foresight it was that all shall be literate and enlightened. At the early age of 4 - in kindergarten - with great pride I pledged allegiance to the American flag and to the republic for witch it stands. One nation, indivisible, with liberty and justice for all. I am the beneficiary of that liberty and justice. Therefore it is fitting and proper that I present to you of FIGHTING TWO the flag I love with all my heart and soul. Commander Dean, I proudly present to you, as skipper of FIGHTING TWO, this flag of the United States of America - the flag you and your gallant men of FIGHTING TWO defend so valiantly. It belongs to you and to the present squadron of FIGHT-ING TWO. I shall give each man a smaller flag, but as their skipper I ask you to be the custodian of this flag for FIGHTING TWO. Guard it and cherish it as well as you have fought for it.

My earnest hope is that we at home, for whom you fought so heroically, pay prove ourselves worthy of FIGHTING TWO. To this I pledge my life in humble gratitude. May God bless you and may the Lord watch between me and Thee while we are absent one from the other.

So endeth an Odyssey of FIGHTING TWO.

Looking back at the success of Fighting Two, it seems to be the magical mix of personalities that the skipper was able to put

Admiral Jocko Clark

together in addition to his strict requirements during training. In Atlantic City where we had 20-plane tail chases every Friday afternoon and anybody that fell out of a maneuver could almost assuredly expect orders back to Norfolk.

The strict requirements of getting hits on the towed sleeve really paid off in combat. Bill Dean was able to make his selection of 42 pilots from about 55 that were assigned during a four-month organizational period but did not have the leeway to select replacement pilots. He had to accept whoever was transferred to the squadron, and it seemed like many of our losses were really the replacement pilots.

Of course a lot of the success was because of Admiral Jocko Clark. He took many risks that other Admirals avoided, like when we detoured to Iwo Jima. Admiral Harrill refused to go along with him and instead went straight over to Eniwetok as ordered for rest and resupply.

It still boiled down to the fact you had to be in the right place at the right time with nerves of steel. You had to have excellent eyesight and be the first to recognize that little blip as an enemy, and have the gumption and nerve to pull the trigger. It was going to be either him or me. Those dogfights of World War II are a thing of the past. Nowadays they have guided missiles and air to air missiles that can be fired from 25 to 50 miles away, letting the missile find the heat source or magnetic source for its success rather than flying your plane within 300 to 500 feet of the target and then estimating the correct lead for your aim on target.

"VF-2 Breaks Up"

It was amazing that orders should take so long to be written. We had been on our way home for a whole month from Manus Island after being relieved from duty on the *Hornet*, and still having to wait for another nine days before expecting to find out where I would head for my next duty station after a thirty-day leave. This leave would be my first in over 2 1/2 years of service. Of course, we enjoyed "Mom" Chung's hospitality and appreciated it very much, but I was anxious to get home and see that my father and sister were surviving OK after my mother's death just three weeks before I was able to make that call home upon arriving Stateside.

It seems like mail delivery was awfully slow in catching up to us once we had left the *Hornet* and I had not known of my mother's demise prior to making the phone call from San Francisco. If I had only known that, I might have tried to throw my bags on the same plane that Adm. Jocko Clark left Manus on within hours of our leaving the *Hornet*.

Although, I had really expected my mother to pass away much sooner for she had been more or less bedridden during the last four years of her life. Doctors and the medical profession did not seem to know anything about treating that disease in those days and could only prescribe aspirin when she was hit by all the different kinds of arthritis and rheumatism, and she had been in severe pain for most of her last seven years.

During the first three years of her bout with arthritis, we were able to get her around in a wheelchair. As her condition deteriorated it became too painful for her to even be helped into the wheelchair. Dad had been able to get a nurse to come in on a daily basis when Yvonne, my sister, and I were in college. But with the outbreak of war, nurses were no longer available and my sister had to give up her college program to help Dad attend to Mother.

I had had orders for the Army induction, which I was able to avoid by one day of grace by my enlistment into the Navy. Although I had not been able to help Dad or my sister in caring for mother, I knew her demise was a big load off their shoulders and they could now go back to enjoy some of the activities of a normal life.

The skipper had sealed orders waiting for all of us at the 0800 squadron muster on the eighth day after arriving back in the States. They really had us scattered around the whole country. A few of us were ordered to ComAirLant in Norfolk, Virginia, for reassignment. Others had orders to ComAirPac in San Francisco for reassignment. Still others had orders directly to various bases in different parts of the country.

It was really amazing for a bunch of guys that had been such a close knit "family," each depending on the other for our lives during the last year and one half, to see 45 sets of orders that spread us all across the country. My orders read to Norfolk for reassignment and included an airline ticket from San Francisco to Chicago. I can't remember when the Navy was so considerate. That airline ticket saved me three days of travel time by train.

The airline ticket was good on the DC-3, which was the standard passenger plane in those days, with 25 seats and a nine-hour schedule from San Francisco to Chicago. Then it was just a three-hour train ride on the Milwaukee Railroad to either Edgerton to see my fiancé, or a three hour ride on the CB&Q (Chicago, Burlington, and Quincy) to Galesburg for Dad to drive up from Brimfield to pick me up at the station.

I had already talked to my father and sister so I flipped a coin and decided to go to Edgerton to see Lori, for I had not received a "Dear John" letter as several of my squadron buddies had. And, I didn't know whether she would still want to get married during my one month of leave, or wait until after the war ended. I was welcomed home with open arms by her whole family, and yes, let's not wait, for in those days it was no sex until after the marriage vows which was the order of the day, at least there in little Edgerton.

Chapter Eleven

MY GIRL BACK HOME

November 1944

Getting Married

We had two weeks to plan the wedding if we were going to have a few days for a honeymoon and then complete the rest of my trip from Edgerton to Norfolk to report on time. It seems weddings nowadays require six months to a year for planning, but because I had not been able to let Lorie know even an approximate date of my return, she had little time to do everything.

As one of the squadron's mail censors I had full knowledge of Navy penalties for allowing mail to leave the carrier if it had any reference to times or dates of action we had been in, or for anticipated action. Granted, some of those letters got to be looking more like doilies from all the deletions that had to be cut out before I could stuff it back in the envelope to be processed as censored mail.

I arrived home before the letters I had written after leaving the *Hornet* got to her. Because of the uncertainty of my arrival, Lorie had made no plans for her wedding. That meant we had to reserve the church and a reception hall, order the flowers that she wanted, find a printer that could schedule immediately the wedding announcements, then mail them out, obtain a wedding dress, and hire a photographer for taking pictures of our big day.

Lorie and her grandmother were both exceedingly good seamstresses, and had usually made all of Lorie's dresses that had kept her appearance looking very charming and very much up-to-date with all the latest styles and fashions. I guess that was one of the reasons I had found her so attractive in addition to her personality. However, there was no time left for them to make her wedding dress, so we went 30 miles up to Madison where she found at Manchesters On the Square an exquisite velvet and lace wedding gown with a short train for the total cost of $65 which included the veil.

What a difference in the prices when I heard that my granddaughter had paid over $3000 for her wedding dress just last year. Lorie's bridesmaid dresses were also very attractive and all for a total cost of $35 which included all alterations. While there in Madison we stopped at the jewelry store to see what rings would be available, with so much of the metal of all kinds going to the war effort. However, that jeweler had a nice selection and Lorie was very satisfied with the rings we were able to pick out. Again, there was a horrendous difference in the price we paid as compared to the thousands of dollars my granddaughter paid last year.

Times sure have changed, for our wedding announcements were printed exactly the way Lorie had wanted them, and they were returned the very next day for us to start addressing the envelopes to all her friends and relatives. I had no relatives other than my father and sister and very few friends, for most of the fellows were now in service and would not be able to attend. In fact, I was not able to find ushers, although my best man would be Hank Ebbott who had been quite a pal all the way through high school days. He had been rejected for service because of an asthmatic condition he suffered even back in school days.

I was able to reserve the church that had been Dad's pastorate all the time I was in junior and senior high school there in Edgerton. But I couldn't get the dining room at the hotel (for those days there were no motels), so Lorie's folks decided to have just a

short lunch in the basement recreation room of the church. As I
remember, that pretty well completed everything that was required.
Except I had packed my dress blues in a shipping crate the carpen-
ter shop aboard the *Hornet* had made for all of us to ship our bulky
and heavy items in. That was so we would not have to carry a lot
of weight in our parachute bags. And it still had not arrived. The
crates had been shipped via freight from Manus Island and apparently had not followed along with us on our way home.

I had packed so much of my bulky stuff in it rather than loading up my parachute bag, which most of us used for short trips. All
my winter sheepskin-lined flight gear and all the handicrafts I had
made in between flights and bridge games were in the crate. My
dairy from the TAD (temporary additional duty) log that I had made
out of teak wood were also in that crate along with my dress blues,
about 6 white uniforms and several khaki uniforms. That had saved
me lugging a lot of weight during the trip home.

We had done amazingly well with our planning in just one
week, when I thought I had better call my father to let him know of
the glad tidings and to request his services in performing our ceremony. He was more than elated to have been asked to perform the
wedding service for his son, but that presented a problem, for he
had now been preaching in Illinois for four years and had given up
his Wisconsin ministerial license. That meant he would have to
make several phone calls to friends back in Wisconsin to find out
about renewing his license again so we would have a validated and
legal marriage ceremony.

I hopped a Greyhound bus from Edgerton heading for
Rockford, Illinois, on its way to Chicago. At Rockford, I had to
change buses and catch one going to Peoria, Illinois. I called Dad
from Peoria and asked him to drive in the 18 miles from Brimfield
for there was no bus service going out there.

When Dad first saw me, tears of joy started streaming down
his face. As he hugged me, I could hear his comment, "Thank the
good Lord you have been able to return," for he had just in the past
few days handled memorial services for the sons of a couple of his
parishioners. He was so embarrassed because of his tears, which he

quickly tried to wipe away. I believe that was the only time I ever saw my father shed a tear, for part of his education to become a minister included training in the ability to control his emotions, especially for a funeral of his friends and parishioners that so often had to be conducted.

While driving back to Brimfield, Dad asked why I hadn't written home more often. My reply was that I really didn't have anything to write about, for I could not allow more in his letters than what I could allow in all the letters I had to censor as one of the ship's censors. Navy regulations required no reference to where we had been, what we had done, or where we were headed next. What else could I say other than I love you all.

He then said he had learned more from reporters from the Peoria Gazette and the Chicago Tribune when they had called asking for his comments on his son's accomplishments that had been in all the radio news flashes and newspaper publications around the country. All he could say was he was proud of his son's accomplishments.

He then said the news had come just days before Mom's death. When he had read the articles to her, he believed she understood the importance of that knowledge and must have died a little happier, not having been able to see her son for the past eighteen months. He also made reference to the more recent publications of LIFE and TIME magazines dated October 23, 1944 with my pictures along with other squadron mates and my skipper.

My sister, Yvonne, had a big welcome home hug for me. She had been busy making supper the whole time Dad had been on his way to Peoria to pick me up. The table had been set and all we had to do was sit down after the hot food had been dished up. While eating, Dad kind of had a little twinkle in his eye when he said you better tell Yvonne about your big news. Her eyes really lit up, when I told her that Lorie wanted her to be one of her bridesmaids the following Sunday when we were going to get married.

Yvonne's first comment was "Oh, I couldn't, I don't have anything to wear!" but I told her not to worry. Lorie already had her dress after guessing the size of all her bridesmaids, and

Grandma Smithback would make any last-minute adjustments if needed. Then the big question was my learning something about being a civilian. Dad said he would have to go to the ration board to get a few extra gasoline ration stamps in order for him to get up to Edgerton and back home.

Then Dad popped a question to me. Would I be the main speaker for his Sunday evening Vesper service in lieu of his sermon tomorrow night? That might in some small way give hope to many of his parishioners that their sons now in combat would also be returning home alive. There were already several GOLD STARS in windows around the community. Dad said he didn't know what I would talk about other than a flight that I would remember most of all, but he would help get a short speech together for me to give at that vesper service. I had never spoken in front of a large audience before, but Dad helped me decide on a topic and then with a few questions, he gave me an outline for the speech.

I don't think I have ever been so nervous, and it kept getting worse during the time Dad was giving the evening prayer and singing the first hymn of the evening. By the time for my introduction my hands were really shaking. Even going into an aerial dog fight had not bothered me as much, for I had been trained to be a fighter pilot, but public speaking had never been part of my education. In the dog fights it was either him or me, and I had survived.

I got so nervous that I could hardly keep my finger moving properly to read the little out line Dad had helped me prepare that afternoon. I gave a short speech on my most memorable flight, which was the long extended flight to the Japanese fleet when we lost so many planes flying back in darkness. Then trying to land aboard the carrier before Adm. Mitscher gave the order to turn the lights on the carrier decks. However, I survived again, even in front of that jam-packed, standing room only, auditorium of Dad's church, and, many people came up to congratulate me and wish me well in whatever my next assignment would be.

The Wedding

The Greyhound bus trip down had taken so long that I thought it would be quicker to take the CB&Q from Galesburg to Chicago and then the Milwaukee Road train that went through Edgerton. Dad didn't know about getting gas to drive me up to Galesburg although it was only 30 miles away. That meant gas for a 60 mile drive for him, which would have used up his gas ration tickets for the next month. However his trip to the ration board proved more generous than he had imagined, for there was no question of giving the father of their "local hero" the gas for Dad to get me to Galesburg and for him to return home.

They also gave him sufficient coupons for the 175 mile trip to Edgerton and back, plus an extra stamp for Dad to be able to drive around and say hello to many of his old friends and former parishioners.

I had three hours to kill in getting from the LaSalle street station which I had come in at on the CB&Q and to get over to the Milwaukee Road train which would leave from the Union station heading to Edgerton. While walking between stations I began to think it might be wise to book a hotel room for our honeymoon. I tried the Palmer House, but sorry, they were all booked up for at least two months. After that rejection, I was more determined than ever. So I tried the Stevens on Michigan Avenue. Again sorry, a whole-week reservation was impossible at this late date. The Bismarck had the same story. Finally, the Harrison had received a cancellation just minutes before I got up to the reservation clerk, and he took pity on me. The room was on 7th floor, if that was all right, and they would need the first night's fee of seven dollars paid in advance to hold the room, which he showed me. It was quite a nice room overlooking some of the rest of the buildings in the loop, so I forked over the $7.00 as required and headed off to the Union Station. What do you suppose the room rental fee for that same roomwould now, several hundred dollars per night?

I arrived back in Edgerton and headed for Hank and Mary

l. to r. Lavonne Prescott, Jane Pearson, Yvonne, Lorie, Lt.(jg) Hargreaves, Henry Ebbott, John Farmer, Ralph Ebbott, and Rev. Theo Hargreaves. The flower girl was Jane Pearson's sister, and the ring bearer was Henry Ebbott's son Rick.

Jane Ebbott's where I had always been welcome as they had a rather large home with several unused bedrooms. Hank, of course was going to be my best man, and their little Richard (then 3 years old) was to be my ring bearer. Mary Jane had just prepared the evening meal, so they pulled up an extra chair and spread the ingredients just a little farther for me to enjoy also.

After dinner Hank showed me a big box that the freight company had delivered just that day. Thank goodness that was the shipping crate I had been looking for, and I would now have the official Navy dress blues for my wedding. I called Lorie to let her know I was back and to find out if there had been anything we had forgotten. She told me her grandmother had taken a couple tucks in her wedding dress and they had been able to fit the bridesmaids' dresses on everybody but my sister, which they would catch when she arrived on Friday.

The wedding went off as planned, and I think we had nearly twice as many in the church auditorium as we had planned on and also at our reception in the recreation room in the basement. And, what a surprise I had to see Mr. and Mrs. George Berquist sitting among the guests. I couldn't believe they had driven up from Park Ridge for my wedding. Conversation with them led to the information that their home had felt so empty after both sons, Jim and George Jr. had been called to service, and that this trip had been a real pleasure to see that I had made it back home again.

They knew that George Jr. and I had been best friends at Knox, and they had enjoyed having me as their guest on so many weekends when I had been a cadet at Glenview. Mr. Berquist was a jovial character, and with his hand over his mouth, whispered an inquiry to me. Do you have enough time now for a honeymoon, and if so, where? I had to whisper back to him my answer, that we were going to be at the Harrison which was the only hotel I could get a reservation at for a whole week. He then looked at Mrs. Berquist and asked if they should reserve a table at the club for next Saturday night. With her affirmative answered he blurted out "You and your new bride will be our guests at the dinner dance at Tam O Shanter next Saturday evening." Lorie was quite amazed to learn she would be going to the place that hosted most of the major golf tournaments held in or around the Chicago area.

The Honeymoon

When those that had come to our reception started to leave, Lorie asked my best man to take her back to her home so she could change from her wedding dress to her going away suit. It was a beautiful Cherry red two-piece that she looked just stunning in and received numerous compliments for looking so beautiful in when she arrived back at the reception. We stayed just a short while before I indicated to my best man that it was time to leave on the short eleven-mile drive down to Janesville. We would have our first night in the Monterey Hotel, which was just a block away from the Milwaukee Road railroad station where we would catch the early morning train for Chicago. We were both so tired by the time we got to our room that we just fell asleep, especially after Lorie had indicated she did not want to get pregnant on her first night, upon learning that I had not come prepared. My father, the preacher, had never discussed methods of protection for his son to use during his earlier years. It seems like sex was never discussed back in those days as it is in more recent times. So poor little innocent me agreed to just cuddle a bit while falling asleep.

We had left an early call for the morning, which gave us time for a leisurely breakfast before having to carry the suitcases one block over to the railroad station. We arrived at the Union station in Chicago and caught a cab taking us to the Harrison. After checking in, my first assignment was to find a drugstore.

Looking back at times I realize much has happened in the 57 years since. We have gone from the experience I had at the drugstore to having school health officials handing out condoms even at schools. This was my experience. The female clerk had asked if she could help me find something, so I asked for a package of condoms. She became so flustered that she ran back to the druggist behind his counter mixing prescriptions. He dropped everything to come out and forcefully get me off to one side. He emphatically let me know when I wanted such products I was to come direct to him without disturbing his female help. He then reached way back under the counter to find my desired product. He came up with a choice of three items as compared to the many items now on open display.

We certainly enjoyed that week in Chicago. We dined and danced at the Palmer House, and the Stevens. Although the Harrison had delicious meals they did not have dancing. We went to the movies or the theatre every evening. We got to see Oklahoma and Annie Get Your Gun and then on Saturday night we caught the Northwestern train shuttling out to Park Ridge where Mr. Berquist met us at the station. We returned to the Berquist home for a cocktail and for Lorie to meet their son's fiancé, Betty, who I had known from the many evenings with Jim and George Jr. during my Cadet days at Glenview. They were both now in service also.

The Bismark Hotel was recommended as the best place in town for dinner so we went there on our last night. The service was terrible and the food was lousy mainly because it had stood on the chef's pick up shelf so long that it was already cold when it was

Carl and Lorie at the Bismark, while waiting for their food that was cold when finally served.

served. Because of our horrible service I left just a 2-cent tip upon leaving. However, we didn't get out of the dining room before we heard, "Call the police, that couple didn't leave a tip, call the police, that couple didn't leave a tip." After talking it over with the head-waiter, he suggested to save embarrassment for all, just throw a dollar bill on the floor and make him pick it up.

Back home in Edgerton, I realized I had transportation problems, for there would be two of us now, not just myself as Lorie wanted to go along with me. I thought there was a good chance that I would draw shore duty for my next assignment. Most likely as an instructor at one of the operational bases for the Ensigns that had just earned their wings. They would be assigned to an operational base to learn something about actual combat flying, which also moved them up to a heavier plane with more horsepower.

Lorie decided she did not want to go by train and then have to use cabs or streetcars for whatever she wanted to do in whatever city we wound up in. The next and only alternative then was to buy a car. I found that all new cars produced two years before had been sold long ago, for the auto plants were now producing tanks, airplanes, or other items for the military. I tried the Ford agency, but they didn't even have a used car. The Chevrolet garage had the same answer.

The Pontiac dealer recognized me from all the gas that I had bought from him back in my high school days after I had just gotten my driver's license. Gas in those days was 5 gallons for a dollar, and occasionally when on a special, six gallons for that dollar bill.

Back in those days I guess I had driven a little more than the average high school student. It was 23 miles up to the nearest swimming hole and 32 miles to Madison for music lessons every Saturday, or other youth functions at the university. Then there were other church activities that Dad would have me as his chauffeur so he could relax somewhat on his way rather than being all tensed up on arrival. With all the activities I had back in those days I hadn't realized how much gas I had been using. The Pontiac dealer's comment to me was, "Carl, I wish I could help you out, but as you can see, the old space in that front window I used for my demonstration car is now the second bay for repairing cars."

The last and only place left for me to investigate was the first place I should have gone to. Hudson Motors had just finished making a few "minor repairs" on an old 1937 Terraplane-Hudson they had received from an estate, which had not been able to sell the car by the time the estate was to be closed.

The garage had not had it very long, but no one had been in to buy it yet because it apparently needed a few "minor" repairs. And, it even had relatively low mileage, for it had come from an older couple that had not driven much. The salesman said it should certainly get me to the East Coast and then some and I could have it for $650 for which I promptly wrote out a check for it before someone else snuck in to edge me out from the scarcity of cars there in Edgerton. He even filled the gas tank for the guy in uniform and gave me an extra gas coupon for five gallons of gas and told me exactly where to go to find the ration board to get enough gasoline coupons to get me to Norfolk, Virginia. I drove home to show Lorie our prized possession, then headed for a ration board to get the gas coupons needed and also other coupons for the butter, meat, shoes, and any other items that we needed ration coupons for.

The big decision then was what could Lorie take along. Even though that Terraplane had an unusually large backseat (in comparison to cars of today) it still boiled down to leaving most of her wedding presents with her folks. We took only a few that could be used in any apartment we would rent at whatever base I would be assigned to. Of course Lorie had always been more or less a clothes horse, so she had quite a number of suitcases packed in addition to her fur coat to help fill all of that enlarged backseat.

That was all accomplished and I still had three days of my leave time and at least three days of travel time left. We decided to head out for a little more leisurely trip with a slight detour to Holton, Michigan, for Lorie to meet my grandparents. We stayed overnight and then headed for Detroit to meet my Aunt Lucille. She was glad to see me again and to meet my new bride. She did not have a second bedroom in that small apartment she was in, so she called the Tuller hotel for a room. Then she suggested we all go downtown, register, and then she would pay for a dinner at the Tuller, for it had an excellent reputation for fine dining.

After checking in, the bellhop took us up to show us the room and warned me that every now and then thieves had been breaking into cars there in the hotel parking lot. He said I should leave the right hand door unlocked so they could get into the glove compartment without smashing the right hand door window. People usually kept the gas coupons in that glove compartment and there in Detroit gas coupons were a very valuable asset. Of course they would take anything of value in addition to the gasoline coupons but they had not usually been looting anything else from the cars.

When I went back down to park the car I made extra sure there were no gas coupons left in the glove compartment and only a few valueless incidentals there in the compartment. We then went down to the dining room and enjoyed a delicious meal with conversation from Aunt Lucille flowing freely and bringing us up to date on some of the family activities.

The bell hop got an extra tip in the morning when he brought our luggage down, for, yes, papers from the glove compartment were scattered all over the front seat. But nothing else was missing even though I had left Lorie's fur coat covering most of the items in the backseat. They apparently didn't know the value of a fur coat, only for the money they would get for gas coupons. I still had all my gas coupons and didn't have the trouble I probably would have had trying to find a garage to replace the window. The weather was getting rather chilly on that first day of December and would have made traveling very uncomfortable with a broken window, if it had taken very long to find and install.

We left the Tuller's parking lot and headed down to Toledo on our final leg of the trip to Norfolk, Virginia. We rounded the western edge of Lake Erie going through Toledo and then headed for the Lincoln Highway (U.S.30), which in those days was the only east-west highway crossing the country. We were in Ohio and headed for Pittsburgh, Pennsylvania, where we could pick up the

Pennsylvania Turnpike, the only super-highway we could use on our entire trip. (Construction of the Interstate highway system that we know today didn't even start until the late 50's and early 60's.)

However, I stopped short of Pittsburgh to take a slight detour up to New Wilmington, just to see the building projects that I had learned the college had started after I had transferred to Knox. I was amazed to see a brand new gym and a residence hall for men and another one for women. Lorie made the comment that she was already farther away from home than she had ever been. Her folks had not been able to do much traveling during those depression days as her father owned the local ice company, delivering 25 to 50 pound blocks of ice twice each week to most homes in the city. (Electric refrigerators did not come on the market 'til well after World War II, when the wartime production of planes and tanks got converted to the peace time refrigerators.) During the winter months when ice got to the depth of 12 to 14 inches, he cut blocks of ice from his spring fed ponds to fill his warehouse before covering the top and sides with sawdust to help insulate the ice from summertime temperatures.

Lorie had been impressed by the size of the Westminster campus, for she had gone to Milton College in Milton, Wisconsin which had a total of only three or four buildings on the entire campus (one of them being her ladies' dormitory). We got back on the road to Pittsburgh and found our way out to the Pennsylvania Turnpike and enjoyed the mountainous scenery all the way before we had to turn south. It had been a long day of driving for me, as Lorie had never learned to drive to help spell me a bit, so we found a motel outside of Hagerstown, Maryland.

After a refreshing night's sleep we headed out again for Norfolk. The drive had become rather slow, for those mountain roads were never more than just two lanes and oftentimes looking down sheer cliffs where attention to the road for me was very necessary. However, we arrived at our destination, registered in the large Norfolk Hotel and then headed for the Naval Air Station to have my orders endorsed showing timely arrival that would start the ball rolling for my new set of orders.

It was late in the afternoon by the time I got my orders endorsed on arrival at Norfolk, so we headed to the officers club for dinner. I couldn't believe my eyes at seeing Dewey Knight having a cocktail at the bar. After a warm greeting and introducing my wife, the obvious question came up, "What have you been doing this past year and a half?"

This started a long tail of woe for both of us. If you remember, when leaving Glenview after carrier landing checkout, I got the orders I wanted for Norfolk in hopes I would get Atlantic Fleet duty, but was ordered to VF-2. I spent the usual four-month indoctrination training on the East Coast, then flew our thirty-six planes cross-country to Alameda to go aboard a carrier headed for Pearl Harbor. Since then, I flew from four different carriers with a total of one year in combat, although only seven months were on the *Hornet* before getting back Stateside after seeing most of the islands in the Pacific Ocean.

Then Dewey started his tail of remembrance. He got orders to San Francisco when leaving Glenview, just as he had wanted, but then got orders to a small squadron. He had the usual four-month organizational training on the West Coast. He then went aboard a Kaiser baby flat top, right down through the Panama Canal and back up to New York for escort duty on all the supply ships and troop convoys across the Atlantic ocean with arrivals at London, Leeds, Southampton, and Liverpool. Those were just the cities I would have given my right arm for, just to see and spend some time with my relatives and grandparents. But switching things around seemed to be the way the Navy operated after getting all those questionnaires to indicate our choice of duty desired every time we advanced to a new training station.

When we arrived back at our hotel, the desk clerk handed me an urgent message to report to room 1009. Not knowing what to expect, I went up alone to investigate. I could hear laughter as I approached the door, and thought I recognized the male voice, but was not expecting to see a prior acquaintance. It was a real surprise to see By Johnson as the door opened, and to meet his new wife. Then the question came up, where is your wife, for you registered as Mr. and Mrs. I then had to go back to our room and get Lorie so she could go up to room 1009 and meet By and his new wife also.

We had quite an evening of chit-chat over a drink or two. Before we called it a night, By, my VF-2 buddy, suggested I drive us on out to the base in the morning, so the girls would have his car to visit whereever they wanted during the day, or just to drive around town. The girls had gotten along famously together and our arrangement for the cars worked out very well during the next few days while By and I were both waiting for orders.

Chapter Twelve

ONE MORE COMBAT TOUR

December 1944 - September 1945

VF-27 logo

VF-27 is Reactivated

My orders came through first and they directed me to NAS Atlantic City. I never did find out where By was sent, but it was not along with me to Atlantic City. I was overjoyed thinking I was to become an instructor, but upon reporting in to the base at Atlantic City, the base commander told me that his quota of instructors was filled and he would have to request further orders for me. He then reserved a room at the Pleasantville Log Cabin motel about halfway between the base and the boardwalk of Atlantic City.

The Log Cabin was a combination of gas pumps out front, a rustic old bar that was quite unique and it was coupled with a restaurant for short orders. Out behind it all were about 25 motel rooms, which we quickly learned were filled mostly by other pilots like me waiting for further orders. None of us could understand why we had been ordered to Atlantic City just to wait for a second set of orders, but that was the Navy way, I guess. Most of us had a hot plate to do a little cooking in the room. Refrigeration was in a box outside the front door where the temperature was usually lower than a normal icebox or a more modern refrigerator, so food did last for a short period without spoiling.

The next week our wives had quite a time with their coffee klatches in the morning and bridge games in the afternoon or an occasional trip down to the boardwalk to visit some of the quaint little antique or specialty stores. The wives had quite a memorable time and even sketched out how they were going to produce an exquisite Christmas dinner on just the hot plates from the various rooms. They had even made arrangements to exchange inexpensive or humorous gifts to celebrate our being so far from home and the ones we loved, and they even had a few decorations strung around the court and our rooms to make it seem more the season it was.

My orders for VF-27 to be commissioned January 1st 1945 at NAS Sanford, Maine, came through the day after Christmas. It would take only about two days driving time so we had three days to spare and headed for New York to see the Big Apple.

We crossed the Brooklyn Bridge and drove around a little to a few of the sites. However, darkness crept up on us although it wasn't even five o'clock yet, the tall skyscrapers seeming to diminish the daylight earlier, and it was time to find a hotel. I lucked out at the first one I tried, and it was well within my budget, for the Navy had placed a $7.00 limit on rooms for the trip. (I wonder how many hundred of dollars that room would be per night now?) We had time to freshen up, and had a very enjoyable dinner before retiring to the room.

The room clerk had given us a room on 4th floor just across the street from the outdoor skating rink of Radio City Music Hall. Looking out the window, instead of seeing just a brick wall of another skyscraper, we had the pleasant sight of the Christmas tree and other decorations all lit up that night. Skaters were enjoying a very good time skating to waltz music. We could even hear it in our room when I cracked the window just a little.

Next day we tried to see the Radio City Music Hall and the Museum of Science and Industry, but after entering the doorway, I found it to have been converted to a Naval Aviation training exhibit for recruiting. There, just above the entrance stairway was a full life size picture of the Navy's "TOP SQUADRON." It was my VF-2,

Enlarged photo of VF-2

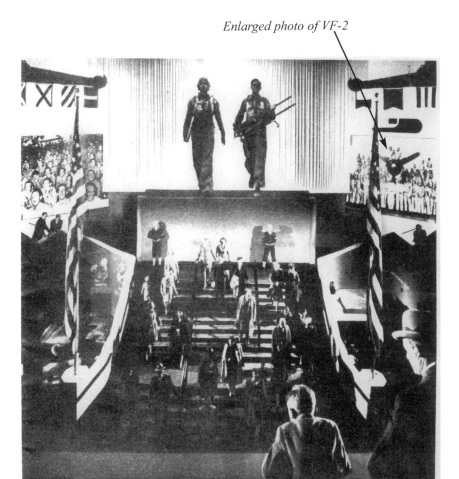

NAVAL AVIATION TRAINING EXHIBIT

AT THE MUSEUM OF SCIENCE AND INDUSTRY, RADIO CITY, NEW YORK, N.Y.
1944   1945

There on the right side was our photo, with me sitting on the hub of our airplane - enlarged to nearly full life size!

taken just after we had run up our totals at Iwo Jima. It pictured Admiral Jocko Clark, Capt. Sample (skipper of the *USS Hornet*), Butch Voris, Bill Dean (skipper of our VF-2) and all my buddies with me sitting on top of the propeller hub. I don't know how the Navy enlarged that picture to such a full size, but there it was! That evening we saw the Radio City Rockettes perform and then Lorie had a full day to browse the large name stores, which I'm sure she enjoyed to no end, although she purchased very little, just enough to prove that she had been there.

We headed for Sanford, Maine which was only a few miles north of the Massachusetts border, and just 60 miles north of Boston. We arrived mid-afternoon to check in at the base. I was the first Air Group officer to arrive and received royal treatment. After signing in, I found the base officers very cooperative, giving me directions to the rental agency and ration board. Lorie liked the first house they showed us, and the landlord lived just four houses away. She said she just had to have $30 per month and we would furnish our own heat and utilities.

It was on a corner lot but had no garage, so the car would have to sit out in the driveway in all the wind and snow and the cold temperatures. However, it was a beautiful house with kitchen, dining room, and living room downstairs, and two bedrooms and bath upstairs. The landlord, a lady whose husband was also in the service, indicated she had been carrying a small bucket of coal each morning to feed the furnace stoker, which gave just enough heat to keep the water pipes from freezing. The weather, however, was turning colder and she thought I should order a whole ton of coal to stoke the furnace for our comfort. As she handed us the keys, she told us the best stores to get groceries at, and said she would order the coal for me.

She'd given us directions to find the ration board and my trip there got us the ration books of stamps that we would need to buy groceries and gasoline for the car. When we got back to the house, the coal truck was already waiting and ready to shovel coal down into the coal bin. The place was nicely furnished and quite comfortable, and after we unloaded the car and placed some of our own wedding presents at strategic points it became our new home. Then it got to be a big rush for Lorie to find the correct dress bag that had her evening gown, and another suitcase that her jewelry was in. We had to get dressed up for the dinner celebration at the inauguration of the new base officers club and a celebration of New Year's eve.

During the dinner a couple more officers and their wives arrived to sit at a table of their own, but were soon introduced as officers to be attached to VF-27. Paul Drury and Red Shirley helped to enlarge the small number attending, for the new base did not even have its full complement of officers yet. The dinner served was very enjoyable along with an occasional dance to the music of a jukebox that the bartender had been instructed to keep going by feeding the required coins when needed.

The women grouped together for a chit-chat and to find out who was from where, while I learned some of the history of Air Group 27. Its first action was against the enemy at Casablanca in North Africa while serving aboard the CVE USS Suwannee. They had an enviable record under the command of Sam Silber in their operations in direct support of amphibious operations in North Africa. By coincidence, Sam Silber was the same skipper that I had when serving aboard the USS Bunker Hill in Fighting 18, which was a full fast carrier task force squadron twice the size of the fighter squadron that had been on the Suwannee.

After that tour of duty the air group was returned to the States to be re-commissioned for a second tour of duty. This time they would have 24 fighter planes to go aboard a CVL. It turned out to be a tour on the USS Princeton where they had another enviable record in support of amphibious operations against Saipan, Guam, Tinian, Peleliu, Anguar, and Leyte.

While serving in the second battle of the Philippine Sea, on 21 September, 1944 the Princeton was hit by a bomb dropped by the Japanese while flight deck crews were refueling planes that had just landed. Ordnance was also on the flight deck ready to be installed for the next flight against the enemy. The Japanese bomb ignited gas lines and with such resultant fires and our own exploding ordnance creating such havoc that the order was given to abandon ship, and all the planes that were in the air were to land on the other carriers. When members of that air group were gathered together again, they were returned to Hawaii for decommissioning and returned to the States. After everyone had a 30-day leave this would be the third time that Air Group 27 had been commissioned for duty.

Paul Drury and Red Shirley had been among the survivors of the *Princeton's* sinking. After talking with them most of the evening, they felt assured that Fred Bardshar would be returning as the air group Commander and skipper of the fighter squadron, although he apparently wasn't going to be there for the January 1st, 8 a.m., recommissioning of the air group. However, between learning some of the history of Air Group 27 on their previous tours of duty, we did enjoy dancing to our favorite pieces, but it just didn't seem the same as when we had a live orchestra.

It was a beautiful, but smaller than normal, base officers club, and the bartender on instructions continued to feed quarters into the jukebox all evening long, we enjoyed the music for what it was. However with such a small number present the evening wore on to the stroke of midnight for us to kiss our wives Happy New Year, and then very shortly afterwards we called it an evening. The three of us pilots would have to be available early in the morning to most likely welcome an Admiral that would probably come flying in from either Quonset Point NAS just outside Providence Rhode Island or from the Squantum Naval Air Station in Boston harbor. The Admiral would formalize the recommissioning ceremony of Air Group 27 to start its third tour of duty and to put it back in official status.

Other pilots started dribbling in later that day and by January 3, we had enough of us Hellcat qualified pilots to get the station pilot to use the station's JRB to fly five of us down to Quonset NAS so we could fly our first Hellcats back to Stanford. We also obtained the handbook for the Hellcat so the new Ensigns would have something to study before we could let them have their cockpit checkout and actually qualify for their solo flights in the single seat Hellcat.

On January 5th Naval Air Station Squantum sent their JRB for eight more pilots to pick up eight more planes for the squadron, and on the sixth Quonset NAS sent an SNB for eight more pilots, which brought us closer to our authorized complement of 24 Hellcats.

We had barely landed back at Sanford when it started to snow. And snow it did! All night long and most of the next day before it stopped and temperatures started dropping to a -25 degrees. There was only one hangar that had no more room to house planes other than just the station's JRB and SNJ. It just went to show the new base wasn't really equipped to handle a squadron operation, for our planes were left outside in the snow and parked on the ramp in front of the operations tower. Drifting snow covered our planes and filled the parking area. It also refilled the taxiways and runways while the snowplows were busy trying to clear everything on their first round, and then the snowplows could start all over again.

When the weather began to clear, temperatures were so low that the oil in the bottom cylinders of the engines of our planes got so stiff that our ground crew could not pull the props through to clear oil from those bottom cylinders. Oil in the bottom cylinders was a natural occurrence when the radial engine was shut down, because the oil was still warm and would drain to the bottom cylinder.

Our crew needed portable kerosene heaters and "hoods" to cover the engines so heat from the kerosene heaters could warm the engine enough to get the oil flowing sufficiently. However, the station had only two hoods available and one heater that first morning. They had to send a rush order to the Navy supply in Brooklyn, New York for additional hoods and heaters, but of course it took a few days before we received the necessary supplies. Our mechanics worked feverishly and we were lucky if they had two planes started by lunchtime. Then two more thawed out by mid-afternoon for our newly reported in Ensigns to gain a little experience flying the Hellcat (after they passed the blindfold cockpit tests), which was all new to most of them for they had their carrier landings check-out in an SNJ. What a place to send a squadron for its four months of operational training! Especially when that squadron would most likely be ordered to the South Pacific for action there.

LCdr Fred Bardshar, who was to be our air group Commander and fighter squadron skipper, arrived before we received our full complement of planes, and he certainly was disgruntled at the availability and flying conditions of that new field. However, he had received a roster of pilots that should be reporting in, and as half of his old squadron that had been on the *Princeton* would now be a nucleus of this new squadron.

He gleefully took a suggestion from one of the bachelor Lt.j.g.'s he had flown with before. He suggested that because of low plane availability the squadron be secured at noon on Friday so we could all head for what was reported to be excellent skiing conditions at North Conway, NH. It was located about a four-hour drive from Sanford, and by getting away at noon on Friday we could have a full weekend of skiing for most of us enjoyed the sport. Especially when we talked the skipper into letting us not report back until noon on Monday when, hopefully, our ground crew would have at least two planes in flyable condition. The skipper took their suggestion with the comment that we might as well enjoy life rather than sitting in the ready room for so many hours waiting for field conditions and plane availability to improve. The gang that had gone down on the *Princeton* certainly deserved the pleasures of skiing when possible.

Needless to say most of the officers and even many of the enlisted men all headed for North Conway for the weekend of skiing, for our planes were still pretty well covered with snow and the base was having a hard time cleaning the runways and taxi-ways. Most of the married couples found one of the very enjoyable bed and breakfast inns, and the bachelors all headed for the dorms where they found themselves to be among only a very few other male occupants. The report was that most of the other occupants filling the dorms were generally attractive young ladies that had come up on the train from New York. Some of the girls were actually there to ski, but the report that came back to the hangar ready room Monday afternoon was that most of the young women were just looking for companionship. So many of the fellows in their home towns were all in the service, but were nowhere near North Conway, therefore, their hometowns were almost void of male companions for them. Needless to say North Conway was a primary activity on the weekends that followed, for the duration of VF-27's assignment in Sanford, Maine.

Most of us enjoyed skiing for the first time in many years, and if we had ski equipment, it was at home and just wasn't available to us then, which forced us to rent. Carroll's ski shop was recommended, and we found prices to be very reasonable. Rental for the skis, boots, and poles came to just $3.00 per day, or $5.00 for the weekend. Of course we had to furnish our own clothing, but when temperatures had been so cold during the week, most of us fellows had brought our own fleece-lined winter flight suits along. We had to then buy a few extra sweaters for our wives, who were able to tuck two or even three pair of slacks into their boots to keep the snow out in temperatures that were still well below zero. The snow was very crisp at those temperatures and made skiing very enjoyable for most of us that had skied in our younger years. The chalet was warm and made an excellent spot for a cup of coffee while we thawed out and rested after every two or three runs on the hills.

As I remember, the squadron had its full complement of pilots during the second week there in Sanford. It consisted of the eleven pilots that had flown in Air Group 27, which had gone down on the *Princeton*, and myself, which was well above the normal assignment of combat experienced pilots. The usual was only five or six pilots with combat experience, and then the balance of the pilots assigned were ensigns, many of whom had just recently qualified in their carrier landings and therefore had not had much time flying a Hellcat.

Some of the ensigns had come from the newly established Navy operational squadrons which were now training pilots for combat before they were assigned to newly commissioned squadrons that would have the usual four months training in the

States before getting orders for combat. Looking back I can understand now how the skipper had such confidence in our training the
inexperienced pilots even with the problems we had on availability
and getting planes started in the morning to train them. That's why
he agreed to the extra long weekends that most squadrons did not
enjoy.

Fortunately the new ensigns did very well on the ice covered
runways, slipping and sliding, for we had only a very few days
when the sun would beat down enough to melt the ice before the
next snow storm would hit the area. The snowplows would clear
the runway but there was always some snow left under their blades.
The sun would hit and melt that snow leaving clear ice before
another day or two of sunshine would continue melting the ice to
provide a clear runway so that we could use brakes again to help
steer the course down runways on either takeoff or landing. The
problem was that if we used the brakes on top of clear ice, our
wheels would lock up and just keep sliding along, but we could still
direct ourselves down the runway using the rudder.

But the major problem was different, when wheels were
locked up and sliding and all of a sudden they hit a bare open spot
on the runway, the plane could be jerked to the side and you would
be headed off the runway and into a snow bank. The other problem
was that if both wheels were locked and sliding from use of the
brakes and you hit a clear spot on the runway, you would probably
nose over and very easily do major damage to the propeller and
engine.

My total flight time for January was just 13 hours, which
included the flight time I had picked up in obtaining our planes
from Squantum and from Quonset Point. It was late in the second
week of January when the skipper assigned pilots into our squadron
divisions, which consisted of the division leader, his wing man, the
section leader, and his wing man. My division was given number
seven and I had Gene Fellows for my wing man, Bob Russell for
my section leader, and Bob Martin as his wing man. The flight
schedules were made not by pilots' names but by division number
so we could learn the flight characteristics of each pilot and what to

Author with VF-27 in Sanford, Maine, February 1945

expect from each other in our division. Although plane availability remained poor, most of the time was given to our ensigns so that they could gather a little more experience and time in flying the Hellcat.

My flight time in February was only a little better, although it included three hours in an SNJ-5 with the hood pulled over my head because the station's pilot had been ordered to give us instrument time to continue our proficiency. Most of the flight time after our ground crews had actually got the planes started each morning continued to be given to our ensigns.

My flight time consisted of leading my division out to the restricted for shipping area over the ocean where our gunnery range was located, for actual live firing practice on a towed sleeve. Sanford was only a few miles from the ocean and it didn't take long to get out to our gunnery range so that my average flight was only about one and a half hours, but it did give us time enough to make many runs actually firing our guns on that target before our ammunition was totally used up. My division did quite well at firing on that sleeve, which was usually riddled with different color holes in the sleeve from the different color paint that our ammunition had been dipped in before the flight, and I think the skipper appreciated our efforts.

Our skipper received orders towards the end of February to move the squadron on March 1st to Creeds, Virginia. This meant that I had to go to my landlady and inform her that we would not be there after March 1st, but that she probably would not have any problem renting the house again for there would be a new squadron moved to the airfield. We had made use of that used Terraplane car in all the trips to North Conway and I hoped it would get us down to Norfolk without problems as it had gotten us this far already. We had enough bachelors in the squadron that could fly the planes down to Norfolk. The skipper authorized those of us with cars to drive and let us leave on the 28th so we would not have to rush our way down to the new airfield.

We had a nice trip south with a few diversions for sight seeing and arrived at Creeds to be utterly disappointed. It was an outlying auxiliary field from the Norfork Naval Air Station. It turned out to be a very small field with just a 2000-foot runway, which had a four foot fence rather close to the end of the runway. That would make takeoffs precarious, especially when we were loaded for bombing practice and/or loaded with the new rockets that I had heard about but never seen until we arrived in Creeds.

There was no bachelor officers quarters or any housing close by, so we had to drive in to Virginia Beach. The Beach at that time of year was pretty well closed down, but we did find one hotel which the skipper and several of the senior officers claimed. Us jg's had to talk a rather aged lady who owned a lovely hotel on the Beach into opening up early for she was a live-in owner doing a few jobs around the hotel for her normal opening on April 1st. However,l she did agree to open up for us if we would agree to pay her $3.50 per room per night during the two months we were there.

We all had a very good time. She even joined some of our evening card games and gave the wives the lowdown on the best of the lower priced restaurants and places to shop while the fellows were out at the base flying. She apparently was so happy to have income a month earlier than usual in the season that every Friday she would go down to the fish market and load up with large fresh shrimp, which she and some of our wives helped boil and then clean for many delicious meals while we stayed there. Of course we were only 30 miles away from main base Norfolk and we would drive over for dinner at the BOQ dining hall one night and then go to the officers club dining room another night, and always tried to make it there for the Saturday night dinner dances.

However, we all felt much safer while flying out to and in our gunnery area for the water below us was much warmer than it had been at Sanford. Chances for survival was 100% better here for we had not heard anything about an air-sea rescue ship or submarine being anywhere close to our gunnery area back at Sanford. Should our engines have developed trouble or quit on us while out some 100 to 200 miles from shore when we were in the gunnery area, we would not have been able to swim for very long before hypothermia would have taken over in our bodies.

Rescue certainly would have been much more probable while flying out from Creeds with so many ships and supply convoys forming out in the Atlantic just out from Norfolk and a little farther north from Baltimore, Maryland and New York City.

We had been flying out of Creeds for only about three weeks when we had a paddle waver (landing signal officer) report in to the squadron. He had been ordered to get our whole squadron field carrier qualified. Even those of us that already had some 140 carrier landings or more to our credit had to show that paddle waver that we knew what it was all about.

The squadron's training syllabus required a trip out to the USS Charger sailing up and down in the Chesapeake Bay. We had to make four daytime landings and then fly back out to the Charger to qualify for two nighttime landings. It was apparent the Admirals had learned from their night landing experience of unqualified pilots after that excessively long flight against the Japanese fleet when we lost so many planes during the first battle of the Philippine Sea, when the first few returning pilots were crashing and fouling up unlit carrier decks.

Admiral Mitscher broke all Navy rules and regulations against lights showing outward on any ship of the fleet at nighttime.

The blackout was for the ship's protection against giving an enemy submarine a lighted target, thus helping it get an easier direction for firing its torpedoes. But Mitscher's command to "Turn on the carrier deck lights" certainly helped pilots remaining airborne to get onto carrier decks more safely, even with the problem of estimating distances in the pitch darkness of night when there were no lights reflecting from clouds as there are when flying over land and seeing the lights of cities and their reflections on clouds.

The night time carrier landing requirement also gave us a chance to show the Ensigns of the squadron how to find a carrier at night when there are no lights to home on or guide you. When a carrier is anticipating landing planes it will boost its speed up so that there will be a minimum of 30 knots of wind over its deck. In doing so, its propellers will increase revolutions per minute, thus churning up much more water that becomes florescent as the fish get swirled around in the wake of the carrier. Every Navy carrier pilot looks for that florescent wake as a homing signal even though it probably would mean nothing to most civilians. With the completion of the two night carrier landings, none of us would ever be able to say we had not experienced a nighttime landing.

We learned of President Roosevelt's death via radio news reports and newspaper articles and pictures, for the mass population hadn't even yet heard of such a thing as TV. However, our training flights went on uninterrupted although we huddled around a radio that one of the pilots had thought to bring from the hotel to the Quonset hut we called a ready room. That is where all flight schedules were posted along with all CAA Notams (government postings of flight conditions and restricted areas for flights).

It was the very next Sunday morning I became so sick I couldn't get out of bed. Lorie called Dr. Sill (our squadron doctor) who also stayed in the same hotel we were in, but he could not diagnose my condition and called main base Norfolk for an ambulance to come out and transport me in to the large main base hospital.

I remained doubled up in total misery the rest of that Sunday, Monday, and most of Tuesday before getting to feel a little better. I couldn't eat or keep anything in my stomach except a small amount of ginger ale, and none of the doctors seemed able to come up with a diagnosis of my ailment. I was awakened at the usual time, 0630, on Wednesday morning for breakfast, which I finally felt like eating a little of. However, before I finished, the hospital doctor making his rounds came in the door, took one look at me and screamed out so everyone within a 100 foot area of my room must have heard, "Why didn't you tell me you had measles!" I must have broken out with all the blotches overnight.

He ran back to the nurses station to order an ambulance, which didn't take much more than 5 minutes to arrive, to haul me way over to the other side of the base where the isolation ward was located. No one was allowed in to visit or even see me from the door to my room. The doctor making Thursday morning rounds came in, pulled up my hospital gown to look at my back, and said all blotches had disappeared. He then wrote orders to clear me out of the isolation ward back to the main hospital for another ambulance ride where the doctor released me for return to full flight duty again.

The only problem then was they could not get transportation for me back to the auxiliary field. I called our hotel and woke up Lorie, who ran down to Virginia Shirley's room to see if she could drive our car over to pick me up, because Lorie had still not learned to drive. Gini said Red was still there and had not left for the base yet, so I lucked out. He would drive over to pick me up.

When he finally arrived he said it had taken him only 45 minutes to get from Virginia Beach to the base main gate. Then it took him at least an hour trying to find someone that knew directions to the well hidden isolation ward only to find out I was back at the main hospital. Then it took at least another half hour getting around to the hospital. He let it be known that he was famished as he had left before having his shower or even having a bite for breakfast and would appreciate driving over to BOQ to squelch his hunger. We consumed a delightful breakfast of eggs, bacon, and toast for a charge of 35 cents, which we had to pay for as we were not members of the Mess that station officers belonged to. They paid by the month for a charge of about $20 dollars for all their meals.

Red wanted to look at the BOQ sign-in register out of curiosity to see if he could recognize a name of anyone he might know that could be staying in BOQ. He found the name of L.E. Slagel and immediately wanted to go up to his room to meet him again for they had been roommates during cadet days. The room was not locked, but we found no one there. Red then reminded me he had not had his morning shower and said L.E. wouldn't mind if he used his towel. Red finished his shower and as he dried off he made the suggestion that I should also take one as it would help make me feel better by getting rid of the hospital perspiration. I did, and as I was getting dressed, a guy came into the room. Red didn't recognize him so we presumed him to be L.E.'s roommate. We carried on a conversation for a few minutes, until this fellow had to use the bathroom. When he came out, we could see he was a little more than perturbed and asked if we had used his towels. Red in kind of a half smirk said yeah, L.E. won't mind, we were buddies back in cadet days. "The hell I won't mind. I'm L.E. Slagel, but I have heard several times that there is another flyer by the exact same name." Well, there was nothing we could say, except we're very sorry and hopefully the maid will replenish your towels when she makes her rounds later in the morning.

There wasn't much more we could say, so after a very short conversation we sheepishly excused ourselves and headed for the car. I heard Red muttering under his breath that he certainly didn't know there could possibly be two L.E. Slagels, both in the Navy and at the same apparent rank. Red was a Lieutenant Senior Grade as was the fellow whose towels we had just used and certainly Reds cadet days roommate would have been of the same rank. Why couldn't one of them at least have been in any other branch of service?

Red headed directly for Creeds as he had already missed his morning hop and didn't want to be late for the afternoon gunnery flight with his division. I checked in with skipper Bardshar after we arrived, but he said he couldn't let me fly until Doc Sill gave his approval for full flight status. Doc was sitting close by playing a game of acey-deucy with some of the other pilots. He said I looked pretty good again, but he had to go get his medical bag from his car so he could at least check my heart and blood pressure after hearing my tale of woe about my hospital stay. I passed the tests and then heard the Doc say he was sorry he hadn't been able to diagnose my condition last Sunday, but it was so rare that anyone my age ever came down with a childhood disease. That was probably the same reason doctors in the hospital had left me lying in bed for three days before seeing all the blotches and then moving me out to the isolation ward.

Shipping Out

It was only a few days later that the skipper received orders to have the squadron and planes moved out to San Diego by May 5. He determined he had enough bachelor pilots to fly the planes even after ordering a few pilots back to Norfolk that had exceeded our authorized complement. He then instructed our yeoman on typing orders for the married pilots to proceed to San Diego, giving us the opportunity to drive our wives home. It had not been my turn to drive to the field on April 23rd when we flew our last gunnery hops, so Lorie had the whole day to carry our possessions down to the trusty old Terraplane.

Other wives were loading their cars, also, and as we had already told our hotel owner landlord we would be leaving before the first of May, she had spent the day shopping and then preparing a delicious meal for the gang. She had so enjoyed our company during the nearly two months we had been guests of her establishment. Although it had been a little too cool for swimming in the ocean, we had often gotten our feet wet in the surf in front of the hotel, and the wives had often been sunbathing on the beach. We all had such a good time at her going away party that most of us slept in rather late the next morning, and we decided to just take it easy for the rest of the day. Except those of us driving cars had to make a special trip to the ration board for enough gas coupons to get us to wherever we called home.

We got to bed early that night so we could set the alarm for an early get-away for home on the 25th. We took a few detours for sightseeing on the way, because we were not rushed for time. We took five days to reach Edgerton, Wisconsin where Lorie would stay with her parents during the time I would be out in the Pacific on combat duty. We had a great welcome home and my mother-in-law, Ilene Amundson, prepared all my favorite dishes during the two days I was able to stay with them before continuing my journey west to San Diego, California.

I hoped our separation would be for just seven months this time rather than the 14 months we had been separated while I had been flying with VF-2. I would no longer be able to drive and left the good old faithful Terraplane that had needed only to be refilled with gas and a couple oil changes during our jaunts in the east. Lorie promised that she would learn to drive it during my absence. I therefore had to catch the Milwaukee Road train from Edgerton to Chicago to start my trip west.

We had a very dolorous parting with tears streaming down both our cheeks when I stepped on the conductor's stool to climb on into the coach. Lorie had her folks, who had driven me to the station, to help cheer her up, but I had only myself to cheer me up and the train was already stopped in Janesville picking up additional passengers before I really got control of my emotions. After arriving in Chicago, I had to ask several people and finally the information desk there at the Union Station for directions and which streetcar routes I needed to get out to Midway airport, the only airport in Chicago in those days that handled passenger flights.

I had to show my orders requiring me to be in San Diego before the ticket agent would even talk to me, for all flights were totally booked, he said, although service men with orders would take priority for seats. There was nothing scheduled direct to San Diego, but he could put me on a flight to Hollywood if I could find my way on down to San Diego. The DC-3 seated 24 people (the only passenger plane used by airlines back in those days) and he could get me a seat on that plane that was about to leave at 1300.

It would be a nine-hour flight costing $99.00 (which is probably the only thing that inflation has not changed in all these years) and should arrive at 2200 hours (l0 PM) when there would most likely not be a room left any place near Hollywood. He offered to wire ahead to reserve a room for me, and gave me the name of the hotel.

I then asked where I could buy a hamburger, for my stomach was growling as it had been a long time since breakfast. He said there was a White Tower down the street, but he didn't think I would have time to get there and back before time to board the plane. Then the information came out that the stewardess would be serving a lunch shortly after takeoff. The airline realized most people had left home before the normal lunch hour just to get to the field on time, and that a dinner would be served at supper time for airlines in those days made sure that passengers never got hungry during those long flights.

With that information I sat down to wait for the boarding call that was announced very shortly afterward. I checked my bag and walked out to the plane to find one of the single seats on the right side of the cabin. (The DC-3 had eight rows of seats, two on the left side and a single on the right, a total of only 24 passengers, with a 25th seat for the stewardess in the very rear of the cabin). What a difference between the twin motor propeller planes of yesteryear capable of only 180 miles per hour ground speed versus the jets of today with up to 500 passengers making a ground speed of some 500 plus miles per hour.

And, yes, we had a delicious lunch within a half hour after takeoff instead of the "complimentary" bag of peanuts served by most airlines now. It was an exquisite steak dinner with all the trimmings served at about 1830 hours, instead of the half sandwich and cookie called a "box lunch" if you get anything more than just the bag of peanuts nowadays.

That ticket agent back at Midway Airport in Chicago sure had estimated the time in the air almost to the minute, even allowing for some strong head winds the pilots kept reporting frequently while we crossed the western states. We landed almost on the nose of 1000 hours as he said we would. Unloading the baggage for only the 24 people that had been aboard didn't take long and it took an even shorter time for everyone to claim their bags, as compared to the half hour to 45 minutes it takes now.

Taxis were waiting just a few steps from the airport terminal front door, and after a short ride I arrived at the hotel. The hotel clerk commented I was lucky I had a reservation, for he was completely sold out and now he could go to bed after putting the sign "No Rooms" out for display. It was a small hotel, just three stories tall at the corner of Hollywood and Vine, if my memory serves me correctly. I was so exhausted after having gotten up so early to catch that early train from Edgerton that I just plopped onto the bed without having had another bite to eat or even a midnight cup of coffee.

The next morning I learned there was no restaurant in the hotel and had to go down the street to find one. After consuming a very filling breakfast of juice, eggs, bacon, toast, and coffee (for a 45 cent tab plus a 10 cent tip as compared to the probable $5.00 charge if you are lucky and a one dollar tip nowadays), I took a short walk to Grumman's Theater to see all the sidewalk Stars of Fame. I then headed back to the hotel for check-out and asked directions to the railroad station that would head south to San Diego for the last leg of my journey.

It wasn't too long a walk to a railroad station for the Atchison, Topeka, and Santa Fe railroad where I purchased a ticket for San Diego. There were so many Marines also waiting for the next train that I couldn't even find a chair or bench to sit on. I wound up in the middle of the push to get aboard when the train finally arrived, but maybe it was a good thing, because I lucked out in getting a seat.

When the train pulled out, there was standing room only until we arrived at the Camp Pendleton depot. Although the coaches nearly emptied out completely of passengers, there were a few more Marines boarding for their day off to be spent in San Diego. It was an interesting train ride along the California coast where I could often see the azure sky meeting the blue waters on the horizon of the vast Pacific Ocean.

We arrived at the Santa Fe depot in downtown San Diego, and after inquiring directions, I learned it was just a short two or three blocks to the Broadway pier where I would have to catch the Coronado ferry to get to Coronado Island. The Navy usually had a bus meeting the ferry that would take us on into the North Island Naval Air Station. There was, and it did get me to the entrance gate to get my orders stamped in, and then on to base operations for endorsement of timely arrival, along with a number of other Navy personnel just arriving for some kind of duty there on the base.

When we all got back on the bus, it started a tour of the base letting passengers off at their desired stop or building they had to get to, and I think I saw most of the base before it finally wound up at BOQ. I went in and registered for a room, which in trying to find it I thought the registration clerk had given me a room about as far away from the desk as he had. I bumped into several other members of VF-27 while traipsing down the long hallway to my room. They said they would wait for me to dump my baggage off in my room and then we could all go over to the dining room together. I sure wish we could get nowadays as good a steak dinner with all the trimmings for the 80 cents the mess steward charged me. We were not attached to the base, just transients, and therefore had to pay cash for the dinner instead of joining the mess for a monthly bill. One of the fellows suggested that we go for an after dinner cocktail drink at the historic and well-advertised Coronado Inn.

Directions to get there indicated we should wait for the station bus for a ride to the base main gate. Then there should be a streetcar every few minutes that would go to downtown Coronado and right past the popular inn. It was a beautiful place with a bar on the lower level, which was decorated very ornately with booths that had such plush seats that made you think you never wanted to get up to leave. However, a couple of our bachelors managed to get up anyway to move over to a table full of young females and never returned to our booth before we decided to call it an evening.

We saw the skipper, who had just beaten me down to the dining room for breakfast, and the gang I was with was then told that our date to report aboard the *CVE Cape Esperance* had been moved back a day. Several of our VF-27 pilots decided to catch the station bus that not only took us back to the base main gate, it also went on the pier for the Coronado ferry to get us back to downtown San Diego. There we could catch the trolley down to Tijuana on the border of Mexico. We wanted to see the bull fights that afternoon, which I had never seen before, and also the HI-LI matches in the evening, which I had never even heard of before.

I joined the gang for a full day of new experiences, which it certainly was. First, I had never been in Mexico before, and then it was a totally new sight for me to see all the merchandisers on the streets hocking their wares, mostly costume jewelry. Strolling up Constitution Avenue and down Revolution Avenue, I saw so many of the carts decorated in Mexican fashion with their donkeys painted to look like zebras on many of the street corners. Some of the donkeys always seemed to have a wooden box ahead of their front feet filled with oats to nibble on.

The owners of the carts and donkeys were all dressed in Mexican style. They offered to let you drape one of their heraches blankets over your shoulders and then you got the 10 gallon sombrero for your head as you climbed up to sit in the cart to have your picture taken, for a fee. Who would ever think the preacher's kid from little Brimfield, Illinois would ever enjoy a bull fight or learn something about para-mutual betting at the HI-LI matches! You win some, and you lose some, but by evening's end I was twenty some dollars richer. Pretty good for a novice.

We slept in quite late after the Mexican trip for it had been well after midnight when we arrived back at the BOQ. We had a leisurely lunch and then went back to our rooms to pack our belongings to go aboard the *Cape Esperance,* for the word had been passed that the gangplank would be pulled very early on the 7th for departure to Hawaii. I think we were all on the flight deck to watch the carrier pull away from the dock and gradually pick up speed as we rounded the northern tip of North Island and headed out into the Pacific Ocean. About an hour and a half later we could faintly see the outline of Catalina Island to the starboard and then I was amazed to realize that we were sailing all by ourselves. I had been

used to looking out and seeing a screen of some 18 to 20 destroyers protecting the carrier fleet from a potential submarine torpedo.
We were all alone without a destroyer, nor even a DE (destroyer
escort) to help prevent a submarine attack. Zig-zagging was our
only defense now. That's what we did all the way to Hawaii making it a six day trip instead of the normal four day passage. We
sailed thirty degrees starboard of the direct course, and then thirty
degrees to the port of a direct course.

I guess the Admirals hadn't heard of any Japanese submarines plying the waters between the west coast and Hawaii for
them to send a carrier so jam-packed with planes that we couldn't
have even catapulted a plane in defense of the carrier should there
have been a submarine scare. The navigator of the carrier had done
an excellent job, for word was passed that we would be able to
enter the channel to Ford Island with outdelay because the anti-sub-
marine gates at the entrance would be opened when the carrier had
rounded Diamond Head corner of Oahu.

The carrier slid easily through the channel and up to the dock
on Ford Island, but the carrier was still some twenty feet from the
pier when the tugboats came up to start pushing the carrier sideways into the pier. Once they got the carrier moving slowly in, they
backed off, but the weight of the carrier so fully loaded kept it moving sideways and it hit the dock's protective pylons with such force
I could see smoke rising from the center of those pylons.

We were to move our luggage from the carrier to the beautiful BOQ that I had stayed in when I was on my way home with VF-
2 just six months earlier. The pleasures of the Ford Island officers
club were ours for the next three days while we waited for the inter-
island passenger ship to haul the whole squadron, personnel and
equipment to NAS Hilo on the big island. I think that base had had
a change of command, and this time we did not have the restriction
of the closed officers club that was in force the last time I had been
on the base.

We were now considered part of, if not all of, the Hawaiian
air defense for the island. We started an intensive training schedule of aerial gunnery firing on a towed target sleeve, dive-bombing,

skip bombing, and rocket bombing on a sled towed on a 1,000-foot line behind a destroyer escort. We continued the gunnery hops in June, but also had a couple hops under the hood of an SNJ to keep our proficiency up in instrument flying.

On the 7th of June we received orders to fly out to the *USS Cowpens*, a CVL qualification landing before packing all our possessions for a flight out to Leyte to relieve the air group presently on the *USS Independence*, also a converted cruiser hull carrier. That air group was to leave all its planes, tools and spare parts aboard the *Independence* for our use, as the air group would be decommissioned once it hit the States, with everyone getting a 30 day leave.

Heading for Combat

We had a whole day to pack up all our belongings for a trip to Leyte and then wait for the R5C-1 (the Navy's designation for the DC-4) coming from Pearl Harbor to fly us up to Ford Island and back to the BOQ we had stayed in earlier. It was just a one night stay, for we had a very early departure on a R5D-1 flight to Johnson Island, a distance of only 700 miles for lunch. That had been just a 4-hour flight and then we were back aboard the plane after lunch for an approximate nine-hour flight to Kwajalein with just a box lunch consisting of a couple sandwiches and an apple. What a difference from the Chicago to Hollywood flight which had an attractive stewardess serving a delicious meal.

We had only a cot provided us to sleep on the sandy beach there, although we did get a sandwich and some hot coffee after landing and a full breakfast for our only overnight accommodations. The next day was a nine-hour flight to Guam and the worst part of the whole flight was we had no seats on the plane, just a wool blanket to soften the hard floor, which normally had freight lashed to it. This time, on Guam, we lucked out with a Quonset hut over our heads for sleeping and a different Quonset hut for a hot dinner served after arriving, although we had had a box lunch midway on the 7-hour flight.

The fourth day's flight from Guam to Samar, Philippine Islands was just under eight hours. Again we had a box lunch about midway, although we received a hot meal on landing before unloading our gear to get on an LCI to take us to Leyte, which turned out to be about a 10 day stay while we were waiting for the *USS Independence* to arrive.

Leyte was something else, for during the night and early morning we normally had 3 to 4 inches of rain every day and then the sun would come out causing a hot steamy humidity for the rest of the day. Fortunately, we had a Quonset hut over our heads at night so we didn't have to worry about getting drenched or soaked with all the water, while we were waiting for the *USS Independence* to arrive, which would be our next home for combat.

The "*Indy*," a nickname we tagged on the carrier because of its lengthy name *Independence*, dropped anchor on the 25th some 500 yards offshore. Its air group waited until the next day to start exchanging their quarters for our Quonset huts. The Captain's motorized gig (small launch) was pressed into service and had to make several trips to accomplish the exchange of personnel, for the planes and equipment remained on the *Indy* for us to use.

I was assigned a stateroom with Buddy Burtch and Bob Zimmerman, a fellow of about my same height but some 50 pounds heavier with muscles strong enough to lift an ox. Zimmerman had been the blocking halfback at the University of Michigan. He had helped so tremendously for Tom Harman to set so many records for picking up long yardage every time he carried the football, and scoring a record number of touch-downs in the Big Ten during the football seasons of 1938, 1939, and 1940.

The *Indy* pulled its anchor on July 1st, and as soon as we got out in the open waters, Capt. Kindall ordered all planes in the air. I think this was to give the LSO a chance to see the capabilities of the pilots of our air group on carrier landings, for it had now been over a month since any of us had flown. Unfortunately, I didn't help that first impression.

I had made a good approach, gotten a cut, and I thought my

landing was a good one. However, I hit the deck and rolled straight forward but I wasn't getting the sudden stop that occurs when my tail hook should have caught a landing wire. I began to wonder if the hook part of the tail hook had sheared off again as it had once done on the *Hornet*. I wasn't floating. I was just rolling on the deck, still straight up the deck until the barrier stopped me with the plane nosing over as the barrier wires wound around the propeller causing sudden engine stoppage and the plane's tail way up in the air. Fortunately my shoulder straps had been locked as required and the straps kept my head from hitting the gun sight.

I felt so bad when crawling out of the cockpit with the help of the deck hand who had been assigned to the plane, for that wasn't the example I had wanted to make. My plane captain had crawled up on the wing waiting to help get me out as expeditiously as possible because a barrier crash often starts a fire. Even though the firefighters, who are always standing by in their silver heat suits with fire extinguishers by their side every time a carrier turns into the wind to receive planes, they didn't have to go to work on my plane.

Down on the deck and walking away from the Hellcat, my plane captain told me it wasn't my fault, that the spring on the tail hook that should have kept it down on the deck did not keep it on the deck. The hook would hit the deck and bounce, hit the deck and bounce over every last one of the landing wires. You should have known long ago that every carrier landing is considered a potential crash. After all landings were completed, the LSO came down to the ready room to say he had never seen a tail hook bounce the way mine had bounced and his report would be to inspect all of the planes for a similar problem.

The next four days were more or less tactical flights for getting familiarized with the ship and its LSO. On July 7th we were in a potential combat area just south of Tokyo and started flying combat air patrols (CAPs) over the fleet as protection against any possible enemy plane that would take to the skies. However, it became evident that Japan had few planes left and apparently very little gas to get what planes they had back into the air. We never even saw a plane in the air during the whole month of July but I soon learned the difference between Fred Bardshar and Bill Dean as squadron skippers.

Back to Combat Air Patrols

Bill Dean often took the combat air patrol flights in an effort to try and keep all divisions and pilots about as equal as possible on the number of strikes flown and the number of enemy planes shot down. As a result, no other squadron in Naval history reached a total of 30 aces during one tour of combat. I had worked up to frequently leading a division towards the end of our VF-2 cruise and had as many strike flights as any of the other divisions, even though being the most junior of all division leaders.

In VF-27, I was the division leader of the seventh division but was outranked by all six other division leaders, and, I was not a member of the previous VF-27 squadron that had survived the sinking of the USS Princeton. Fred Bardshar seldom, if ever, flew a combat air patrol. He seemed to have an idea that he had to lead all missions and strikes. He along with the more senior division leaders were scheduled to fly to targets on Honshu as the fleet moved north along Japan's eastern coast.

Our pilots flew to targets all the way up to the northern island of Hokkaido and hit targets there in all kinds of weather before the fleet turned around and headed south for targets back on Honshu again. My division was assigned nothing but CAPs during most of the month of July.

That is, until the last week of July when my boys and I got an assignment to fly a cover mission over the rescue submarine, which we found with no problem. Some of the other divisions reported they never could find the sub, leaving it unprotected should the enemy have sent any planes out to do it harm. I am afraid some of their navigating wasn't quite what it should have been, for I had no trouble in finding the submarine, and allowed it to stay on the surface rather than being submerged during the peri-

VF-27 Hellcat formation on way to target

od of those assigned flights. My division was on station when word came that a Sub Lt. Wells from the *HMS Formidable* had made a water landing and we were able to direct the sub to his rescue on the 28th of July.

We were assigned to fly CAPs again until my second hop of the day on July 30th when my four planes were each finally loaded with a bomb for an unspecified target, just trying to find anything to destroy. We did.

We found a train moving north on the railroad tracks close to the eastern shoreline of Honshu and made several strafing runs on it. We must have hit its boiler for it looked like an awful lot of white steam bursting out from its engine. The train gradually slowed to a crawl before it could reach one of the tunnels that the railroad bed had been cut through to make a level track line along the coast for its safety.

We flew around looking for another target of opportunity for a few minutes and then returned to the track. The train had not made an exit on the other side of the tunnel and as we still had our bombs, we effectively used them to destroy the railroad tracks on both ends of that tunnel. The tunnel had been cut through a small mountain that extended right to the eastern coast of Honshu. I believe it was called Mont Sonomiya if my memory serves correctly. I believe it would have required many days if not even weeks before they could move any military equipment or supplies on that rail line again.

Then we were back to flying CAPs again for the next nine days before we got a change in assignments. During all those CAP flights we never once saw a Japanese plane in the air and it had become very monotonous flying those wide circles around our task group waiting for a vector out to investigate anything that never came. Finally on August 9th our planes were loaded with bombs again to be dropped on the Koriyama railroad center or any other target of opportunity we could find.

The next day we were back to flying CAPs again. It was only a few minutes after our landing aboard that the *Indy* received an honorary message from Admiral Radford, Commander Task Force 38.4. It read, "Give that division of fighters from VF-27 that just landed a WELL DONE. The task force was in the wind for less than one minute with all four fighters having landed."

I felt rather proud of my division and myself for having timed my landing cut while the carrier was still some 6 to 7 degrees from true straight into the wind direction. The LSO had learned by that time that I could make whatever final correction or adjustment that was needed to make a successful landing. That early cut enabled my wingman Gene Fellows, my section leader Bob Russell and his wingman Bob Martin to make perfect landings for an average of 19-second intervals.

That was a pretty good landing interval, for each pilot would have to make the needed final adjustments to get squared away for a straight up the deck landing while he was in descent to the deck after getting a cut from the LSO. It required the pilot to be nearly in the center of the deck for the tail hook to engage the landing wire and not jerk the plane sideways.

Being off center made it much harder for the carrier's deck hand to crawl under your tail fins to disengage the hook from the landing wire. Then a second deck hand would give a thumbs up to the pilot to hit the switch to raise the tail hook and then give the clear to taxi signal. The pilot would go to full throttle for a second to get his plane moving forward fast enough to taxi past the barriers. When clear of the barriers, another deck hand would hit the control to raise the barrier. The pilot would then look for additional taxi directors to park his plane.

The LSO's assistant had to see the barrier on the rise before he could signal the LSO that the deck was clear for the next landing. Then the LSO could give a cut to the next plane that was fast approaching for its landing. The whole procedure was repeated three more times for the division to land.

It was a combined effort not only by the pilot but by the deck crew as well to establish such a landing interval, and the Admiral's "Well Done" belonged to the deck crew as well as my division pilots. Capt. Kindell sent down a big cake for us to enjoy at dinner that evening in honor of his carrier being in the wind for less than one minute. He also noted that many times he would receive a division of planes that would take up to six minutes to land. I presume the captain had his personal chef make several more cakes for the deck crews also. A carrier heading into the wind to recover or launch planes is a perfect target for submarines to unleash their dastardly torpedoes. Just ask the crew of the USS Saratoga how many times she was back in dry dock for repairs from torpedo hits.

The War Ends

During the time my division suffered through the monotonous CAP flights, the skipper and other senior divisions were escorting our torpedo bombers on very successful flights in putting the battleship Nagato out of commission. Returning pilots stated they had experienced heavy antiaircraft bursts. Those black puffs were extremely damaging if any of them would hit your plane.

The *Nagato* was anchored at the Yokasuka naval base some 30 miles southwest of Tokyo. The battleship *Haruna* was bombed well beyond immediate repair at the Kure naval base, which was way over on the southwest side of the Japanese home island of Honshu. The carrier *Ryuho* and the heavy cruisers *Tone* and *Oyoda* were targets that were also anchored at Kure naval base.

During July our torpedo bombers also sunk the battleships *Hyuga* and *Ise*. When all the smoke cleared and our pilots had returned, our skipper had gotten pictures of the destruction accomplished and a special picture of the *Oyoda* resting on its side on the bottom of Kure Bay.

I really do believe Bill Dean would have mixed the divisions up on all the different types of flights, so each division would have had some participation in the destruction of the Japanese Navy that our air group had accomplished rather than the total exclusion of my division from all the escort duties of our torpedo bombers in their successful flights. Though there certainly would have been a lot of risk in making the strafing dives ahead of the bombers and torpedo planes, it was part of a fighter pilot's duties to strafe enemy gun emplacements to reduce the amount of antiaircraft fire coming up at the dive bombers or the torpedo bombers on their low-level approach to their release point for the deadly torpedoes.

I lost both roommates during the past few weeks, although Buddy Burch was able to nurse his plane out close to the rescue submarine that was on station, after being hit by antiaircraft in one of his dives on a battleship. Word was the sub was able to pick him up and was treating his injuries to the best of their ability while the sub remained on station, and Buddy would become a submariner at least until the sub returned to port or was able to get to its mother ship, before getting transportation back to our *USS Independence*. Bob Zimmerman was hit by antiaircraft, and those that saw him said he went straight on in and never pulled out of his dive. I certainly missed Bob, for he was quite a jokester and kept things on the lively side wherever he was.

August 14th was to be a day of relaxation or sunbathing as

our task group had backed off the combat area and its usual routes of up and down Honshu. The tanker fleet was some 220 miles away and we covered that during the night to a point option to meet them for refueling. Some of us were in ready one just relaxing and listening to Tokyo Rose and her wonderful music, when the skipper came in and asked two of us to go over to the *USS Thetis Bay*, a CVE that had replacement planes. They would be taken back to Pearl Harbor if we didn't get them now while we were with the tanker fleet before it headed back to Pearl Harbor.

The *Thetis Bay*'s only purpose was to supply replacement planes for those lost in combat. It was a ship that did not have near enough speed to join the fast carrier task forces. The planes were just waiting to be asked for, but pilots from the carriers needing them had to come over to the *Thetis Bay* to fly them off for return to our own carriers.

That meant my buddy and I had to get into our flight suits and go to the aft port side quarters of the carrier for a breeches buoy ride to a destroyer. Then a breeches buoy ride from the destroyer to the *Thetis Bay* where we had to turn in the paperwork to the carrier's air officer to claim two planes that were needed as replacement for the two roommates I had lost.

I had thought these planes were to be new, for we had brand-new planes when I served as a replacement pilot back in February of '44 on the *USS Kalinin Bay*. However when the launching officer gave me the signal to wind up to full power for the catapult shot, I couldn't get the RPMs needed for full throttle and had to cut back and give a thumbs down signal to the launching officer.

The flight deck officer then came over and must have been a bit ticked off with me, because he climbed on the wing of my plane to talk to me. However, I wasn't about to take that plane when it wouldn't go to full RPM. He then begrudgingly gave the signal to unhook me from the catapult and taxi me off to the side. A pilot always has the right to fly it or down it if something isn't up to snuff.

That is when I learned these were not new planes but they were supposed to be the best of the planes from some carrier that had orders to head back to Pearl Harbor for repair or air group replacement and left these planes on the beach to become replacements. So, they were loaded on the *Thetis Bay* to come along with the tanker fleet this time.

Anyway, I got out of the deck officer's hair by taking the second plane, which gave satisfactory full power when I had wrapped it up to full power and then gave the forward head nod indicating I was ready for the catapult shot. After my buddy also got in the air from our catapult shots we had to fly around for 2 1/2 hours waiting for the *Indy* to finish refueling and re-spotting the deck for landings. All the planes had been moved to the rear of the flight deck for ready take off but then had to be moved to the front of the flight deck to make room for planes to land.

On August 15th I was scheduled to lead my division as air cover for the rescue submarine so it could stay surfaced and available to rescue any pilot in trouble without having to worry about a Japanese plane coming out to attack it. The threat of a kamikaze pilot willing to fly a one way flight for a ticket to honor his Emperor was still on our minds. What better target would a kamikaze have than hitting a submarine on the surface just out of small arms range from the shores of Honshu.

The sub was stationed about five miles off the coast of Honshu and would be available to rescue any pilot in trouble. We found it on station without any problem, but the weather was none too good and we waited and waited for our replacement division to show up to relieve us. However when our gas supply dwindled to only enough to get us back to our carrier, I radioed the sub that I was leaving and for them to determine whether they should stay surfaced or go submerged, and started back for the *Independence*. Halfway back, we heard on the radio that the war was officially declared over. This was the first time I could remember, that our task group had ever opened up on radio for fear that Japanese listening stations could get bearings to our fleet and know what direction to send its planes to hit our task forces. This, then was the day in history that we had all been waiting for.

We had heard about the two atomic bombs and all the

destruction they had caused. A news flash that we had received on the carrier indicated we were not to fly within 50 miles of the two locations for it would be years before anyone could possibly venture into either of those locations for fear of radiation contamination.

But, we had also seen Tokyo with its burned-out rubble amongst the canals that wound around in the midst of ashes. The damage that the B-29 raids had made when dropping their fire bombs, that had killed twice the number of people in the Tokyo area that had been reported as deaths in both Hiroshima and Nagasaki. Yes, Tokyo had been completely demolished except for the Imperial Palace, which had been put on the restricted targets list and we had been well warned never to bomb or strafe. Just stay away from it with the threat of a court-martial if we disobeyed.

The Japanese were such fanatics about their Emperor and his palace that our admirals and generals were afraid our American losses would go even much higher than the estimated over one million deaths upon our invasion of Honshu, their home island, which was scheduled to happen in just two months. Yes, it was unfortunate that 250,000 civilians had to die as the result of the atomic

Author's August 15, 1945 log book entry -
"The WAR was officially declared over..."

bombs, but those 250,000 probably saved many millions of lives and even more millions of injuries on both sides, had President Truman not had the fortitude to approve the dropping of those two bombs. Japan had not been able during the last month and a half of the war to launch any planes to challenge us fighter pilots, but they still had plenty of antiaircraft ballistics as we found out with the loss of my two roommates.

Flying Over The Missouri

It was a whole week after we had learned that the war was officially over, that the 16 first line carriers and remaining 8 CVL carriers from all four task groups were ordered to launch at least a half deck load of planes to fly over Yokohama and Tokyo. This was to be a show of strength to squelch any Japanese person or group from thinking of reversing the decision that their military commanders had made in ending the war. All ships and carriers within each of our four task groups had to be capable of making speeds in excess of 30 knots in order to be eligible to join the fast carrier task forces. Each task group now included four major first-line carriers, each capable of doing 33 knots, along with two CVL carriers.

This had been an amazing buildup of our naval strength during the previous 3 1/2 years. The war had started with only six first-line fleet carriers, but four of those had been sunk in various combat situations. The *Lexington* (CV-2) was sunk at Coral Sea, the *Yorktown* (CV-5) at the battle for Midway, the *Wasp* (CV-7) went down at Guadalcanal, and the *Hornet* (CV-8) was sunk at Santa Cruz. That left only the *Saratoga* (CV-3) and *Enterprise* (CV-6) still active although the *Sara* had taken several fish (torpedoes) in various conflicts and had spent much of the war in dry dock for repairs.

The ship building companies back in the States really went to work, with so many civilians showing their patriotic duty by going to work in ship building yards and factories all across the

Half the planes from all the carriers near Japan flew over the Battleship Missouri *in a show of strength while the Peace Treaty was being signed. Over 1800 carrier planes took part. These photos show some of the armada en route.*

United States. They ground out and assembled over 100 carriers including many Kaiser CVEs that were used to cover the Marine landings in the Pacific, or in escorting troop and supply convoys crossing the Atlantic. The Essex class was all new during the war years starting with the *Essex* itself as CV-9, which was commissioned in late 1942, the new *Yorktown* as CV-10, the *Intrepid* as CV-11, the new *Hornet* as CV-12, *Franklin* CV-13, *Ticonderoga* CV-14, *Randolph* CV-15, the new *Lexington* CV-16, *Bunker Hill* CV-17, the new *Wasp* CV-18, *Hancock* CV-19, *Bennington* CV-20, *BonHomme Richard* CV-31, and the *Shangri La* CV-38. In addition we had nine carriers of the Independence class that were converted to carriers from cruiser hulls, except the *Princeton* (CVL-23) that was sunk at the battle of Leyte in October of '44.

The weather was anything but agreeable and we had at least 1200 planes in the air launched from our carriers to impress the Japanese people that the decisions their military officers had made to end the war should not be reversed in any fashion. It was a precarious flight for us to stay in place in that large a formation with so many planes. Some of us had to convert to instrument flying when clouds obscured our vision, trusting that our flight leaders would not change throttle settings before we got out of the clouds. The battleship *USS Missouri* and her escorting ships had gone into Sagami Wan to anchor close to Tokyo, and it would be on the deck of the *Missouri* where delegates from Japan and our United States officers would eventually sign the peace treaty. I think our large flight was really to cover the *Missouri* as she moved in position to drop anchor for the business ahead.

After the peace was actually signed, one of the four task groups would move into Tokyo Bay to drop anchor for a week and each day would allow half of the ships crew a day of liberty to go ashore to visit the sites of Yokohama and Tokyo. Our task group was not scheduled to go in 'til the fourth week, so our flight assignments were to cruise around the Japanese home island of Honshu to locate prisoner of war camps, which by then were supposed to have large white "PW" painted on the roof of the buildings of the camps. When we found a camp with the PW on its roof we were to mark our chart boards with the location, then try to locate some of our torpedo bombers that had been loaded with packages of clothing, shoes, food, candy, and cigarettes in lieu of the bombs that they had previously carried.   It was such a thrill to see our American men that had been prisoners, waving a thank you as they opened the packages, for they were still being treated as prisoners even weeks after the war ended. I could never understand whether the Japanese were just reticent to acknowledge the camps' existence or whether they just didn't know themselves, or have proper records as to the location of the many PW camps.

Winding Down Still Had Its Dangers

September 1st turned out to be a rather sad day. Weather was zero zero, with a very low ceiling, and almost solid clouds, but

Our task group searched Japan for POW camps such as this.

we were launched anyway to continue our assignment for the day. It was to fly around Mount Fuji to look for more PW camps. We twisted and turned trying to stay clear of the clouds, flying one direction and then another direction to avoid them, although trying to stay on my basic course of heading to Mount Fuji. But the clouds kept getting closer and closer with distance between them getting almost non-existent the higher we got. We had gained altitude to about 12,000 feet in an effort to get over and on top of the clouds, but they were solid even to a much higher altitude. I had to gain another 1000 feet to make sure we would clear Mount Fuji without slamming into the mountain. Ground reference had become almost negligible and navigation had been totally lost with all our twisting and turning, but I thought we had flown fairly close to the mountain.

All of a sudden we were in total soup, as this cloud was very dense with the grayish mist that restricted visibility to a mere few feet in front of us making formation flying very hazardous. When you can't see more than just a few feet you normally fly a lot closer to the next plane than you would when weather was good and you have unrestricted visibility. But in this soup, I had to go on total instruments and I am sure my wing man and section had been straining their eyeballs for several minutes before we broke free of that cloud. When we did, my section leader got on the radio saying, "Gene's gone."

I started a slight turn to port to stay clear of the next voluminous cloud and called for Gene, but there was no answer, and he didn't join up while we were in the clear between clouds. I began to remember the many times I had struggled to stay in formation-while peering through the soup when I was a wingman. Getting disoriented when visibility is low to none, makes it is most difficult to switch over to instruments, but I prayed that Gene could have done that most improbable task.

Bob Russell radioed that he was breaking off to fly on instruments himself for it was just too difficult trying to stay in formation. He said he was going to head back to the carrier because it was nonsense flying in such soup, for it had not cleared as the weatherman aboard the carrier had indicated it should.

I was on total instrument flying all the way back to the carrier, but maintained my altitude for quite some time, not knowing where Bob Russell was, although I felt sure he had been letting down from the moment he had broken away. I had turned around to flying the opposite course from what we had flown trying to get to Mount Fuji. It was a good thing the carrier had installed the ZBX homing system of radio direction finding already, for in all the twisting and turning on the way out, my opposite direction back would never have gotten me back to the carrier.

If I hadn't had the code for the ZBX that day for the compass heading back to the carrier, I never would have found the *Independence*. Thank goodness Bob Russell and his wingman, Bob Martin, had used the same homing ZBX to find the carrier and we all had been able to safely let down from the 12,000 foot altitude we had been at when the decision was made to return to the carrier.

Weather had not cleared, but the skipper thought we should go out and search for Gene as he might be floating in his life raft. Fred and I were catapulted off the carrier and headed for the area Gene should have been in. The weather was now totally overcast and we had to fly the whole distance with a ceiling of no more than 800 feet. We spread out for a little wider search line but saw nothing, no raft, and no oil slick that should have been left from a water landing.

We even made many passes over Nii Shima hoping to see Gene on the small island, but then went back to searching the water again. However, the luck we had hoped for totally avoided us. Gene had apparently become totally disoriented flying in that soup, and it is anybody's guess as to what really happened to him. However, he had not returned and there had been no information coming in that he was able to make a landing anywhere and eventually return to the squadron.

Gene had been one of the first few ensigns to report to the squadron back in Sanford, Maine, in January. All who knew him loved him for his genial manner, his thoughtfulness toward others, and, with it all, his high devotion to duty, and I sure missed him as all the other squadron mates did.

We were back on reconnaissance flights again for the next two weeks, finding an occasional roof with the white PW on it. Just our flying over brought our American prisoners climbing to the top of the roofs and waving for a fare-thee-well, trying to make sure we saw them. Our torpedo bombers always dropped packages to them and the prison guards now seemed to be a little more lenient letting our Americans open and unpack the boxes themselves without supervision judging by what we could see from the air in the first few drops.

Our task group pulled in to Tokyo Bay on September 16th after 78 days at sea, but the *Independence* dropped anchor at the Yokasuka Navy base, where we would have to take the trolley up through Yokohama to Tokyo. We had a few blocks to walk from the Navy Pier to catch the trolley and I couldn't believe the living conditions of the Japanese residents. Each block had its urinal ditch, and we would see men walk up to the ditch and pee. We would also see women come out occasionally to bring their chamber pots to dump the contents in the ditch. Sanitation was almost non-existent in the whole area, every unpaved street had its ditch, and odors coming up just weren't the best.

We had been warned to take our own lunch and canteen for water, which proved to be a blessing for it was a very accurate statement. We found no restaurant and no streetcars to ride in order to see some of the city. After walking a few blocks we had to remember how we had gotten there, for there were no bridges to continue our walks across the canals, and we would have to backtrack and head out a different direction. It was easier to catch another trolley to a nearby city than it was to find our way to see where Gen. MacArthur had set up shop.

We enjoyed seeing some of the countryside that had not been bombed out as the cities had been that had war production industries. We arrived back at the trolley station just after the normal day's business ended. We caught the trolley and headed back to Yokasuka Navy base. Seated just behind us were two well-dressed

Japanese fellows speaking in English. I introduced myself and had quite a nice conversation with them on our ride down to Yokasuka. One of them had graduated from UCLA medical school, the other had received his law degree from Harvard.

They had both gone home to see their parents after graduation and had their passports and visas lifted at the start of the war, and had been required to go to work in Tokyo. They had been there for the duration and couldn't quite understand why the Americans had created such destruction in Tokyo and Yokohama and then released the atomic bombs so shortly thereafter.

They did however understand that Japan had started the war with its attack on Pearl Harbor. Their next comment was, "Why did your government allow Russia to enter the war just eight days before dropping the atomic bombs?" Why? Why hadn't we continued our efforts and gone right on straight into Moscow? They both were afraid of Russian requirements that might be placed on Japan. They could see many problems developing from Russia's actions, even for the United States.

I stayed aboard the *Independence* for the rest of the week as I had seen enough of Japan. I just relaxed, sunbathing on the flight deck or down in the metal shop where I had not quite finished some ash trays from expended 40-millimeter shells. It was just a hobby, but I was glad to get them much closer to being finished. I enjoyed working on them more than going ashore and taking the trolley up to Tokyo and seeing all the burned-out rubble from our B-29 raids.

After a week at anchor in Tokyo Bay, we pulled anchor. I thought we were going back on patrol trying to find more PW camps, but we soon found out we were headed for Saipan. There, as we understood, was another group waiting to relieve our air group, even though we had been aboard only three months when the usual tour of duty was for six months. However, with the end of the war, most of my squadron had indicated they wanted to be released from active duty. Because only the skipper and three others, as I remember, were going to stay and go regular Navy, the rest of us were to be discharged back to civilian life.

Congress had already passed legislation requiring the down-

Aircraft from Air Group 27 passing over the carrier U.S.S. Shangri La, one of several carriers in Task Group 58. Note the destroyer on the carrier's port side. It is most likely transferring mail to and from the carrier.

sizing of the whole war department, which included the Army, the Navy, and the Marine Corps. It had established rules for each person's separation back to civilian life if they so desired, or to just let your skipper know that you would take the option of going regular Navy. Those that had gone through the academy, or one way or other had obtained their status as regular Navy, would be expected to stay in the uniform.

Congress had established points for discharging those that wanted to go back to civilian life. The first option was the number of months in service. The second option was number of months in direct combat. The third option was point values Congress assigned to decorations we had been awarded while in service.

All three methods were increased somewhat if you were married or had a family to support. Most of our whole air group qualified for discharge under all three methods of computation except a very few of our junior ensigns that had been ordered to the squadron after we had suffered losses, had missed all three calculations.

We headed straight south from Tokyo for an overnight trip to Saipan. When we arrived, we left the *Independence* after gathering our baggage and found two buses just waiting for us to land and to transport us to Asleto Airfield. What a change in the airfield I had first seen over a year ago when Griffin and I had escorted the TBF that Chief Tweed had been a passenger in. Admiral Clark had interrogated him and found very important information about Guam and relayed it back to Pearl Harbor. Admiral Nimitz had then sent orders for Clark to expedite Tweed's trip back to Hawaii as fast as possible by getting him to Asleto Field for Nimitz had already dispatched a DC-3 to arrive at Asleto within a few hours.

That time we were within hearing distance of gunshots when the Marines were still fighting to take the island and Tweed was on his way back to Hawaii. Griff and I had exchanged taking pictures of each other sitting in the cockpit of a Japanese Zero that was still on the field. The field had now been doubled in length and had an R4D waiting to fly us down to Guam. We landed on Guam and had buses to shuttle us over to the East Coast R & R camp. There we had to wait for transportation back to the States.

The R & R was certainly a misnomer. Although we were on the East Coast, I don't remember a sandy beach for swimming for it was pretty much just stones rather than a nice sandy beach. That was probably due to currents, waves, and the tides. The only exercise we could participate in was on the volleyball court and bending an elbow at the O'Club where drinks were certainly cheap enough. Anything you could name costs only one ticket. We purchased 20 tickets for one dollar, which made it a grand total of five cents per drink and they were really loaded. Two or three had most of us staggering back to the Quonset hut to hit the sack.

We waited and waited some more and after two weeks the skipper heard about the *Independence* heading back to the States for Navy Day celebrations. He was able to persuade the powers that be to have the *Independence* come back to Guam for us to board for our transportation back to the States. The new air group that had replaced us had moved into all our former staterooms so we were relegated to cots set up on the hangar deck. But, it was a means of getting back to the States, and we were fortunate to even have those cots when there was ever so many troops all waiting for transportation home.

The *Independence* headed back to Tokyo Bay where a few more passengers were loaded and with of them having to use cots along with us on the hangar deck. When we left Tokyo Bay, we started the great circle route to home, and after passing the Aleutian Islands extending southwest from Alaska and by only 200 miles we saw the carrier's armory department start de-arming the ship.

I saw belts of 2400 rounds of 50 caliber machine gun bullets taken from each of the 24 Hellcats we had flown in combat and just dumped all overboard. Ammunition from the TBFs twin 50 caliber guns went next, and then all of the unbelted rounds from deep in the carrier's ammunition hold were brought up to the flight deck for tossing overboard. Bombs and depth charges were next to go over the side for us to be totally disarmed by the time we reached the mouth of the Columbia River. What a waste of the taxpayers money to have dumped all that ammunition over the side and now it rests on the bottom of the ocean. But, we've just fought the war to end all wars, we thought.

When we entered the channel to the Columbia River a small boat came out to meet us with the special pilot to guide the carrier through the narrow channels of the river leading to Portland, Oregon. We had a great time watching our progress up to the river and enjoyed a lot of interesting scenery while progressing up the river. At times we wondered how the special pilot was able to keep the carrier from running aground on some of the sharp turns in the river, but that was what he had come aboard to do and we made it all the way up to Portland without a problem.

Several of the fellows we had picked up as passengers when we entered Tokyo Bay got impatient and went back to their cots to obtain their duffel bags or parachute bags in their haste to exit the carrier. The gangplank that should have come up from the pier seemed to be taking an unusually long lime to come over to the hangar deck.

Those fellows that had been passengers had spotted a way that they could toss their bags from the carrier onto the pier and then jump over to the pier. It was on the same level, even with the railing of the starboard gun turret, and in their haste to get on the pier, they all lucked out without any of them falling to the water below.

Several of our own gang could see the Red Cross tables lined up on the pier, loaded with small cartons of fresh milk and a variety of apples, both of which we had not enjoyed for a long, long time. They also jumped ship and we never did find out whether they came back for orders or just went AWOL, although our pilots did wait for us at the Red Cross tables.

Chapter Thirteen

BECOMING A CIVILIAN

I was so thankful to have survived our combat and grateful to the Lord that I was so lucky. I was particularly lucky in that I had survived all my combat flights, the three barrier crashes during my 179 carrier landings, and had been able to return to the states. I joined several other pilots that were looking for good old terra firma, USA. We went right on through the warehouse behind the wooden dock looking for some actual ground to bend down to kiss before we could do anything else. That accomplished, we returned to the Red Cross tables to enjoy the fresh milk and apples they were handing out.

I had no regrets for the three and half years that I had just spent in serving my country, for I had seen an awful lot of the world that I would not otherwise have seen. After milling around on the dock a while longer and enjoying some cookies that had been brought out in addition to the milk and apples, we went back aboard the carrier to see if the skipper had gotten any further orders for us. But he had nothing, and no news as to where we would have to report for separation. We would not have to stay on the carrier, but had to come back and be there on the carrier for an 0800 muster in the morning. He was certain he would have more information for us by then.

The next thing we did to help celebrate our return to the United States was to find a liquor store, which didn't take too long to do. However, the clerk/store owner wouldn't sell us even one bottle without a liquor card which he told us was a requirement all over the state of Oregon. Then he told us the office that issued those cards would already have closed for the day. Standing near-by was one of his customers and heard our conversation. He took pity on us and gave us the password for his Portland club with the comment that if we would buy dinner there, he was sure the bar-tender would serve a few after dinner drinks for us. We had a love-ly dinner and yes the bartender did serve enough drinks so that get-ting back to the carrier required each of us helping one another stumbling along, feeling just a little bit happy.

We had our bags out on the pier at 0800 for muster and then a bus ride was ordered for us to go up to the Naval Air Station, Seattle, Washington for further orders. A couple Navy buses from NAS Seattle arrived very shortly thereafter. We had a very congen-ial driver who on his own took us a bit out of his way to give us a better view of the majestic Mt. St. Helens and then Mt. Rainier, which very few of us had ever seen before. That is except B. J. Sample whose home was in Seattle and was thrilled to be getting back to his home turf.

The weather had been turning cloudy and rain started and lasted for the rest of the trip. We soon found out why everybody had been telling us "You'll just love Seattle." But B. J. thought it was just wonderful, for he had grown up in it and was used to that type of weather.

We had to use our raincoats for the next few days before it cleared enough so that I could go down to station operations and have enough of a ceiling to request an NSJ to get my flight time for the month and also to see Seattle from the air. Bill Condon went along with me and at the end of my hour, I landed to give Bill the stick for the last hour of air time. We barely accomplished that before the next rain storm came along. But we both had accom-plished two hours air time and that was all that was needed to keep our flight pay coming for the month.

It seemed like the Navy operated usually on a ten day basis for orders for squadrons coming back from combat, for again it was the tenth day before I received mine along with most members of the squadron. My orders read for me to report to the Navy base, Great Lakes, Illinois, for separation. A Milwaukee road pullman car berth ticket was provided for the three-day trip, along with my orders. I had the rest of the day to visit ships' service on base, to see if I could get a few gifts to give the wife and my mother-in-law upon arriving at home.

Lorie had complained so much in her letters that she could get only silk stockings and was waiting for the day that she could purchase some of the new nylon stockings which had been so very elusive during the war years. All nylon had been reserved for making aviation parachutes for us flyers. I lucked out at ships' service, for they had just received their first shipment of the new nylon stockings and I was able to purchase a few in different colors for my gifts to the family. Those were not large items and would easily fit in my duffel bag.

I then had a leisurely lunch and still had the afternoon to do some sight-seeing around Seattle and to get to the railroad station to change my ticket. The usual route between Minneapolis/St. Paul and Chicago went through Eau Claire, Wisconsin, Fond du Lac, Milwaukee, Racine, Kenosha, and then to Chicago. I wanted to switch my ticket for a change of trains at Minneapolis for the train that went down the Mississippi River to LaCross. There it would cross the river and head for Portage and Madison, and then down through Edgerton where I could stop and see my wife for a couple days on my proceed orders that had allowed a little extra time for possible casualties on the trips. I then could catch the train at Edgerton before continuing on through Janesville, Beloit, and Rockford, Illinois, and then to Chicago. I had really thought I would be able to drive that trusty old Terraplane car from Edgerton straight over to Great Lakes instead of having to go clear down into Chicago and then back up along the shores of Lake Michigan to Great Lakes.

It was a glorious arrival back home and everyone was certainly glad to see me. They had not really expected me, as I had not been able to phone home to give them even an anticipated time of arrival, and no one was there at the train station to meet me. I got off the train and just parked my bags there in the station office and walked the three blocks down the tracks to Lorie's place.

My mother-in-law went right to work making some of my favorite foods again. And, when I inquired where the car was for I also wanted to go to see Hank Ebbott who had been my best man at our wedding. I learned it had been sold as it had been in the way of her father's trucks, but Lorie had never written in her letters that the car had been sold. He insisted she sell it for he did not want it taking up one garage space that was needed for one of his trucks. I had to go to the railroad station to get another train ticket when Lorie let it be known she wanted to be with me. I did not think it would take more than one day to fill out papers for my separation from service.

We took the early train from Edgerton to Chicago and then back up to Evanston where I got us a room for the night at the Edgewater Hotel on the shores of Lake Michigan. I could easily catch the North Shore train up to Great Lakes from there. I couldn't believe the personal attention the Edgewater extended us. A beautiful room with a bouquet of flowers, a box of candy, and the bed turned down for the night with a mint chocolate on the pillows after we had enjoyed a wonderful dinner and dance in the adjoining ballroom. All that attention had been extended for a total charge of just six dollars per night. (Guess what the charge would be at today's inflated prices.)

I got up early the next morning and caught the North Shore train for Great Lakes. They had big signs at the North Shore station and along the route to the base and then directions to the building for those people coming for separation. People were very ingenious at giving us directions, but we still had to wait in line for our turn to see the interviewing officer. I filled out the forms required of me to list all my times, dates and places of training. The next space was for all my duty stations, squadrons, and carriers I had served on. Then I was informed to come back the next day when the yeoman would have my separation orders typed.

I think I had already signed where I was supposed to sign on the separation papers and handed it to the officer who would then sign to make the separation official. However, when he was about to sign the papers he noticed my date of rank. He said just a minute, let me go check something. When he came back he said he had remembered correctly, that they had just received an ALNAV and if I wanted to go over to Glenview for a full flight physical I could be discharged as a full two-striper rather than just as a JG. My serial number of 250902 fell within the numbers eligible for promotion. Of course I wanted that flight physical and had to wait for the noon bus that would head to Glenview Naval Air Station.

A return bus would not get back to Great Lakes until too late for him, as he was able now to maintain strict office hours. He authorized me to see him again the next morning when I would become a Lieutenant Senior Grade and a civilian in the same day. I took the bus and got to Glenview and found the new hospital and medical station. The corpsman got started on my schneider for exercise and heart condition, and then drew some blood for testing. When it was all returned, the doctor came in to listen to my heart. He gave me no trouble about passing the flight physical and signed the physical forms and also the promotion papers.

I was able to get back to the main gate in time to catch the bus back to Great Lakes and then the North Shore south to Evanston for a second night at the Edgewater Hotel. We enjoyed the same service that night, except that bouquet of flowers had not been changed for they were still looking fresh and nice.

I got out early the next morning to catch the North Shore again, going north to Great Lakes. I found the lieutenant commander that was acting as a separation officer and he had had the yeoman retype my separation paper showing I was a lieutenant rather than a JG. I had just become a full senior grade lieutenant and a civilian in the same day, and was handed a ruptured duck emblem that everyone received when leaving service. I was able to catch the North Shore south bound to Evanston. Lorie and I checked out and caught the North Shore going south, although we had to walk a couple blocks to the Union Station to catch the afternoon train back to Edgerton.

Dad had thrown out most of my civilian clothes by now and as Lorie had always enjoyed nice clothes, she insisted I go up to McNeil and Moore in Madison, which was an exclusive men's store, for my new civilian suit. We found a beautiful three-piece tan gabardine that fit me pretty well for $48. (I wish I could buy a suit for that same price nowadays.)

But at McNeil and Moore you don't leave the store with a suit the fits just pretty good. They have to get the tailor to come out, measure the exact length to make the cuffs (which were in style back in those days), and also adjust the back of the coat if the coat showed the least little wrinkle. He said it would take a couple hours to make the adjustments for he had other work ahead of mine. With that amount of time, I decided to go over to the University of Wisconsin office to find out about registration, which would also include signing up for married housing. Lorie had not wanted me to make use of my military flying education nor even apply for an airline pilot (probably would have been a co-pilot slot) for they were paying just $200 per month back in those days before the horrendous increase in civilian passenger flying.

I was still wearing my light winter leather jacket, which the University registrar noticed and said you are eligible for the GI Bill of Rights. He said I would get $90 per month, and because I had already signed up for married housing I would be one of the first to get residence in one of the very recently moved mobile homes that they had brought down from Badger Ordnance. The ordnance plant had thousands of employees making gunpowder during the war and had set several hundred of these 26 foot trailers making a small village across the highway from the ordnance plant, which was midway between Sauk City and Baraboo.

The trailers there at Badger Village were now mostly all vacant because the ordnance plant had been shut down after our victory over Japan, and the former employees had left for their homes, whereever they might have come from across the country. The University would bring down as many as could be placed on camp Randall right next to the Field House and the football stadium. Any student registration for married housing after those trailers on Camp Randall were filled would have to commute to the trailers at Badger City, which would be about a 45 minute drive. These trailers would be the only solution for married veterans.

The University had never had to provide for married couples before and just didn't have rooms for married veterans in such numbers, although they still had rooms for singles in the dorms. The registrar let me know that I was lucky to have signed up as soon as that afternoon, the trailers were filling up in a hurry with all the former GI's coming back for the next semester. Most of the veterans that signed up before Christmas vacation were able to get married housing there on camp Randall. After the Christmas vacation if former GIs were married they would pay the same rent as we would have to, but make the drive by bus or in their own cars on days when they might have only one or two classes scheduled.

Although the commuters would be charged the same $25 per month as our Camp Randall homes, it was so much easier for me to walk the three blocks to class, as all but one of my classes would be in Sterling Hall. Living on campus also made it much easier to take advantage of our student activities tickets. Basketball games in the Field House that next semester were virtually out our side door, as were all the boxing, wrestling, indoor track, and the Wisconsin State High School basketball tournament games the next March. Football games the next fall were just a stone's throw away. Now all I had to do was settle down to study for all the classes my days' in service had interrupted. I transferred credits from my first semester at Wisconsin back to Knox College, which then awarded me my Bachelor of Arts degree, but I still had to work for my BBA from the University of Wisconsin. (Madison, for we had just about 12,000 students on campus that first semester I was back and the administration hadn't even dreamed registrations would go so high that it would be necessary to establish all the extension campuses.)

It was amazing to see so many ex-military men (mostly men, that is although there certainly were a few women that took advantage of the GI Bill provisions for education). Professor Elwell was head of the School of Business and thought I should take all the accounting courses over again as it had been four years since I had done any accounting work while I was flying in the Navy. So instead of just two more semesters as a senior, it took four to complete all the courses that Elwell insisted I take to receive my BBA, and several of the courses were required simply because the textbook for the courses had been written by you know who!

Mid way through the fourth semester we had many corporate personnel managers come for interviews to select employees for their companies. Nearly all of them were offering a salary of $200 per month except Firestone Tire and Rubber, which offered $220 (quite a change from today's starting salaries for college graduates!)

Lorie knew my heart was still in flying, but she quickly eliminated all airline potentials as they were only paying $200 per month for former Navy pilots, and the decision came down to Firestone to be assistant stores accountant for the Milwaukee district. We had three TBA (tire, battery, and accessories) stores, one tire retread shop, eleven TBA stores that also pumped gas and the storage farm for all the gas supplies. To keep the farm supplied, I had to order gas for delivery in railroad tank cars that carried approximately 8,000 gallons. We had no tanker trucks back in those days.

John Cerjance was my senior accountant and between us we had to do all the accounting work including keeping a running inventory of all tires (car, truck, and earth mover) in all stores and then we each would head out to a store at the end of the month to take an actual inventory. That meant counting every nut, bolt, and tire in the place. We had to price out everything we had counted and then apply that inventory to the earnings report for that month. From that we calculated the earnings for the particular store which then determined the bonus that store manager would receive for that six month period.

The accounting for the whole mid-west area was transferred to the Chicago office in about two years and I received a promotion to be in charge of the Peoria, Illinois district. However, Lorie would have no part of Chicago and would not even go down to look at a few apartments I had selected, and after about six months of commuting from Milwaukee to Chicago and staying in a hotel five nights a week it was time for a change.

Lorie had a cousin that I never should have listened to, for, he made financing to buy the Rock and Walworth County Nehi, Party-Pack, Royal Crown distributing agency so easy that I was paying almost twice what I should have. But Lorie wanted to get closer to home (Edgerton) and this business was just twelve miles away in Janesville, Wisconsin. That was my first lesson in business for myself. Besides the excessive price, I really wasn't ready for handling the 40 pound cases all day long. However the profit wasn't too bad, I purchased each case for 55 cents and sold it to the merchants for 80 cents. That way the merchant made 40 cents when the price of soda was still 5 cents.

I did stick it out for a year and a half before seeing an advertisement in the paper for an assistant examiner for the Federal Deposit Insurance Corporation. The requirement was that you have a college degree in either accounting or law. I qualified and received a nice recommendation from the local banker. With that, Bill Hammill (assistant supervising examiner) saw to it that I got to the proper place for the federal examination so he would not have to interview others that might have taken the exam elsewhere.

I served the usual four years as an assistant during which I was continually studying for the examination for senior examiner. It would be a one-week exam consisting of four days written and then a Friday quiz in front of a three-man panel. One of the panel was always there to distract you any way he could to see if you could handle a Board of Directors meeting, which would have some of the most influential business men of the community. And I am sitting there telling them they have to change their ways or I will have to close their bank. That would probably arouse their dander if not even create quite a commotion. I must have said the right things for Bill Hammill congratulated me on passing the exam on the first try, which he said doesn't happen very often. Most fellows get too rattled on Friday to convince the panel that you could handle a bank board meeting with an adverse topic to discuss.

I was transferred to the Lansing, Michigan, office for my first three years as a senior examiner. As such I was the junior of the senior examiners and had to take my crew to every place that the seniors preferred not to take. That meant I would be in Battle Creek one week, then up to Soo St Marie, then Bad Axe, then up to Calumet,and then maybe down to Chelsea and then probably up to Cadillac for an endless crisscrossing of the state. All that traveling and still trying to commute to Milwaukee at least two weekends per month to see my two boys.

Lorie would not come over to Michigan to even take a look at a couple excellent places I had selected for her to choose from out in Birmingham, a rather exclusive suburb of Detroit. It had a magnificent layout with wide streets and well-kept homes. However, with no residence in the Detroit area, the boss insisted I find something in the Lansing area for it had already been six months and he just couldn't continue to carry me on full per diem.

A small cottage was found out on Lake Lansing for me to call home. Here I could stretch out on the porch and watch the fish jumping, or the loons or other ducks landing on the water. I now had to pay the cost of seeing my boys two weekends a month by

flying via Capital Air Lines from Lansing to Milwaukee. And for the drive from whereever I happened to have been working during the week, down through Michigan City, Gary, and Chicago on my way for the weekend Navy drill at NAS Glenview on Chicago's north west side.

Of course that made a rather late Sunday evening drive back to Lansing after we were secured at 1700 (5 p.m.) from the weekend drill. Which was okay because I still enjoyed the flying, espe-

Three generations - The author with his father, Rev. Theo Hargreaves and his son, Jeff in 1951.

cially when former squadron mate Butch Voris would bring his newly formed Blue Angels up to Glenview, for a weekend show over Chicago's water front.

My Naval Reserve status had never been extinguished, and when living in Janesville a Bill Henke had colluded to establish the Navy's Ninth District Reserve organization 9-1. We were able to accrue points for retirement along with the monthly lessons we had to submit to the ninth district headquarters at Great Lakes education center. After moving to Milwaukee, I bumped into Howard Strochin at a Navy affair after which we got together and had a Navy unit formed for Milwaukee. The only hitch was one or the other of us always had to drive down to Glenview to get an SNJ to fly back to Billy Mitchell Field for us to have a plane to fly during the weekend. We operated from the original one-room terminal on the north side of the field and the original control tower for instructions on taxiing, takeoff, or landing on the 4,000-foot runways. As the unit grew with more Navy pilots learning of the unit we had to have Glenview fly a twin-engine Beech up for our pilots to bring more SNJs for our weekend flights.

Large construction crews were seen out in the middle of the field in late 1952 or early 1953 when the new terminal was put under construction. To us pilots it seemed like a wild venture, because what pilot would ever consistently want to taxi from the mid-field terminal and operations desk to the end of runway for takeoff. But that was the start of what now has had even more expansions with runways lengthened considerably.

Our unit had grown so fast that orders came through CNARTC (Chief Naval Air Reserve Training Command) for us to move the unit to Glenview and fly the old Able Dog, a plane with a crew of three - Pilot, radioman, and gunner. It was an easy plane to fly and had been used in Korea. It carried more destructive armament than the famous B-17s that flew bombing missions from England to targets in Germany. It was the plane we had flown from Glenview to Miami Opa Locka in April 1954 for our annual two weeks of active duty. Although the rest of us had no trouble, Howie Lentz somehow or other tromped on the brakes so viciously in leaving his parking spot that he nosed up the plane, requiring a complete change of engine and propeller. Even though he was a master at swinging out on the piano for us to listen to the latest music, or to harmonize in the evenings in the BOQ, we never quit calling him "Nose up."

In 1955 we were checked out in the bent wing F4U Corsairs. In 1956 we had the usual early spring cruise (two weeks active duty) in the bent wings. Then a month later, the Navy required us to take a second cruise for transition to the F9F Grumman Cougar.

Everything had to be doubled, or cut in half. Ground speed and air speed doubled. We now had to read fuel in pounds rather than in gallons, that would be sucked through that engine in little over an hour if we couldn't get clearance to 30,000 feet immediately. There the air was much lighter with a fuel air mixture much lower. Back in those days jets flamed out quite frequently, so we bad to learn how to try to restart before you lost too much altitude, as those beasts came down rather fast without an engine. Takeoff and landing speeds were quite different than what we had been used to, and you always kept 92% power on for the landings until after you had crossed the end of the runway.

1957 saw us transitioned to the S2F, which was used primarily for anti-sub search. It was a two pilot plane with a navigator and a utility space for another person. We carried sono-bouys for dropping to more accurately determine location of potential enemy submarines.

We assembled for the usual June weekend drill on Saturday morning and at the close of weekend duties Sunday afternoon we left saying, "See you all next month." We stood for the usual Saturday morning muster for the July weekend drill and retired to our usual ready room. At that point I had to make pilot assignments to planes with takeoff and landing times. But there was no list of plane numbers and no planes on the tarmac.

I had to run over to base operations to find out which planes we would be using for the weekend and was told they had no request for planes for our squadron and if I wanted to find out anything further I would have to go up to see CNARTC. I did, and when stepping into his office I recognized Admiral Parnell who had been the task force admiral with his flag on the *Enterprise* when we were aboard at Tarawa and Kwajalein some 15 years earlier. However, he still called me by name and asked what he could do for me.

The Admiral seemed quite amused listening to the reason for my visit, and when I completed he called for his yeoman who came in from his desk in front of the Admiral's door, he exclaimed Admiral didn't you send those orders out? What orders? You know, the orders BUNAV sent out to disband all squadrons that are heavy on LtCdrs for that was not the usual or normal personnel complement for a squadron. OH, there they are, in that stack on your desk, and the Admiral's face turned bright red.

Please have a seat while I sign them, and you can take them all down to the squadron. That meant we would not even collect pay or expenses for July 1958 in the War department's haste to down-size the military personnel and bases.

After relating the demise of my military pay, Lorie accused me of deliberately resigning from the squadron to reduce her spending money, as I had previously warned her that we just couldn't keep up with the Gerbers (who we had met at a church dance back in 1954). But she liked the parties Gerber hosted at his home and the lush meals I had to pay for when Lorie would accept invitations to join them at Carl Rasches or Heiney's Supper Club on 76th Street, or several other expensive supper clubs.

Remembering back to those times it was probably less expensive for me to pay my way back to Milwaukee twice a month than it would have been for me to pay for all the expenses of joining the Gerbers at all the supper club invitations Lorie would have accepted, had I been working out of Milwaukee headquarters.

My boss had probably surmised by this time that Lorie had become a problem for me and when the Madison East sub-district had become available he transferred me back to Madison. I suppose he thought Lorie might at least move to a town closer to her home. But NO. She then filed for a divorce in 1959 and got the newer car, the house, and the furniture and I had to rent a room in

Madison. The nicest room I could find was in a beautiful home on the shores of Lake Mendota, and owned by a charming little old Jewish lady. Once she found out I had no animosities against her race, we had many enjoyable evenings discussing worldly matters. I also got invitations to many delicious dinners that she prepared for her family that arrived for every holiday.

FDIC (Federal Deposit Insurance Corporation) had already reserved a spot for me at Rutgers University for the two week in residence for American Bankers commercial banking course. It then required a written problem once a month for the balance of the year. And, during my senior year I had to research and write a thesis on any topic related to banking. What else. I picked the topic of financing the purchase of a plane. It got accepted and I added another degree to the list. The BA from Knox, the BBA from University of Wisconsin, and now the Commercial Banking from Rutgers, and the American Bankers Association.

It was quite a change from the Michigan routine. After the three years of roaming that state from one end to the other it was a real god-send to have my own sub-district. It started with a line drawn north and south through Madison to the Illinois border and north to Waupon and from Madison east to Oconomowac for all the state banks within that area that were not members of the Federal Reserve system. Those were examined by examiners from the Fed. But I certainly had more time to research for my thesis for Rutgers when not on the road driving such long distances.

All banks in my district had been completed in 1959, but the boss ordered me to help the Eau Claire district in northwestern Wisconsin finish its '59 schedule, which we had accomplished by late January. My assistants had completed their part of the examination and I had excused them for their drive back to Madison. The bank's CEO had been tied up most of that Friday afternoon, but I still had to have some discussion with him before I could wrap up the exam. It was nearly 7 p.m. by the time I could get his assurance that certain corrections would be made. By the time I got packed up and driven down to Baraboo I was getting rather hungry. Scots Highway House, a well known supper club would help ease that hunger, for I had eaten many meals there when I was Mac MacNamera's assistant in the early days with FDIC.

Scot had always served a delicious meal at reasonable prices, and I forget now what I had ordered but when I had eaten about half the meal a group of ladies entered the bar section and started playing the nickelodeon. Scot came over to say, "You better ask them to dance - The floor is empty." So I asked one of them and got turned down, although she said I should ask the gal at the other end of the bar. I did and had a wonderful time on that dance floor with a partner that followed every move and step I could think of. She was also an excellent gourmet cook and even became the President of Madison's gourmet club for several years.

Scot kept plugging quarters into that nickelodeon which at that time played five songs for each quarter and we danced the night away. When the other ladies (all married) felt it was time to head home from their night out with the girls, they asked if I could give Jeanette (recently divorced) a ride home. Yes, of course I could and my food got even colder while we continued to dance, getting only a bite here and there between pieces on the jive box.

Jeanette Palenshus Kovick quickly became my steady date whenever I could swing around to Baraboo on the way home, back to Madison on Friday night and often for a home cooked dinner on Saturday night before we headed out for an evening of dancing week after week. We were married just before Christmas and had 41 years together before she passed away, which has now given me time to gather my thoughts to complete this manuscript.

This, then, is the account of my service for my country. Every generation has its history. But if a record of that history isn't preserved, future generations won't have anything to learn from. We therefore must struggle every day to preserve it for posterity.

INDEX

Grimes, Bob: 184, 189, 214
Guam: 158, 180, 183, 184, 190, 222, 230, 285, 305, 324
Guantanamo Bay: 235

H

HaHa Jima: 221
Halmahera: 246
Hammill, Bill: 335
Harbert, Charlie: 96, 97, 101, 102, 104, 180, 191, 238, 240, 250
Hargreaves, Rev. Theo C.: 1, 30, 267
Hargreaves, Yvonne: 268
Harman, Tom: 305
Harrigan, Nol: 144, 158, 184, 188, 251
Harrill, Adm.: 203, 212, 262
Harris, L. E. "Tex": 124, 142, 166
Harris, L.E. "Tex": 183, 184, 185, 214, 250
Harrold, Wayne: 128
Harshbarger, Ensign: 50
Haruna: 311
Heisel, Lt.: 60, 61
Henke, Bill: 337
Heyer, John: 66
Hickum Field: 114
Hilner, Ralph: 58, 61
Hilo NAS: 303
Hiroshima: 314
HMS Formidable: 308
Hokkaido: 307
Holladay, Lt. Jack: 89, 91, 98, 108, 143
Holmgaard, Evald: 246, 250
Holton: 3
Honshu: 307, 311, 312, 313, 315
hoosegow: 140
Hyuga: 311

I

Ice, Bill: 19, 20

IRON, Operation: 164
Ise: 311
Iwo Jima: 186, 187, 203, 211, 214, 220, 227, 229, 230

J

Jenkins, Col.: 6, 21
Johnson, By: 118, 122, 144, 186, 214, 218, 221, 231, 238, 246, 279
Johnson, LtCdr. Roy L.: 89, 178
Jones, George: 248

K

Kaiser flat top carrier: 151
kamikaze: 313
Kaneohe Marine Air Station: 116, 140
Kerlee, LtCdr.: 217
Kindall, Capt.: 305, 310
King Neptunus Rex: 155
Knight, Dewey: 81, 279
Knight, Louis: 58
Knox College: 21, 29, 30
Kure: 311
Kwajalein: 135, 174, 176, 180, 237, 304

L

Lake, Kenny: 189, 211, 214, 227, 228, 246
Lanigan: 2
Latimer, Lat: 211, 221
LeForge, Shorty: 137, 148, 185, 212
Lentz, Howie: 338
Levering: 190
Leyte: 240, 285, 305, 317
Little Rippers: 153, 156
Lloyd, Demi: 142, 143, 147, 166, 170, 184
LSO: 70
Luzon: 245, 249